FREE COMRADES

ANARCHISM AND HOMOSEXUALITY IN THE UNITED STATES, 1895–1917

FREE COMRADES

ANARCHISM AND HOMOSEXUALITY IN THE UNITED STATES, 1895–1917

Terence Kissack

AK
PRESS
EDINBURGH • OAKLAND • WEST VIRGINIA

Free Comrades: Anarchism and Homosexuality in the United States, 1895–1917

© 2008 Terence Kissack
This edition © 2008 AK Press (Oakland, Edinburgh, West Virginia)

ISBN-13 9781904859116

Library of Congress Control Number: 2006933528

AK Press
674-A 23rd Street
Oakland, CA 94612
USA
www.akpress.org
akpress@akpress.org

AK Press
PO Box 12766
Edinburgh EH8 9YE
Scotland
www.akuk.com
ak@akedin.demon.co.uk

The above addresses would be delighted to provide you with the latest AK Press distribution catalog, which features the several thousand books, pamphlets, zines, audio and video products, and stylish apparel published and/or distributed by AK Press. Alternatively, visit our web site for the complete catalog, latest news, and secure ordering.

Printed in Canada on acid free, recycled paper with union labor.

Cover by Chris Wright (www.seldomwright.com)
Interior design and layout by ZB

CONTENTS

ACKNOWLEDGMENTS

This book began as my dissertation in United States History which I completed at the City University of New York in 2004. The friends I made at CUNY—most especially Erica Ball, David D. Doyle Jr., Megan Elias, Cindy Lobel, Kathy Feeley, Marcia Gallo, Kerri Jackson, Delia Mellis, Jason Tougaw, and Peter Vellon—were enormously helpful to me and were by far my best teachers.

At CUNY I had the privilege of working with Martin Duberman, who served as chair of my dissertation committee. Marty's knowledge of the history of radicalism and sexuality in the United States proved to be an invaluable resource. I am equally indebted to the other members of my committee. I spent some of my best days as a student in seminars run by David Nasaw and Thomas Kessner. As committee members they were masters of the art of academic tough love. Thankfully, David and Tom both have a wicked sense of humor; difficult lessons were taught without too much bruising of my ego. Blanche Wiesen Cook was both a sartorial and an academic influence in my life. I was fortunate that Lisa Duggan agreed to serve on my committee even though she was not CUNY faculty. I am grateful for her careful and insightful comments and for her quick wit.

A number of friends, colleagues, and teachers honed my thinking and lifted my spirits. Special thanks to Paul Avrich, Carol Berkin, The Boys at Bolerium Books, Marjorie Bryer, Joey Cain, Phillip Cannistraro, Jack Diggins, Betty Einerman, Jeffrey Escoffier, Michael Helquist, Kevin Jenkins, Hubert Kennedy, Brigitte Koenig, Jon Kaufmann, Gerard Koskovich, Regina Kunzel, Barbara Loomis, Molly McGarry, Martin Meeker, Kevin Murphy, James Osborne, D. Sachs, Susan Stryker, Randolph Trumbach, Nancy Unger, Jim Van Buskirk, and Willie Walker. I owe an enormous debt to my editor Zach Blue and to Barry Pateman, whose dedication to the exploration of anarchist history and willingness to give his time and insights is truly remarkable.

A number of institutions and organizations assisted me during my research. CUNY's History Department, the CUNY Graduate Center, and the Colonial Dames of New York all awarded me much needed financial support during my days as a student. The archivists and staff at the New York Public Library, the Tamiment Archives at New York University, the Houghton Library at Harvard University, the Emma Goldman Papers Project of U.C. Berkeley, the Hatcher Library, University of Michigan, Ann Arbor which houses the Joseph Labadie Collection, and the volunteers and staff of the Gay, Lesbian, Bisexual, Transgender Historical Society were all very generous with their time and assistance.

I am enormously thankful for the love and support of my parents, Alfred Kissack and Micheline Maccario, who never wavered in their enthusiasm for my work. Sadly, my mother passed away in late 2007. I dedicate this book to her. My brothers, Alec, Lyle, and Bruno; their respective partners, Laura, Clemmie, and Maureen; and my niece and nephews, Allie, Mitch, Diego, Ramsey, and Tyson deserve my thanks for putting me up and putting up with me during research trips.

Finally, I want to thank my partner Mark Coleman. Mark was not in my life when this book was in its infancy, but I would not have finished it without his love and support.

INTRODUCTION:

ANARCHISM AND THE POLITICS OF HOMOSEXUALITY

IN THE LATE-NINETEENTH AND early-twentieth centuries, activists living in the urban, industrial West began to articulate a politics of homosexuality. Though various early-nineteenth century political thinkers, like Jeremy Bentham and Charles Fourier, touched on the question of homosexuality and its place in the social order, same-sex love enjoyed increased attention in the late-nineteenth and early-twentieth centuries due to a quantitative and qualitative shift in the political and sexual cultures of the West.[1] This development is best documented in Northern Europe, especially Germany and England. In these countries, intellectuals and reformers including Karl Heinrich Ulrichs, Edith Ellis, Anna Rüling, Edward Carpenter, Helene Stöcker, and John Addington Symonds published and circulated defenses of same-sex love. In 1897, the German sexologist and sex radical, Magnus Hirschfeld formed the Scientific-Humanitarian Committee (SHC), the world's first homosexual rights organization. The SHC published a journal, sponsored lectures, did outreach to media, clergy, and other professionals, and lobbied for legal reforms. The members of the SHC and other contemporary activists were radical intellectuals, producing new forms of knowledge and political ideas. They created new understandings of homosexuality, forged new political terms and goals, and articulated sharp critiques of oppressive social norms and values. These activists constructed new forms of political and social consciousness that shaped the lives of millions of people.[2]

Historians have not documented a similar movement in the United States during this period. This is not to say that Americans in the late-nineteenth and early-twentieth centuries were silent on the moral, social, and cultural meanings of same-sex love. As in the rest of the developed world, America witnessed a dramatic increase in the level of interest in homosexuality. Sexual behavior and identity were the subjects of a number of discussions and investigations based in law, psychiatry, journalism, and literature.[3] Few Americans, however, produced political defenses of same-sex love similar to those being penned by European sex radicals.

The only pre-World War I era American work comparable to those being produced in Europe at the time is Edward Irenaeus Prime-Stevenson's *The Intersexes: A History of Simisexualism As a Problem in Social Life*. *The Intersexes* engages with the texts of other reformers and seeks to add new perspectives and information to the unfolding debate about the place of same-sex love in Western culture. But Prime-Stevenson published his book only after moving to Italy. There were 125 copies of Prime-Stevenson's work printed in 1908 by a small, private English-language press in Rome. There is very little evidence that Prime-Stevenson's work had much impact in the country of his birth.[4]

In this period, there were no political groups organized along the lines of the SHC in the United States. There is mention of one small group, but the veracity of the account describing its existence is questionable. In an autobiographical narrative published in 1922, Earl Lind claimed to have been a member of a New York group called the Cercle Hermaphroditos that formed "to unite for defense against the world's bitter persecution of bisexuals."[5] By "bisexual" Lind meant men, like himself, who were sexually attracted to men. According to Lind, members of this group, which "numbered about a score," met at "Paresis Hall," a resort located in New York City's Bowery and well-known as a hang out for "fairies," or effeminate homosexuals.[6] Though members of the group shared their experiences of job discrimination and their risk of random street violence, they did not take any action beyond coming together for mutual support. At best, then, the group—assuming it existed—was, in the words of George Chauncey, a "loosely constituted club" offering support and recreational opportunity to its members.[7] The Cercle Hermaphroditos published no pamphlets, journals, or books; sponsored no lectures; and left no evidence of any activity outside of Paresis Hall. In fact, other than Lind's account, there is no evidence that the organization actually existed, and as historian Jonathan Ned Katz notes, "it is difficult to know exactly where Earl Lind's accounts pass from fact to fiction."The story of the Cercle Hermaphroditos, Katz writes, may well be "apocryphal."[8]

Of course, there were individuals who carved out a place for themselves by claiming social space within cities, and refusing to conform to normative gender and sexual codes. Chauncey's work on gay life in New York City (as well as the work done by others), offers a window on the lives of some of these brave souls. Their "immediate, spontaneous, and personal" struggles are part of what historians Elizabeth Lapovsky Kennedy and Madeline D. Davis have identified as "pre-political forms of resistance" within gay and lesbian communities.[9] By gathering in small social groups and living a life that visibly contradicted gender-normative behavior, thousands of gay men and lesbians asserted the validity and value of their lives and loves. But these efforts did not result—at least not directly—in the creation of a body of political ideas and rhetoric that engaged the legal, social, and cultural social norms that regulated homosexuality. Resistance to homophobia at the individual level was largely evanescent, limited, and easily rolled back. "Pre-political forms of resistance" cannot substitute for a critique that challenges the actions of the state, as well as other regulatory bodies and agents, in a sustained and rational manner.

The absence of a group like the SHC or a figure on the order of Edward Carpenter sets the United States apart from the overall pattern of Western culture. But this apparent exceptionalism is just that—apparent and not real. There was, in fact, a vital, engaged, political discussion of homosexuality in the United States in the late-nineteenth and early-twentieth centuries. Unlike Europe, however, these politics did not emerge from a nascent homosexual rights movement, nor was it articulated by homosexual intellectuals. Rather, the first sustained US-based consideration of the social, ethical, and cultural place of homosexuality took place within the English-language anarchist movement.

From the mid-1890s through the 1920s, key English-speaking figures of the anarchist movement debated the subject of same-sex passion and its place in the social order. Among Americans, they were alone in doing so; no other political movement or notable public figure of the period dealt with the issue of homosexuality. Anarchist sex radicals like John William Lloyd, Emma Goldman, Alexander Berkman, Leonard Abbott, and Benjamin R. Tucker published books, wrote articles, and delivered lectures in cities across the country that addressed the subject of same-sex love. It was a complicated issue at the time, and their lectures contained contradictions and limitations. While the anarchists were guided by their belief that women and men had the right to pattern their intimate lives free of interference from outside authority, they struggled at times to understand how same-sex relations fit into their analysis of sexual relations.

The anarchist sex radicals in the United States were well aware of the homosexual political discourse going on in Europe. Anarchists like John William Lloyd and Emma Goldman, for example, were profoundly influenced by the ideas and work of Carpenter, Hirschfeld, Havelock Ellis, and other European sex radicals. The anarchists were avid readers of the work of sexologists who they identified with the overall project of sexual reform. In their travels overseas, these anarchists met with their European counterparts, sharing ideas, and becoming a conduit through which the ideas percolating in Europe could reach an American audience. The European sex radicals were equally well aware of the work by anarchists in the US. Hirschfeld praised Goldman as "the first and only woman, indeed one could say the first and only human being, of importance in America to carry the issue of homosexual love to the broadest layers of the public."[10] The anarchist sex radicals were eager participants in a transatlantic sexual politic that sought to end the legal and social oppression of homosexuals and reveal new forms of scientific knowledge. The anarchists brought their own passionate belief in the possibility of revolutionary social and cultural transformation to this transatlantic reform movement.

The politics of homosexuality outlined by the anarchists was unprecedented and unique in the United States. The anarchists were alone in successfully articulating a political critique of American social and legal rules, and the cultural norms that regulated same-sex relations. Anarchist sex radicals developed and sustained a far-ranging and complex critique of "normal" social and sexual values, which circulated across a relatively broad public. Due to their ability and willingness to draw on the resources of the anarchist movement, these sex radicals made homosexuality a topic of political discourse and debate. In doing so, they helped shift the sexual, cultural, and political landscape of the United States. They threw themselves into a fractious debate about homosexuality that has only grown in volume and salience over the hundred years since it first began. While the contemporary homosexual rights movement is not the lineal descendent of the anarchist movement, the turn-of-the-century sex radicals examined in this book raised many of the questions that continue to be at the heart of American sexual politics.

The politics of homosexuality articulated by turn-of-the-twentieth-century anarchist sex radicals grew out of their overall political ideals and goals. The men and women active in the anarchist movement wished to rebuild all aspects of life according to the principles of liberty and self-rule. They worked to bring about a revolution where all forms of human association and desire would be transformed. Work, love, friendship, consumption, art, literature, patterns of settlement, and almost all other aspects of life would all be born anew. In the words of Emma Goldman:

> Anarchism…stands for the liberation of the human mind from the dominion of religion; the liberation of the human body from the dominion of property; liberation from the shackles and restraint of government. Anarchism stands for a social order based on the free grouping of individuals for the purpose of producing real social wealth; an order that will guarantee to every human being free access to the earth and full enjoyment of the necessities of life, according to individual desires, tastes, and inclinations.[11]

The scope and seeming audacity of the anarchists' goals meant that no subject was off limits for discussion. Though Goldman does not specifically discuss sexuality in the passage quoted above, the fundamental principle applied to the politics of homosexuality by herself and other anarchist sex radicals is expressed here. The anarchists insisted that there should be no external authority governing people's personal or public associations; all "desires, tastes, and inclinations" should be respected and given room to flourish. Social attitudes, laws, and religious doctrines that condemned love between members of the same sex was critiqued by the anarchist sex radicals as part of a vision of complete and far-reaching social change.

The anarchists were in profound conflict with the values and rules of the society where they lived. They denounced the heavy hand of law and tradition as, in the words of Alexander Berkman, "the greatest impediment to man's advance, hedging him in with a thousand prohibitions…weighting his mind down with outlived canons and codes, thwarting his will with imperatives of thought and feeling, with 'thou shalt' and 'thou shalt not' of behavior and action."[12] Anarchism, at least in the eyes of those who espoused it, was an attempt to clear away the dead weight of the past in order to permit new growth. The anarchists pursued a social revolution that would free all aspects of life from the control of hierarchal relationships. All persons would be free to establish living, work, and social relationships of their own choosing. This utopian bent forced them to question the rules of the world they lived in. The anarchists, according to Margaret Marsh, "of all the radicals and reformers during the latter half of the nineteenth century [and early-twentieth century], came closest to a total renunciation of not only law and government but also traditional cultural values and social norms."[13] The movement's dissident culture fostered and enabled the challenge of social taboos, including those surrounding same-sex love.

Various anarchist sex activists outlined different positions on the question of homosexuality; the politics of homosexuality they articulated was essentially an intellectual and cultural debate carried out by individual activists within the movement. In part, this reflects the nature of the movement. "The essence of anarchism," James Joll pointed out, "was freedom of choice and the absence of central direction making."[14] An attempt to enforce a false unity among the various voices in the movement would obscure more than it revealed. Benjamin Tucker, for example, framed his politics of homosexuality as an abstract discussion of individual rights, rather than a defense of persons who were homosexuals. He made no reference to identity, either individual or community-based, and avoided use of sexological terminology. Emma Goldman, on the other hand, spoke of homosexuals as a persecuted minority, like others, deserving better treatment. She corresponded regularly with sexologists and was greatly influenced by their ideas. "As an anarchist," she told the German sexologist Magnus Hirschfeld, "my place has ever been with the persecuted."[15] Though both Tucker and Goldman agreed on the larger principles of absolute individual autonomy, the style of their delivery and their political rhetoric was markedly different. No single position on the ethical, cultural, and social place of homosexuality emerged from the anarchist movement. There was broad, never-ending, and impassioned debates about any number of critical questions, including issues dealing with sexuality. This book captures and analyzes the specific ways that the anarchists dealt with the question of same-sex love.

This is not a book about gay anarchists. While some of the anarchists discussed below were attracted to members of their own sex, for the most part, the anarchist sex radicals did not identify as homosexual, nor did they claim to speak for all homosexual men and women. Although I do consider the individual psychology of the activists I examine, for the most part, the focus is on the politics initiated and advanced by the anarchists. This is a study of public pronouncements, not private actions or feelings, except as they relate to the creation and shaping of political discourse.

The anarchist sex radicals were interested in the ethical, social, and cultural place of homosexuality within society, because that question lies at the nexus of individual freedom and state power. What use a person can make of his or her body is a fundamental question of any social or political order. The anarchist sex radicals examined the question of same-sex love because policemen, moral arbiters, doctors, clergymen, and other authorities sought to regulate homosexual behavior. This fact was most clearly demonstrated to the anarchists by Oscar Wilde's trial in 1895. In the decades that followed, the anarchists found a number of opportunities to revisit the critical questions raised by the state's attempt to restrict personal life. They reacted against the state's control and suppression of the free expression of erotic desire and individual autonomy.

While there has been some work done on the sexual politics of a number of European anarchists, historians of American anarchism have not fully appreciated the importance of the anarchists' politics of homosexuality.[16] This is not to say that the phenomenon has gone completely unnoticed. Several studies of anarchism, in particular biographies of Emma Goldman, have noted that the anarchists spoke out against the unjust treatment of gay men and lesbians.[17] For the most part, however, these studies do not examine the homosexual politics of Goldman and her comrades in any depth. More often than not, the anarchist discussion of homosexuality is noted briefly, just another example of anarchists defending individual rights. Of course, any study of anarchist sexual politics must begin with this basic truth, but it cannot end there. This book gives greater texture and richness to the largely anecdotal evidence that currently constitutes our understanding of the relationship between American anarchism and the politics of homosexuality. In the pages that follow, I examine why the anarchists began to address the social, ethical, and cultural place of homosexuality; how they went about doing so; what discourses—including sexology and literature—shaped their thinking on the matter; and to the extent we can know, what effect these efforts had.

Historians and political scientists working in the field of American gay and lesbian studies have also overlooked the work of the anarchist sex radicals. This is largely because the anarchists do not fit into the models of gay and lesbian identity and politics that have come to dominate historical and political discourse in the post-World War II era. Anarchists and the politics of homosexuality they produced are not easily assimilated into current social, cultural, and political categories. They were not "gay activists," nor did they operate within the bounds of liberal, civil rights discourse.

Those who study the history of the politics of homosexuality have tended to focus on those organizations and individuals who share the largely liberal, reformist outlook and tactics of post-World War II gay and lesbian politics. Hirschfeld, Ulrichs, and other European activists, for example, are easily assimilated into modern narratives of political progress and community-building, and their politics fit within the context of contemporary strategies for social change. Anarchists did not seek to reform legal codes, nor did they lobby politicians in order to get the police to stop raiding the clubs and bars frequented by homosexuals. Their vision for change was something more fundamental—a radical alternative to the principles of the established rules of the American social order. The sexual politics of anarchist sex radicals was embedded in the larger political discourse of anarchism—they wrote as anarchists, not as homosexual rights activists. This is not a study of gay and lesbian anarchists, rather it is an examination of what anarchist sex radicals had to say about the legal, cultural, and social status of same-sex love.

That historians have not fully documented the work of anarchists in relation to this issue is also due to the way that the Left developed in the United States. From the late-nineteenth century through the early decades of the twentieth century, anarchism was a vital force in the United States. Thousands were active in organizations that ranged from experimental schools to labor unions; anarchist journals, including *Liberty* and *Mother Earth*, enjoyed considerable readership; and thousands attended lectures by noted anarchists. But the anarchist movement in the United States never recovered from the suppression it endured during and immediately after World War I, when most of its journals were shut down and several of its most important activists were imprisoned and deported under the Sedition Act of 1918. In the 1920s and 1930s, what remained of the movement was overshadowed and dogged by the ascendant Communist Party (CP). The CP came to dominate the Left in a way that excluded and marginalized the ideas and perspectives of the anarchists. For many Americans the history of the Left is synonymous with the history of the CP or its various Marxist-Leninist critics. There is little room in the American historical imagination for libertarian socialism. As anarchism faded from collective memory, the accomplishments of those who fought for a more equitable social, economic, and sexual order languished in the archives. Though there was a resurgence of interest in anarchism and other forms of libertarian socialism in the late 1960s and early 1970s, many Americans—even those engaged in radical sexual politics—remain largely unaware of the rich political history forged by those who dedicated their lives to the anarchist movement. It is my hope that this book recovers and gives proper attention to the important role that anarchist sex radicals have played in the history of the Left and in the history of the politics of homosexuality.

Before outlining the chapters of the study that follows, I must address the question of language, terms, and definitions. Turn-of-the-century American anarchism was complex; there was no party platform that delineated the shared goals and methods that anarchists espoused. The anarchists were united in their defense of individual freedom and in their opposition to the state, but they were divided over the questions of ultimate goals, means, and methods. Anarchists passionately debated questions such as: Who should own the means of production? Is syndicalism compatible with anarchism? And what is the nature of free love? Most scholars consider anarchism a variant of socialism. It is important to remember, however, that while most anarchists are socialists, not all socialists are anarchists. When I use the term socialist I am more often than not describing those on the Left who did not reject government as a useful tool for social change. These would include members of the Socialist Party and the Communist Party, all of whom sought to achieve their goals by the seizure—though peaceful or violent means—of the state and by state appropriation of the means of production. Anarchists overwhelmingly rejected this strategy. "We do not," wrote Emma Goldman, "favor the socialistic idea of converting men and women into mere producing machines under the eye of a paternalistic government. We go to the opposite extreme and demand the fullest and most complete liberty for each and every person to work out his own salvation upon any lines that he pleases."[18] Opposition to the state is the fundamental principle upon which anarchism rests. I also use the term libertarian, which has a distinct set of meanings in the context of post-World War II American political thought. When I use it, I do so in the spirit that the turn-of-the-century anarchists used it—that is, to indicate a politics that rejected all forms of hierarchy and domination.

If anything, the language I use to describe same-sex sexuality is even more loaded. What might be called the terminology problem—whether to use the word gay, lesbian, homosexual, queer, homogenic, invert, sexual deviant, bisexual, or something else entirely to describe the subjects of one's study—haunts the study of the history of sexuality like no other field. Entire library shelves are filled with studies that carefully excavate the genesis, dispersion, and social effects of sexological, popular, and legal categories naming same-sex love. One can credit or blame the influence of post-structuralist theory for the fascination with language within queer studies. The question of terminology is made all the more difficult since there was no shared language used by those writing about same-sex sexuality—anarchists or otherwise—at the turn of twentieth century. The *mélange* of language employed at the time reflects the fact that there was a wide and oftentimes conflicting variety of ideas about the nature, cause and morality of same-sex behavior and identity. For some it was a horrible sin, one "not to be named." For others, it was a scientifically curious anomaly. For still others, it was a deeply rooted set of feelings and desires. The anarchists drew promiscuously from the wide array of terms available to them. Rather than attempting to impose a false unity on what was a fractured and often contradictory ideological landscape, I have decided to preserve the variety of terms used to describe same-sex love in this period. Of course it is impossible to not rely on any term to describe the subject of one's study, even if only for heuristic purposes. I have decided to rely mainly on the term "homosexual," a word that was coined in the late-nineteenth century, as a neutral descriptive term. I only rarely use the terms gay and lesbian. In instances where I employ the terms used by the person whose politics I'm examining, I submit them to analytic pressure. The somewhat unstable set of terms used in this study may be confusing, but in that, it reflects the temper and culture of the time.

The chapters of this book are organized thematically, rather than strictly chronologically. The first chapter is a broad introduction to the anarchist movement with particular emphasis on anarchist sexual politics. One cannot understand why the anarchists would be interested in the question of same-sex love without understanding who they were and what they stood for. The purpose of this chapter is to identify the variants of anarchism that existed during the period, as well as to describe the rough scope and reach of the movement, and place it within the context of American culture. I argue that sexuality was a key concern of English-language anarchists in the United States, which reflects the fact that their particular movement was more middle-class in composition than the non-English speaking sister movements in the United States and abroad. In the course of my discussion, I identify the main figures within the movement who wrote on the subject of homosexuality. I compare the anarchists' politics of sexuality with that of the socialists, and discuss early—pre-1895—treatments of homosexuality by English-language anarchists.

The second chapter examines the role that Oscar Wilde's trial played in the formation of a politics of homosexuality on the anarchist movement. Wilde's conviction and imprisonment brought a new and sharp focus on the issue of same-sex relations to a broad public; the imprisonment of one of the world's best-known celebrities was a scandal of enormous proportion. Conservative moralists on both sides of the Atlantic saw in Wilde's fall, a sign of incipient moral decadence that could only be held back by more diligent policing.

Nearly alone among their contemporaries, the anarchist sex radicals rallied to Wilde's defense. Benjamin R. Tucker was an especially keen defender of Wilde during his most desperate hours. Wilde made homosexuality a political issue for the anarchists in a way it had not previously been. What had been a very minor concern of anarchist sex radicals was transformed into an issue that received increasing levels of attention. The Wilde trial highlighted the way in which the state sought to control and regulate the free expression of erotic desire. In the years after the trial, Wilde remained a key figure in anarchist discourse on homosexuality.

The third chapter examines how Walt Whitman's work played in anarchist discussions of the moral and cultural place of same-sex love. In the late-nineteenth century, anarchists discussing Whitman's work in regards to sexual politics did so with reference to heterosexuality. But by the early-twentieth century this began to change, indicating and reflecting the increased awareness and salience that the issue of same-sex love was developing in the larger culture. In this chapter, I am particularly interested in the work of an anarchist named John William Lloyd. During much of his life Lloyd described himself as a "Whitmanite." He saw in Whitman's poetry and prose—and the work of Whitman's emulator and admirer, Edward Carpenter—a language with which to model same-sex love. But the rapidly changing cultural and sexual landscape of the early-twentieth century made Lloyd's rhetorical assertions problematic as we shall see. The last part of this chapter examines how Emma Goldman used Whitman to address the issue of homosexuality. By comparing the various ways that different anarchist sex radicals used Whitman's writings in their politics I will examine how culture and politics inform each other.

The fourth chapter examines the way that anarchist sex radicals used discussions of prison as a framework for their politics of homosexuality. Prison has been, and remains, a key institution through which Americans seek to understand homosexual behavior and identity. As early as the 1820s, American prison reformers and prison authorities discussed homosexual behavior among inmates. Overwhelmingly, these reformers and administrators were concerned with stamping out what they perceived to be a vicious and immoral practice. What is striking about the anarchists' discussion of prison homosexuality is their refusal to see it simply as an emblematic manifestation of a repressive institution. The anarchists understood the phenomenon of sex in prison through the prism of their larger sexual politics. In this chapter, I spend considerable time examining Alexander Berkman's *Prison Memoirs of an Anarchist*, one of the most important texts to emerge from the pre-WWI anarchist movement. While this book has rightly been appreciated as a political work concerned with prisons and the larger ideas of anarchism I argue that its sexual politics—specifically the way in which it examines same-sex love—is under-appreciated. Berkman's memoir is among the most important texts dealing with same-sex love written in the United States in the first half of the twentieth century.

The fifth chapter examines how the anarchists drew upon and helped shape the discourse of sexology. The anarchist sex radicals were drawn to the work of those sexologists—like Magnus Hirschfeld and Edward Carpenter—that they felt reflected their own views. Anarchists believed that the clear light of rationality, when applied to the question of sexuality, would sweep away the vestiges of "Puritanism" in the United States. In this chapter I pay special attention to the speaking tours of Emma Goldman, who, from 1913 onwards, regularly included talks on homosexuality in her lecture repertoire. Goldman's speeches were part of her effort to educate about the nature of homosexual desire and to inform the public about what life was like for homosexual men and women. Her lectures and their goals were part and parcel of the sexological project, which contended that, through sex education and the scientific study of desire, social values and mores could be reshaped. Goldman's lectures were unprecedented in their scope and reach and were a critical part of the anarchist politics of homosexuality. She was an extremely charismatic speaker and her discussions of the social and moral place of homosexuality were very popular. I will examine how Goldman framed her discussions of homosexuality and how her talks were received.

In chapter six I examine the terrible impact that WWI had on the anarchist movement. During the war, anarchist journals were shut down and, in the immediate aftermath of the war, several anarchist sex radicals were deported. The rise of the Communist Party also damaged the anarchists, as CP activists went out of their way to marginalize them. The communists succeeded in seizing the Left. The anarchist work being done around sexual politics was a casualty of this political and cultural calamity. But despite the devastating impact of the war, a number of anarchists tried to continue their work, and the ideas generated by the pre-WWI anarchist sex radicals persisted as important influences on the lives of intellectuals, bohemians, and activists. The lives and works of Kenneth Rexroth, Elsa Gidlow, Jan Gay, and others are examined as a way to capture these patterns of persistence.

In the late 1960s and early 1970s, Anarchism enjoyed a revival in the Western World and that is explored in my conclusion. This second wave of activism constitutes a new phase in anarchist history that lies beyond the scope of this study. Nonetheless, I hint at the complex relationship that the "New Radicals," as George Woodcock called them, had with their predecessors. I am, of course, particularly interested in how the sexual politics of anarchism intersected with the politics of homosexuality. I analyze this intersection within the context of the dramatically different sexual and cultural realities of pre-WWI and post-Stonewall America. In the contemporary political world, "gay" and "lesbian" are the dominant terms to relate the politics of homosexuality, whereas in the world that I am concerned with here, "anarchism" was the key term. This reversal of terms—and the massive social, political, and cultural changes that this reversal signals—complicates any claims for simple continuity between the two periods. The gay liberation and lesbian feminist politics forged in the late 1960s were certainly influenced by the work of the pre-WWI anarchist sex radicals, but they represent a distinct and new phase in the politics of anarchism and homosexuality.

CHAPTER ONE:

"THE RIGHT TO COMPLETE LIBERTY OF ACTION": ANARCHISM, SEXUALITY, AND AMERICAN CULTURE

IN 1912, WILL DURANT left a Catholic seminary and joined the teaching staff of the Ferrer Center, an anarchist school and cultural center located in New York City. The Ferrer Center, which opened in 1911, was an early countercultural institution created by turn-of-the-century anarchists who sought to construct a new world in what they saw as the decaying and corrupted body of the existing order. Durant would eventually become one of America's most popular historians, but at the time he was a young man in search of himself. Durant was drawn to the political and intellectual life of the Ferrer Center, a perfect counterpoint to the seminary life he turned his back on.

In addition to his teaching duties, Durant was asked to deliver a series of lectures on the topic of sex. His talks included a presentation on free love as well as lectures titled "Prostitution, Its History, Causes, and Effects," "Homosexualism," and "Sex and Religion."[1] Durant's lectures proved to be quite popular. For example, his discussion of "Sex and Religion" attracted a crowd of "some sixty anarchists, socialists, single-taxers, and free-lovers," a diversity of political opinion and perspective that reflected the heterodox ideological culture of the anarchist movement. His argument was provocative: Christianity and other religious traditions were shot through with erotic currents and symbols. According to Durant, audience members "were glad to hear me dilate on sex as one of the sources of religion, and to learn that the phallus had in many places and forms been worshipped as a symbol of divine power."[2]

Unlike the people at the Ferrer Center, the leaders of the Catholic Church, with whom Durant was so recently associated, were not amused. Shortly after his talk, Durant's brother, Sam, called to tell him that the *Newark Evening News* "has a story, on the front page, about the Bishop excommunicating you because of your lecture last Sunday."[3] Durant's interpretation of scripture did not amuse the Bishop and he acted to expel this newly minted heretic. By choosing to speak at the Ferrer Center, Durant forfeited his respectability and joined the ranks of anarchists, bohemians, disaffected intellectuals, and others interested in exploring new ways of living and loving.

We do not know what the Bishop thought about Durant giving a lecture on "Homosexualism," because in his public comments regarding Durant's ex-communication, he remarked only on the lectures about religion. Unfortunately, there is no known transcript of Durant's address, though he did draw on a number of discourses and was inspired by others as he drafted his speech on same-sex love. He seems also to have had a personal interest in the subject of same-sex eroticism—his choice of the topic is proof enough of that. In one of his memoirs, Durant recounts that just prior to taking the job at the Ferrer Center, he shared a room with "a handsome Neapolitan, with the figure of Michelangelo's David." His admiration for his roommate's body later struck him as having an erotic component: "There must have been a trace of the homosexual in me," he mused, "for I enjoyed looking at him, especially when he undressed for a bath." The living David that he shared a room with was not the only man whose beauty Durant remarked upon: "I must have surprised my intimates," he confessed, by the frequency with which he voiced his "admiration for the male body."[4] Whether or not Durant acted on his feelings is unclear, but he was interested enough in the topic to have informed himself and to be willing to speak to an audience about it.[5]

In constructing his speech Durant may have consulted with some of the leading figures associated with the Ferrer Center, a number of whom—including Emma Goldman and Alexander Berkman—had already or would shortly deliver public presentations on the topic of same-sex love. There were many anarchists, as well as those drawn to the anarchist movement, who were interested in the social, cultural, and ethical status of homosexuality. For example, Alden Freeman, himself a homosexual, donated frequently to anarchist causes and paid Durant's salary at the Ferrer Center. There were many people at the Ferrer Center who could have spoken knowledgeably with Durant about his lectures.

We do know that Durant drew upon the nascent science of sexology in exploring his topic. His use of the term "homosexualism" indicates as much. Durant's neologism is a variant of the word "homosexual" itself, a new term coined in 1869 by the Hungarian sexologist Karoly Maria Benkert, and not introduced into English until the 1890s.[6] Emma Goldman, Leonard Abbott, or other Ferrer Center figures may well have introduced Durant to this relatively new scientific literature. It is highly doubtful that he had encountered sexological discourse at the seminary. Durant felt comfortable in using such new terms because he could expect that his Ferrer Center audience, interested as they were in the subject of sex, would be familiar with the new terminology being coined by sexologists.

Durant's talk on "homosexualism" did not elicit a particularly strong reaction from the Ferrer Center audience. No one moved to excommunicate the eager new faculty member for bringing up the subject of same-sex love. By contrast, Durant's other presentations sparked lively discussions. Following Durant's talk on "Sex and Religion," for example, his audience asked "hundreds of questions" of him, but when it came to the lecture on "homosexualism," the Ferrer Center audience had relatively little to say.[7] The idea that "almost every symbol in religious history, from the serpent of paradise to the steeples on the churches in nearby Fifth Avenue, had a phallic origin" was a novelty for Durant's audience.[8] The fact that two people of the same sex might love each other and seek to express that love through sex was not, apparently, remarkable.

The relatively sedate reaction of his audience indicates that Durant's lecture was not the first time that anarchists had publicly discussed the issue of homosexuality—it was a topic common enough to be unremarkable. For decades before Durant came to the Ferrer Center, anarchist sex radicals had defended the right of men and women to love whomever they wished. Nearly ten years before Durant gave his lecture, Emma Goldman—one of the era's best know anarchists—stated plainly in a talk she gave in Chicago, that "the sex organs as well as all the other organs of the human body are the property of the individual possessing them, and that individual and no other must be the sole authority and judge over his or her acts."[9] This was a commonly held position in the English-language anarchist movement. The 1895 trial of Oscar Wilde gave the issue of homosexuality a salience it lacked among American anarchists, and it was at least from that point onward that the basic principle that each person was "the sole authority and judge of his or her acts" was applied by anarchists to the question of same-sex relations. In the aftermath of the Wilde trial, anarchist sex radicals argued that as long as the sex was consensual the gender of the participants was beside the point. Talk of homosexuality was old hat for those who attended lectures at the Ferrer Center—nothing to get worked up about and certainly not a topic that generated scandal or disapproval.

The blasé attitude of Durant's Ferrer Center audience that night stands in stark contrast to how the topic of homosexuality was greeted in other forums of the day. That is, when it was discussed at all. Durant's lecture was, in fact, a rather rare occurrence. Outside of anarchist meetings and lecture halls, there were few public venues where the topic of homosexuality was discussed. More importantly, the political, social, and cultural context of the public discussions that did occur, was radically different than that atmosphere in which Durant spoke.

In 1907, for example, Dr. Georg Merzbach, a colleague of the German sexologist and homosexual rights activist Magnus Hirschfeld, traveled to the United States and delivered a series of lectures on what he called "our area of specialization." In March of that year, Merzbach spoke before the New York Society of Medical Jurisprudence. His "select audience" included lawyers and doctors, as well as "three ministers" that he took pains to invite. Merzbach spoke before doctors, psychiatrists, lawyers, and clergymen because these professions had a vested interest in the topic of sexuality; they crafted policy and practice that shaped the lives of people whose emotional and erotic commitments revolved around members of their own sex. Despite the novelty of his address—or perhaps because of it—Merzbach was able to tell Hirschfeld that he "made a truly sensational impression" on the gathered professionals. Unlike the members of the Ferrer Center, Merzbach's audience spent nearly two hours asking questions of their visitor. Though some audience members advised their colleagues to act with tolerance when dealing with homosexuals, others felt homosexuality called for drastic countermeasures. Merzbach fielded questions from doctors and other professional eager to fine-tune their methods of intervention.[10] These included: "Doesn't homosexuality lead ultimately to paranoia or other psychoses?" and "Can homosexuality be eradicated by castration?"

The people who founded the Ferrer Center were opposed to the kind of power wielded by those who attended Merzbach's lecture. Merzbach's audience was made up of professionals who operated the regulatory institutions that meted out judgment, penalty, and cure to patients, prisoners, and supplicants seeking redemption from illness, crime, and sin. Merzbach's audience members made their living by establishing and enforcing norms of human behavior. Durant's Ferrer Center audience approached the topic of sexuality, politics, and education from a radically different perspective—one grounded in the political ideals of absolute freedom of individual expression and association. The anarchists had a critique of the kinds of power exercised by the elites who helped formulate and enforce the punitive, negative view of same-sex love, as expressed in the questions posed to Merzbach by some of his audience members. The "sex act," according to Goldman, "is simply the execution of certain natural functions of the body," and since "we do not pay or consult a preacher or politician" when choosing to breath, walk or otherwise use the body, why should people do so when using the sexual organs?[11] The anarchists would reject the idea that the professionals that attended Merzbach's presentation should have the power or authority to make decisions about the most intimate parts of lives other than their own.

Durant's talk on "homosexualism" reflected the larger mission of the Ferrer Center. The men and women who visited the Ferrer Center attended lectures on sexuality in order to better appreciate and understand the diversity of human life and expression. The activists who ran the Ferrer Center sponsored lectures on a wide variety of topics in the hopes of furthering the coming of a society in which no one would govern the life choices of others. By rejecting all forms of authoritarian hierarchy, the anarchists hoped to craft a world in which work, culture, and love were freely expressed and enjoyed. They envisioned a world where each person was her or his own master, where no outside authority would constrain the actions of others. Durant's audience attended his talk not because they had a professional stake in the subject of the lecture, but because the topic of sex, variation, and free expression interested them. When it came to the exploration of the ethical, social, and cultural place of same-sex love in American culture, there was a sharp divide between the libertarian atmosphere of the Ferrer Center and the more censorious lecture halls of organizations like the New York Society of Medical Jurisprudence.

The anarchist sex radicals addressed the subject of homosexuality in the context of a radical political movement. Homosexuality was not the only aspect of sexuality that the anarchists debated. In accordance with their ideas about self-rule, for example, they rejected marriage, which they viewed as a coercive institution policed by both church and state. Rather than be forced to submit passion to the cookie cutter pattern of marriage, the anarchists argued that individuals should have the possibility of creating their own relationships. "Commonly calling themselves free lovers," writes historian Margaret Marsh, "anarchists believed that adults could decide what type of sexual association they desired and were capable of choosing the nature and the duration of that association."[12] Unlike many of their contemporaries, the anarchists did not insist that the only legitimate sexual relationships were those between a man and woman bound to each other in holy matrimony. Nor did the anarchists tie sexual expression to reproduction. At a time when it was illegal to circulate birth control information through the mail, the anarchists were early and loud supporters of women's right to control their fertility. More than a few anarchists—among them Goldman and Ben Reitman—spent time in jail for their efforts to end what they saw as the injustices of the American system of laws and values that regulated sexual behavior. It was in the context of their overall critique of American sexual mores and rules—and in particular their rejection of marriage and their advocacy of free love—that the anarchists considered the question of homosexuality.

In order to understand how it came to pass that homosexuality was a topic of political debate and discussion amongst the anarchists, one must first understand what the anarchists stood for and what their movement looked like. What follows is a brief overview of the main characteristics of the movement, with a special emphasis on the sexual politics developed by the anarchist sex radicals. Later chapters examine the issue of how these men and women dealt with the issue of homosexuality in more depth, here the reasons for the topic's relative importance to the anarchists will be outlined. No other movement in the period was as focussed on exploring and defending the social, cultural, and political rights of men and women whose erotic lives were focused on members of their own sex. The anarchist sex radicals were unique among their contemporaries because they dealt with issues of burning importance for people whose voices were seldom heard and little respected. They were the first Americans to articulate a politics of homosexuality.

The sexual politics of the anarchists reflected the larger political values and goals of the movement. Anarchists, writes Richard Sonn, "sought freedom from domination and the right to determine his or her own destiny in workplace, family, and school, while rejecting all forms of hierarchy—that of the academy, of the church, of social class, of 'correct speech' as defined by elites—as well as those coercive arms of the state, the army, the police, and the judiciary."[13] Writing in 1910 for the *Encyclopedia Britannica*, Peter Kropotkin, a Russian nobleman, who renounced his title and became one of the best-known anarchists of his time, attempted to define anarchism for a general readership: Anarchists, he wrote, advocate a "theory of life and conduct under which society is conceived without government—harmony in such a society being obtained...by free agreements...constituted for the sake of production and consumption, as also for the satisfaction of the infinite variety of need and aspirations of a civilized being." This would be a society run according to the lights of those who constituted it; they would obey no authority other than their own consciences. In Kropotkin's words, "man would not be...limited in the exercise of his will by

fear of punishment, or by obedience towards individuals or metaphysical enti-
ties, which both lead to depression of initiative and servility of mind." Freed
from religious and secular law and other regulations, people would be able to
construct lives that best reflect and fulfill their desires. Like most anarchists,
Kropotkin does not give any concrete guidelines for what an anarchist society might look like. Future arrangements, he contended, would "result from
an ever-changing adjustment and readjustment of equilibrium between the
multitude of forces and influences" in society.[14] According to the anarchists, all
manner of needs and desires would find expression in the future society operated under anarchist principles.

In the United States, two variants of anarchism attracted significant membership: communist anarchism and individualist anarchism. The two strains differed from each other in several ways, most notably in their ideas about property ownership and in the means of bringing about social change. Communist
anarchists—such as Emma Goldman and Alexander Berkman—believed that
property should be held in common, while individualist anarchists—like Benjamin R. Tucker—believed that individuals should have control over the means
of production. Crudely put, Goldman and Berkman advocated the shared life
of the commune, while Tucker's ideal world consisted of a network of rug-
ged individualists. What also set them apart was that some communist anarchists countenanced the use of political violence, while individualists tended
to eschew violence entirely. Not all anarchists can be fit into such neat categories. Though the distinctions between communist- and individualist-anar-
chism was of utmost importance to some, a number of anarchists, including
figures like John William Lloyd, downplayed the differences between the two
camps. Lloyd's ideas were a mixture of communalism, individualism, and ideas
drawn from other strands of reformist and radical thought. Though the varia-
tions among communist and individualists were important, the basic principles
of self-rule, freedom of individual expression, opposition to hierarchy, and the
defense of social and individual dissent were the essential heart of anarchism.

It is difficult to construct a simple profile of those who joined the anarchist
movement—anarchists found converts among the poor and the wealthy, native-born Americans and recent immigrants. Some generalizations, however,
can be made with relative certainty. Anarchists were concentrated in cities in
the Northeast, Midwest, and Pacific Coast areas, though there were pockets of
activism along the industrial frontier in the Western states. In the United States,
communist anarchists tended to be immigrants and more often from the working class, while individualist anarchists were often native-born, middle-class
Americans.

The anarchists typically enjoyed limited success among organized, native-born workers, but what they lacked in numbers was offset by the ideological influence they were able to exert. According to political scientists Seymour Martin Lipset and Gary Marks, prior to World War I, many American labor activists "regarded the state as an enemy and felt that government-owned industry would be much more difficult for workers and unions to resist than private companies."[15] Samuel Gompers, the legendary leader of the American Federation of Labor (AFL) much of its early history described himself as "three quarters anarchist."[16] Gompers was notoriously anti-radical and was no fan of the anarchists, but his statement indicates the degree to which antistatist thought circulated in labor circles. The historian J. F. Finn argues that anarchists played a role in pushing the AFL to ban "party politics from the deliberations of the [union's] conventions."[17] Ideologically, if not numerically, anarchism was a force among labor's advocates.

There were few anarchists in the South. The southern states were not a hospitable environment for anarchism or any other form of radical politics that threatened the racial and class order established in the post-Reconstruction years. Because the South attracted few immigrants, violently suppressed activism by African-Americans and other working class people, and had a relatively small and unsophisticated middle class, there was not the same constituency for anarchism as there was in cities of the North and West. Emma Goldman, for example, very rarely ventured below the Mason-Dixon Line during her many years as a public speaker. With this in mind, it is unsurprising, given the concentration of African-Americans in the South, that there were few black anarchists. In this, anarchists were no different than the Socialist Party or other Left groups of the pre-WWI era.

Compared to other branches of the Left during the period, women were well represented among the anarchists. This was especially true in the English language anarchist movement. Women served both in leadership positions and among the rank and file. Rather than being relegated to "women's auxiliaries," as they were in so much of the turn-of-the-century Left, women were at the center of the anarchist movement.

Anarchist women were especially important in the construction of the idea of free love and in the critique of oppressive gender patterns. At the heart of anarchist sexual politics, was a sharp rebuke to the notion that women were less sexual than men and that they were incapable of making decisions for themselves. This was largely a sexual politics constructed by anarchist women, but it resonated across gender lines and was popular among anarchist sex radicals. For example, when the idea that women had little sexual passion—certainly far less than men—had great currency, the journal *Liberty* rejected that assumption and made no distinction between female and male sexual agency. Tucker and his largely male contributors readily acknowledged that women were quite capable of lustful thoughts and deeds, and that, furthermore, such actions did not call into question their moral standing. They explicitly rejected the notion that women were morally superior to men by virtue of their supposed lack of passion. Historian, Margaret Marsh writes of *Liberty* that it "stood consistently behind the campaign to eliminate the double standard and to remove any social stigma from the women who chose to exercise their sexual freedom."[18]

In addition to taking a positive stand for women's right to pursue sexual pleasure, the anarchists were sharply critical of the hierarchical and patriarchal nature of marriage. Anarchist, Voltairine de Cleyre, compared the life of a married woman to that of a "bonded slave, who takes her master's name, her master's bread, and serves her master's passion."[19] According to historian Hal Sears, "The word 'free' in free love held two meanings for woman: the freedom not to surrender her vagina to anybody, regardless of their relationship or supposed duty, and the freedom to offer it at will."[20] The radicalism of anarchist sexual politics—the very thing that made it open to the defense of same-sex love—is grounded in a feminist analysis of sexuality.

While the various ethnic groups active in the anarchist movement did cooperate at times, for the most part they remained divided along linguistic and cultural lines. For example, in 1900, when activists from the United States attended an anarchist convention in Europe, they discussed the different ethnic groups separately, acknowledging the distinct dynamics of each community. In her report to the general assembly, Emma Goldman carefully distinguished between what she termed the "American" movement, meaning the English-language movement, and the "foreign," or immigrant movements, in the United States. James F. Morton told his European comrades that "the methods of propaganda differ greatly according to the place, language, and nationality" of the anarchist groups.[21]

The immigrant anarchists largely conducted their political and cultural activities in their native tongues. To illustrate, there were Spanish, Russian, German, Yiddish, Italian, and English anarchist journals published in the United States, and leading figures within the respective language groups largely communicated in the language of their birth country. This meant that the movement was effectively separated into language groups. Though Emma Goldman and Alexander Berkman delivered lectures in a variety of languages their audience members would have been lost had they come to the lecture hall on the wrong night. With few exceptions—Voltairine de Cleyre, the most notable—the native-born anarchists were linguistically separated from the newer immigrant groups, like the Italians, Eastern European Jews, and Russians. While some key figures like Goldman bridged the movement's linguistic divides, most anarchists had limited contact with comrades from other language groups.

Though the decades of the late-nineteenth and early-twentieth centuries were—in the words of historian Richard Sonn—the "heyday of the international anarchist movement," it is difficult to arrive at hard numbers of anarchists.[22] Margaret Marsh estimates that in any given year between 1880 and 1920 "there were at least fifteen- to twenty-thousand committed anarchists in the United States, and perhaps an additional thirty- to fifty-thousand sympathizers."[23] Since there was most likely a high rate of turnover in the movement, hundreds of thousands of people became familiar with the ideas, goals, and leaders of the movement.

But the influence of anarchism cannot simply be measured by tallying up numbers of activists. The anarchists' influence on American social and cultural thought was disproportionate to the size of the movement itself. Writers, artists, bohemians, radicals, intellectuals, and reformers—among them Jack London, Alice Hamilton, Eugene O'Neill, Margaret Sanger, Hutchins Hapgood, Frank Harris, Robert Henri, William James, and Margaret Anderson—were all drawn to the ideas and passionate spirit of the anarchists. In this regard, the anarchist movement of the turn-of-the-century can be compared to the Communist party of the 1930s. Like the Communists, the anarchists "considered themselves revolutionaries, marching...along the path of human liberation." Their "deep faith in their cause and its ultimate triumph" created a powerful attraction.[24] Such dedication and idealism drew the attention of many outside the movement; fellow travelers lent their support and helped magnify anarchism's influence. The dedicated core of anarchist activists was complemented by a much larger shadow-movement of people who might not have been willing to embrace the full scope of anarchist ideology, but nonetheless acknowledged the impact and relevance of its critiques of power.

The participation of a few anarchists in some of the more spectacular acts of political violence strongly colored their reputation. Anarchists, for example, were blamed for the Haymarket Tragedy of 1886, a confrontation in Chicago between workers and police that resulted in the death of eight police officers and an unknown number of demonstrators. Eight anarchists were arrested and convicted for their alleged participation in the incident. One of those convicted committed suicide in prison, four were hanged, and three spent years in prison before being pardoned by Governor John Peter Altgeld. The figure of the anarchist as a swarthy, deranged bomb-throwing terrorist was commonplace in Western culture at the time. Some, like psychiatrist Cesare Lomobroso went so far as to argue that "anarchists like other criminals suffered from hereditary bodily anomalies," comparing their movement to "a form of epidemic disease."[25]

The Haymarket Tragedy and the ensuing trial engendered a wave of anti-anarchist and anti-socialist feeling. Anarchism's influence among members of the native-born working class suffered a severe setback. Middle class and elite Americans were even more horrified by the thought of what might happen should the anarchists succeed in their nefarious plots. The reaction of many Americans can be gauged by the behavior of the young Theodore Roosevelt, who was in the Dakotas trying his hand at ranching at the time of the Haymarket Tragedy. When news of Chicago's events reached the range, Roosevelt gathered together his cowboy friends and burned the accused in effigy. According to Paul Avrich, the reaction to the Haymarket Tragedy constitutes the first Red Scare in American history.[26]

This would not be the last time that Roosevelt fulminated against the anarchists. In 1901, a young anarchist named Leon Czolgosz assassinated President McKinley, and though he insisted that he acted alone, his actions set off another wave of anti-anarchist hysteria, which resulted in the arrest of a number of anarchists. Theodore Roosevelt, now president of the United States, attacked what he viewed as a dangerous threat to the nation: "The anarchist," he declared, "is a criminal whose perverted instincts lead him to prefer confusion and chaos to the most beneficent form of social order… The anarchist is everywhere not merely the enemy of system and of progress, but the deadly foe of liberty." Roosevelt called for vigorous repression of anarchism. "No man or body of men preaching anarchist doctrines should be allowed at large …Anarchist speeches, writings, and meetings are essentially seditious and treasonable." In order to stem the spread of these seditious ideas, Roosevelt called for changes in the immigration laws. "We should aim," he proposed, "to exclude absolutely not only all persons who are known to be believers in anarchistic principles or members of anarchistic societies, but also all persons who are of low moral tendency or unsavory reputation."[27] Roosevelt's view of the anarchists as a kind of political and moral infection that required containment and drastic surgical cure was commonly held. Margaret Marsh argues that, "Americans viewed anarchists as the harbingers of chaos."[28]

In order to understand Roosevelt's outrage with the anarchists it is important to understand that, in addition to presenting a physical danger, the president felt the anarchists were a threat to the nation's moral fiber. Along with political disorder, the anarchists were associated with sexual chaos. The idea that anarchism would bring about an erotic revolution was both fascinating and deeply frightening to many Americans. Newspaper accounts denouncing the anarchists rarely missed the opportunity to note that they were "free lovers," whose ideas threatened the sanctity of the home and hearth. Writing in the *American Law Review* in 1902, James Beck described the anarchists as "mental and moral perverts." In his 1901 address, Roosevelt portrayed the anarchists as a moral danger to the country and associated them with sexual disorder; the anarchists, Roosevelt thundered, were "perverted" and equal to "persons who are of low moral tendency."[29] Of course, Roosevelt and Beck's statements came immediately following McKinley's assassination, but their words also reflect the fact that the anarchists devoted considerable resources—in lectures, publications, and political organizing—to addressing how power operates at the most intimate levels of human life. In their attempt to construct a new sexual ethics, anarchists addressed a wide variety of topics including birth control, marriage, obscenity, and homosexuality. "The sex question," Emma Goldman believed, was "one of the most vital of our time."[30] Goldman and her comrades challenged the notion that the only legitimate form of erotic expression was sex between married people, ideally for procreative purposes. To those who felt that sexual conduct outside the bonds of marriage was a danger to the social order, the anarchists were not merely harbingers of political violence, they were, themselves, symptoms of moral decay and sexual chaos.

Roosevelt was not alone in noting the anarchists' interest in sexuality, though not all observers were as critical as he was. The writer Hutchins Hapgood, who was a great admirer of the anarchists, wrote that they were "extreme rebels against sex conventions."[31] A good deal of his attraction to the anarchists was due to their rejection of what he felt were the stifling sexual norms of his upbringing, against which he was rebelling. Some accused the anarchists of doing little else but seeking sexual liberation. Hapgood's contemporary, Floyd Dell, observed that the anarchists, unlike the state socialists, "have left the industrial field more and more and have entered into other kinds of propaganda." They "have especially 'gone in for kissing games.'"[32] The anarchists, according to Dell, "seemed to lay more stress on the importance of Freedom in the relations of men and women than in the other relations of human society."[33] Dell's comment regarding anarchist "kissing games" was made as an epigrammatic criticism, but it reflects a basic truth: Anarchism was the only political movement of the time to treat issues of sexual liberation as fundamental to the project of human emancipation. The anarchists, according to historian David Kennedy, "demanded not only political but also aesthetic and especially psychological revolution. And the cutting psychological theories the anarchists consistently invoked aimed at one central fact of life: sex."[34]

The fact that anarchists were associated with revolt in matters social, as well as political, constituted part of their appeal. The mixture of sexual transgression, political upheaval, and idealism was a powerful draw for middle-class people wanting to experience psychological freedom. Young Durant felt a frisson of liberation when, shortly after leaving the seminary, he found himself delivering talks on sex at the Ferrer Center. The breathless description of adventures that appear in his autobiographical works give ample evidence of the excitement Durant felt when he joined the anarchist ranks. Others felt similarly.

In the autobiographical novel, *A Girl Among the Anarchists*, Isabel Meredith describes the appeal of anarchism in terms that illustrate the degree to which it was seen as a path to personal liberation. "The right to complete liberty of action," Meredith writes, "the conviction that morality is relative and personal and can never be imposed from without…and that consequently no man has a right to judge his fellow; such and similar doctrines which I heard frequently upheld, impressed me deeply."[35] Meredith was the pseudonym of Helen and Olivia Rossetti, the nieces of the English painter Dante Gabriel Rossetti, who were active in the anarchist movement in their youth. The Rossettis edited *The Torch: A Revolutionary Journal of International Socialism* that featured contributions from Emma Goldman, George Bernard Shaw, Emile Zola, and Ford Maddox Ford. The Rossettis, Durant, and other men and women on both sides of the Atlantic were attracted to anarchism because it served them, in the words of the Rossettis, in their attempt to "free [themselves] from all the ideas, customs, and prejudices which usually influence [their] class."[36]

The volatile mixture of personal emancipation, sexual liberation, and political radicalism also colored Hutchins Hapgood's interest in anarchism. Hapgood wrote several works on anarchism and befriended leading figures in the movement. Goldman wryly commented that her friend would not have known what to write about were it "not for the radicals." Hapgood writes "well enough," she teased, "but is so poor in material."[37] Hapgood was drawn to the anarchists because they symbolized revolt in all facets of life. Hapgood wrote so often and so favorably of the anarchists that Mabel Dodge Luhan claimed that "he did a great deal to make their cause weaker, in a way, because by writing sympathetically of them, he helped remove the terror of them from people's mind."[38] But it was precisely anarchism's aura of transgression that drew Hapgood. "People who are regarded as evil," Hapgood wrote, "have often had for me a strange and haunting appeal."[39] Mary Berenson, who like Luhan gathered artists and intellectuals around her, claimed that Hapgood was "seeking for God and the

Absolute among thieves, anarchists, prostitutes, and pederasts."[40] Berenson's juxtaposition of anarchists, with prostitutes and pederasts indicates the degree to which political revolt was associated with sexual deviance and how both phenomenons were linked to anarchism. The mixture of social revolt, sexual deviance and idealism associated with anarchism was a powerful psychological resource for those seeking to escape conventional lives. It was precisely this complex mix of associations that drew Hapgood to the feet of Goldman and her colleagues.

We should not, however, confuse the ways that the anarchists were perceived—even by some of their admirers—with how the anarchists saw themselves. Anarchist sex radicals did not believe they were acting to bring about disorder—they wished to construct a new social and sexual order, and dealt with issues of sexuality in a serious and sustained way. Nor were all anarchists enthusiastic about pursuing sex and gender politics. In fact, some of the most famous anarchists of the nineteenth- and early-twentieth centuries were extremely conservative in their sexual politics. The mid-century, French anarchist Pierre-Joseph Proudhon, for example, thought women's emancipation and birth control would usher in a "Pornocracy," and his unpublished writings contain frequent condemnations of sodomy.[41] Johann Most, a leading figure in American's German-language anarchist movement and a contemporary of Tucker and Goldman, equaled Proudhon in misogyny and antipathy toward sexual liberalism.[42]

Peter Kropotkin, though hardly as vehement as Proudhon or Most, shared their suspicions of sexual politics. When Will Durant, then on a trip to Europe, told Kropotkin that he intended to visit the eminent sexologist Havelock Ellis, Kropotkin advised Durant not to go, warning that "the detailed study of sex... always led to morbidity and perversion."[43] Kropotkin issued a similar warning to Emma Goldman when she was visiting London. In both cases Kropotkin spoke in vain; neither Durant nor Goldman heeded his advice to avoid the likes of Ellis.

In the United States, class and ethnicity—themselves largely overlapping categories—often indicated whether or not a particular anarchist chose to put sexuality at the heart of her or his politics. In general, working-class, immigrant anarchists were less interested in sexual politics while their largely middle-class, English-speaking peers were more enthusiastic in their advocacy of free love and more expansive in their interpretation of what that might allow. Leading individualist anarchists, like Ezra and Angela Heywood and Moses Harman, for example, devoted much more attention to the subject of sex, the rights of women, and the politics of culture than did communist anarchist leaders like

Johann Most. Though this is a somewhat large generalization and therefore limited in its veracity. Some immigrant, working-class anarchists cared passionately about the application of anarchist principles to private life. Robert Reitzel, for example, the editor of the Detroit based, German anarchist publication *Der arme Teufel* (The Poor Devil) was, according to his biographer, "one of the first in America to speak positively of homosexuality."[44] And leading communist anarchists in the English language movement, including Berkman and Goldman, devoted considerable resources to the pursuit of questions of sexuality. Goldman, in fact, was one the most famous sex radicals of her day, a name to shock, delight, and conjure with.

In the United States, many of the English-language anarchists—whether communists or individualists—shared an interest in the politics of sexuality. This distinguished them from most of their peers in Europe and from their non-English speaking comrades in the US. Harry Kelly wrote in *Mother Earth* about this disjuncture between the "European" and the "American" movements. "The sex question," Kelly wrote, "is probably more in evidence in the American Anarchist movement than in the European." Though Kelly described the ideological division as being one between the continents, it applied perfectly well to the different language groups within the United States—"European" meaning foreign-born, non-English-speaking anarchists, and "American" meaning the largely native-born, English-speaking movement. Kelly, who titled his essay, "Anarchism—A Plea for the Impersonal," was not altogether pleased with this development. He was troubled that the foreign-language anarchists "concern themselves more with the mass movement than we do; they fight the capitalist; we fight Comstock."[45] While a number of English-language anarchists shared Kelly's misgivings that so much attention was being devoted to sexual politics, the majority of Kelly's comrades were less troubled. The pages of *Mother Earth*, where Kelly's piece appeared, are filled with essays exploring various aspects of the "sex question," including articles on birth control, free love, sexual jealousy, and homosexuality.[46] In spite of Kelly's "plea," the English-language anarchists in the United States were noted for the resources and time they devoted to applying anarchist principles to the politics of personal life.

The issue of homosexuality proved to be a particularly contentious one among the various anarchist communities. Goldman, for example, was constantly fighting what she called the "'respectability' in our ranks." Her Italian and Jewish anarchist comrades "condemned me bitterly," she wrote, "because I had taken up the cause of the Homo Sexuals [sic] and Lesbians as a persecuted faction in the human family." Goldman rejected their criticism as stemming from an overly "economic" view of life. "Very few of them," Goldman felt,

"have come within miles of the intricacies of life that motivates human action."[47] From the perspective of her anarchist critics, Goldman was wasting
critical resources speaking on topics of secondary importance. For them, the
issue of economic injustice was of paramount importance. And since most immigrant anarchists were men, there were fewer women to advocate for gender
equality in love and life. Goldman's anarchist critics were also wary of what
they saw as the negative publicity that such action generated. "Anarchism,"
in their view, "was already enough misunderstood, and anarchists considered
depraved; it was inadvisable to add to the misconceptions by taking up perverted sex-forms." The disapproval of her comrades deterred Goldman little,
and in fact, had the opposite effect. "I minded the censors in my own ranks,"
she wrote, "as little as I did those in the enemy's camp. In fact, censorship from
comrades had the same effect on me as police persecution; it made me surer of
myself, more determined to plead for every victim, be it one of social wrong or
moral prejudice."[48] If Goldman's comrades thought that they could silence her
they were profoundly wrong.

None of this is to say that English-language anarchists did not engage in
what now might be called homophobic outbursts. In 1915, for example, *Mother
Earth* published an essay by Robert Allerton Parker attacking "Feminism in
America." Parker, who may have coined the term "birth control," was a teacher
at the Ferrer Center.[49] In his essay Parker described feminism as "an amusing and typical instance of feminine intellectual homosexuality," a description
which belittles the goals of feminism and imputes a negative value to same-sex
love. By this point, this was a tired accusation, one already made by conservative critics of the women's movement. Ironically, Parker's attack focused on
the sexual conservatism of the turn-of-the-century women's movement. He
criticized the leading figures of the movement for choosing the side of "organized morality" and accused them of being "clean-handed slaves of the State,
the Charities, The Churches, and the 'captains' of industry."[50] Though Parker's
analysis of the women's movement was widely shared by other anarchists, his
language and style of attack were not. Parker's contribution to *Mother Earth* is
not indicative of a broadly shared feeling against homosexuality. *Mother Earth*,
which at the time was edited by Alexander Berkman, carried essays that represented a diversity of voices, and not all statements or sentiments that appeared
in its pages were shared by all of the people associated with it. Nevertheless, examples such as Parker's essay complicate any effort to assert that the pre–World
War I anarchist sex radicals were wholly and completely "gay positive." Even
anarchists who expressed support for the right of men and women to love
members of their own sex made statements that contradicted those claims.

Whatever their shortcomings, anarchist sex radicals' views distinguished them from their contemporaries on the Left. The non-anarchist Left held to what has come to be called the Victorian sexual code. It was wedded to notions of female purity and insistent on the need to curb the supposedly baser instincts of men. Historian Mari Jo Buhle describes the majority of Socialist Party members as being "social purity-oriented," people who "hoped to stave off the invasion of capitalism into personal life and attempted to preserve the ideals of a presumably preexisting sexual morality."[51] Daniel DeLeon, the leader of the Socialist Labor Party from 1890 until his death in 1914, absolutely rejected the notion that socialism implied the end of marriage and the sexual liberation of women. Following the demise of the capitalist mode of production, women would be safely ensconced in the home. "Accordingly," writes L. Glen Seretan, "she would be excluded from work outside the home and no longer 'unsexed' by having 'to compete with men in unseemly occupations,' while the dross of capitalism's morally corrosive environment—promiscuity, adultery, and divorce—would not again degrade her."[52] Though he was a political rival of DeLeon, Eugene V. Debs, the SPA's best-known leader, shared some of his foes conservative views regarding women's place. "Debs," writes Nick Salvatore, "saw women as subsidiary to his main concerns, in orbit around and tangential to the leading actors...their fathers, husbands, and brothers."[53]

The anarchists were quick to note that the sexual and gender politics of most American socialists did not differ significantly from those of their capitalist rivals. Emma Goldman held that those radicals who refused to engage "the sex question" were hardly worse than the mainstream moralists she struggled against. She bemoaned the fact that it was possible to meet radicals "permeated with bourgeois morality in matters of sex, thanking the Lord they are not like the other fellows."[54] Goldman was a sharp—if not always consistent—critic of radicals who could not or would not include sexual freedom in their politics. Goldman was continually frustrated with what she perceived as the conservative nature of American radical culture.

Benjamin R. Tucker's essay, "State Socialism and Anarchism" illuminates just how far the anarchists and the Marxian socialists diverged on the question of sexual politics. In it, he discusses how the two schools of thought differed and how they were alike. Unlike the socialists, the anarchists—according to Tucker—were not timid in dealing with the subject of sexuality. Adopting a mocking tone, Tucker writes that while socialists did not wish to dwell on "so delicate a matter as that of the relations of the sexes, the Anarchists do not shrink from the application of their principle" in whatever arena of life. Tucker asserts, that sexuality, like all other aspects of life, should be governed by individual desire in free association with others. Anarchists

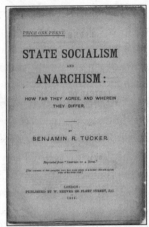

STATE SOCIALISM AND ANARCHISM:

> acknowledge and defend the right of any man and woman, or any men and women, to love each other for as long or as short a time as they can, will, or may. To them legal marriage and legal divorce are equal absurdities. They look forward to the time when every individual, whether man or woman, shall be self-supporting, and when each shall have an independent home of his or her own, whether it be a separate house or rooms in a house with others; when the love relations between these independent individuals shall be as varied as are individual inclinations and attractions.[55]

Benjamin Tucker's *State Socialism and Anarchism*, published in 1895 by W. Reeves, London (courtesy of the Kate Sharpley Library).

Although Tucker's language—"relations between the sexes"—assumes a heterosexual couple, the logic of his analysis undercuts such a narrow reading. Tucker's analysis does not rule out a homoerotic reading of his sexual politics, in fact, quite the opposite is true. Tucker was careful not to set up arbitrary boundaries for sexual behavior. Nowhere, either in this passage or elsewhere, does he list what is not permitted in sexual relations. According to Tucker, anarchists furnish no "code of morals to be imposed upon the individual." And it is the attempt to regulate the lives of others that is itself the problem. Prefiguring the argument that he would make when discussing the Oscar Wilde trial of 1895, Tucker wrote that "Anarchists look upon attempts to arbitrarily suppress vice as in themselves crimes."[56]

It is difficult to know how a contemporary reader would have interpreted Tucker's passage in regards to the matter of homosexuality. His phrasing allows for the possibility that two or, indeed, more than two men or women would enter into consensual relations with members of their own sex. Tucker's gender-neutral wording reflects his intention of treating women and men with absolute equality. Neither sex has a monopoly on sexual desire or greater inclination toward acting out on those desires. But the result—grammatically as well as politically—is the creation of the grounds for a homosexual reading of his sexual ethics. This reading is most clear in a passage that states that anarchists, "look forward to the time...when the love relations between...independent individuals shall be as varied as are individual inclinations and attractions."[57] Here the gender of the people involved in sexual relations disappears, and neither is the nature of their desire specified. It might be a man attracted to other men or a woman attracted to both men and women. In any case, Tucker was willing to accept their desires as legitimate and worth pursuing. The emphasis on the right of individuals to pursue their desires and attractions as they see fit was the bedrock on which anarchist sexual politics rested. Consenting individuals are perfectly within their rights to do whatever they desire. Should two "independent individuals" who share "inclinations and attractions" wish to pursue "love relations," then no one has the right to interfere with their choices. As historian Laurence Veysey notes, Tucker's sexual politics implies the right to explore "the full range of sexual experiments."[58]

The anarchists understood that love and sex were not innocent of power. They worked to expose the exercise of hierarchy and domination that lay behind moral codes. Some viewed sexual repression as a tool of political, social, and economic oppression. Arguments against the suppression of birth control, for example, were often framed as attempts by the ruling elites to manipulate demographics with an eye toward extending their power. Anarchist writer C. L. James attacked President Roosevelt's call for large families, as well as his vehement opposition to birth control by arguing that the "social view...that propagation...is a duty" was merely a ploy to ensure that "food for gunpowder should [not] fail."[59] Roosevelt's dreams of an American military colossus, James implied, could only be achieved with an abundant supply of soldiers, administrators, and workers. The president's admonitions against family planning were the perfect prescription for a growing military and economic power. James insisted that Roosevelt's sexual politics were intimately tied to his dreams of creating a rival to the European empires.

Challenging normative ideas about sex seemed, to some anarchists, to be a revolutionary act in and of itself. William Thurston Brown, a member of the SPA who was active in anarchist circles, argued that in "the sex question is bound every human right, every human possibility, every human fulfillment. And you can't deal with [the] sex question sanely, manfully, effectively, without finding [yourself] under obligation to completely overturn this whole system of things, and build a new society from the ground up."[60] Rejecting the argument that agitation on the sex question was a waste of time better spent on more serious matters, James S. Denson believed that "emancipation from sexual superstition will bring economic reorganization much more quickly than economic reorganization will bring emancipation from sexual superstition." This is so, Denson wrote, because, having tasted the fruits of sexual liberation, a free woman or man will chafe under the burdens of "present economic institutions," and as a consequence "the energies of that sex radical are likely to be

called into play to help on progressive industrial movement."[61] An anonymous
writer self-titled "Ego" wrote, "Free love will gradually undermine existing
economics."[62] Sex, in other words, was the key to social transformation—an
idea that neatly turns the crudely materialist analysis of the relationship between sex and gender relations and economic structures on its head. Sex, according to Denson, Brown, and their colleagues was not an epiphenomenal
bubble, but a powerful set of relationships, desires, and behaviors that structured
the cultural, economic, and cultural life of all Americans. As such, it deserved
careful consideration and should be treated with
seriousness.

Anarchist sex radicals challenged the code
of respectable reticence that dominated middle-
class culture. Angela Heywood, who published
The Word, an anarchist, free-love journal with
her husband Ezra Heywood, argued that rather
than engage in literary evasions people should
make use of plain language when speaking of the
sexual organs and the sex act. Among the terms
that Heywood suggested were the terms "cock,"
"cunt," and "fuck." Needless to say, Heywood's
enthusiasm for what she called "sexnomencla-
ture" was not widely shared outside the anar-

Ezra Heywood (courtesy of the Kate
Sharpley Library).

chist movement.[63] But her desire to speak plainly
about the body was widely shared among the
anarchists. John William Lloyd, for example, wrote a poem entitled "Finger
Eleventh, Finger of Love" in praise of the penis, and another entitled "Love-
Mouth," which honored the vagina. When the body is "reckoned obscene,"
Lloyd insisted, "life reeks" and "love rots." He condemned those "ashamed of
the beauty of the animal form" and rebuked those who denied the use of "the
passionate words of sex-admiration."[64] While many Americans declined to discuss homosexuality on the grounds that it was obscene—a crime not to be
named among Christians—the anarchist sex radicals felt that censoring sex talk
was the true obscenity.

Anarchist sex radicals rejected the notion that sexuality was bestial and that
morality was a product of divine authority. In another of his poems, entitled
"O Passionate Ache," Lloyd defended what he characterized as the "animal"
act of sex, stating, "would God that we were all more animal for no animal
knows lust or sins against the liberty of its mate, or condemns the natural as
vile." Sexual desire, writes Lloyd, is "as pure as the hunger and thirst in your

stomach." Lloyd neatly inverts the theological arguments used against so-called crimes against nature. "It is not the animal we are to fear," he wrote, "it is the perverted human, it is that which *rapes*, that which vindicates the conventional as more holy than Nature."[65] Similarly, Michael Monahan argued that though "the animals are frankly unmoral," they "do not die of paresis, or syphilis or any of the disorders mentioned in the *Psychopathia Sexualis*."[66] Monahan's reference to the diagnosis of paresis and his mention of *Psychopathia Sexualis* is an indirect naming of same-sex eroticism. Paresis was a form of mental illness associated with homosexuality, its name used most infamously in the naming of New York's Paresis Hall, a dance hall frequented by "fairies."[67] Likewise, *Psychopathia Sexualis*, Krafft-Ebing's tome on sexual deviation, was a *locus classicus* of homosexuality. Monahan's discussion of the "natural" is ironic in that animals, held to be much closer to nature than humans, are free of the supposed sexual illnesses that plague humanity. Both Monahan and Lloyd are playing with the idea that animals are freer in their sexual liaisons. The problem with sex isn't that it is innately immoral, but that people believe it is immoral and they are therefore racked with guilt when they pursue erotic pleasure. Animals romp with wild abandon, unplagued by modern psychosexual ills. Rather than condemn certain acts as "unnatural" or "bestial," Monahan and Lloyd appeal to the "unmoral" laws of nature to justify a wide variety of pleasures and to rebuke those who, in their minds, shore up oppressive, man-made sexual norms.

One of the key elements of anarchist sexual politics—if not the most important one—was a critique of marriage. Their antagonism to marriage placed the anarchists squarely in opposition to sexual American norms. They saw marriage as a binding institution, policed by the state and sanctioned by religious authority. In 1888, the Supreme Court asserted that wedlock "is more than a mere contract. The consent of the parties is of course essential, but when the contract to marry is executed by the marriage, a relation is created between the parties which they cannot change."[68] Divorce was difficult to procure, though the number of divorces rose in the late-nineteenth and early-twentieth centuries. This development was bitterly opposed by those who "clung to the view of marriage as a lifelong, sacred commitment, and considered divorce a 'contagion.'"[69] The concern expressed by the justices in 1888 did not diminish with the coming of the new century. In 1905, President Roosevelt "issued a special message to the Senate and the House alerting members that a growing number of Americans believed that the sanctity of marriage was held in 'diminishing regard' because 'the divorce laws are dangerously lax and indifferently administered' in some of the States."[70] Roosevelt, and those who shared his opinions, viewed marriage as the bedrock upon which the moral and social order of America rested.

While Roosevelt lamented the apparent collapse of marriage, the anarchists were among the institution's most fervent critics. Women, the anarchists claimed, were the main victims of the tyranny of the marriage bed. Though "man...pays his toll" in marriage, Emma Goldman wrote, "as his sphere is wider, marriage does not limit him as much [as it does] woman."[71] Voltairine de Cleyre described the married woman as "a bonded slave, who takes her master's name, her master's bread, her master's commands, and serves her master's passions; who passes through the ordeal of pregnancy and the throes of travail at his dictation—not at her desire; who can control no property, not even her own body, without his consent."[72] De Cleyre was disdainful of the conservative defense of the sanctity of marriage and the home. In a speech entitled "Sex Slavery," de Cleyre denounced both "the Church" and "the State" as twin pillars of authoritarianism. She mocked those who sang the praises of the good wife: "Stay at home, ye malcontents! Be patient, obedient, submissive! Darn our socks, mend out shirts, wash our dishes, get our meals, wait on us and *mind our children!*"[73] The anarchist critique of marriage was premised on the idea that women as well as men deserved to live their lives free from the authority of others, whether police agents, priests, or husbands. "All our social institutions, customs, arrangements," in the words of John William Lloyd, "should be expressions of the motive that the woman must always be free."[74]

The principle of equal treatment of women and men had a direct impact on the anarchist sex radical's homosexual politics. Rather than attempt to enforce a single standard of behavior—that of sexual restraint—anarchists wished to extend to women access to sexual pleasure that was enjoyed, if only ideally, by men. In 1899, Emma Goldman gave a lecture in San Francisco in which she defended women's right to seek out love whenever and wherever they might find it. "Why," Goldman asked, "should not the woman enjoy the same right if she so pleases?"[75] As historian Margaret Marsh has shown, Goldman and other anarchist women "forged an explicit link between sexuality and self-realization" and in so doing rejected the notion of women as asexual guardians of purity.[76] Having eschewed the role of moral guardians, anarchist sex radical women were more willing to accept non-normative sexual contact and relationships including those between people of the same sex, as valid and worthy.

In place of marriage, the anarchists championed what they called "free-love unions." When Durant spoke at the Ferrer Center on the subject of free love in 1912, one of those in attendance remarked that many of his audience members "were living in free love at the time."[77] Free-love unions were consensual relationships unsanctioned by church or state, which either party could leave at will. One of the more famous—not to say infamous—advocates of free love during the late-nineteenth century was Victoria Woodhull. Though an inconsistent anarchist at best, Woodhull's view of free love expressed in her speech, "The Principles of Social Freedom," is a succinct statement of the principles of free love. "To those who denounce me," Woodhull proclaimed, "I reply,"

> Yes, I am a Free Lover. I have an inalienable, constitutional and natural right to love whom I may, to love as long or as short a period as I can; to change that love every day if I please, and with that right neither you nor any law you can frame have any right to interfere. And I have the further right to demand a free and unrestricted exercise of that right, and it is your duty not only to accord it, but as a community, to see that I am protected in it. I trust that I am fully understood, for I mean just that, and nothing less![78]

Though she did not address the possibility that her choice of lover might include women in her speech, the logic of Woodhull's argument did not preclude it. Quite the contrary, the principle of free love implied the defense of any and all consensual relationships regardless of the gender of the individuals involved. Because of their critique of marriage, the anarchists found themselves able and willing to speak on other issues of sexuality, including homosexuality when, as it did with the case of Oscar Wilde, the issue came to the fore. Their critique of marriage opened up a space within which same-sex eroticism could be legitimated. The anarchist discourse of free love produced a sexual politics radically different from that pursued by those who wished merely to reform the institution of marriage. The radical potential of their critique of normative patterns of heterosexuality can be measured by the extent to which the anarchists dealt with same-sex relationships.

On questions regarding the politics of sexuality the Socialist Party was far more conventional than the anarchists. This is especially true in regards to the question of same-sex eroticism. While some socialists—particularly intellectuals like Charlotte Perkins Gilman and Crystal and Max Eastman—wrote about sexuality, no American socialist addressed homosexuality to any meaningful extent when they articulated their sexual politics.[79] In the first decades of the twentieth century, one of the few times the socialist press examined the subject of homosexuality was when the Eulenburg Affair broke in Germany. Named after Philipp Eulenburg, a member of Kaiser Wilhelm II's inner circle, the scandal involved "a series of courts-marital concerned with homosexual conduct in the army as well as five courtroom trials that turned on the homosexuality of prominent members of Kaiser Wilhelm's entourage and cabinet."[80] The scandal was precipitated by a series of scandalous revelations by Maximilian Harden, the publisher of *Die Zukunft* (The Future), an independent weekly. Harden had known for some time about the sexual tastes of some of the Kaiser's entourage but had restrained from making the information public. A series of sharp disagreements with imperial policy led Harden to use the information about Eulenburg and others to attack the Kaiser. Harden was also motivated because he believed that "homosexuality was becoming rampant" and that, unless exposed, this vice would eat away at the German nation.[81]

German socialists saw the Eulenburg Affair as a golden opportunity to smear imperial rule with the taint of sodomy. The sexual behaviors of the country's leaders provided the socialists with ammunition they could use to delegitimize the regime. American socialists also used the Eulenburg Affair as a cudgel with which to beat their opponents. In 1908, for example, an article which appeared in the socialist publication *Wilshire's* reveled in the "staggering blow" delivered to the "ruling classes of Germany." The publication reproduced a cartoon that had appeared in the German press, which showed Harden pulling back a curtain to reveal a dinner party presided over by the emperor. The partygoers are depicted as pigs and the caption reads, "Ladies, and gentlemen, behold the set that ruled Germany." Also reproduced in the article are the words of August Bebel, one of the leaders of the German Socialist Party: "How hideously disgusting are the things brought to light at this trial; how disgusting are those who have met ruin in this investigation and must bear the responsibility!"[82] Bebel's words give some indication of the vituperation that the Eulenburg Affair engendered. *Wilshire's* eagerly reproduced this acidic tone for its readers. Without making direct accusations, the implication that the ruling elites of both countries were decadent, corrupt, and rife with homosexuality was a key to the socialist papers interest in the scandal.

Emma Goldman's journal, *Mother Earth*, also reported on the Eulenburg scandal revealing that "his Majesty's most intimate friends have a strong penchant for the charms of—their own sex." However, the tone of *Mother Earth's* reportage on the scandal is significantly different than that featured in *Wilshire's*. Rather than using the Eulenburg Affair as an opportunity to tar the emperor and his court as a pack of "hideously disgusting" animals exposed by the clear light of day, *Mother Earth* pokes fun at the outrage of the supposedly upright German people, the "good faithful subjects of the Fatherland," who "stand aghast" at the conduct of their nobility. *Mother Earth* argues that the mindset of those who look for moral leadership from their rulers was at the heart of the scandal. That the Germans countenanced an Emperor is at issue, not the fact that the Emperor or members of his court had relationships with other men. If the "good, faithful subjects of the Fatherland" didn't place their emperor on a pedestal then there would be no occasion for scandal. The public condemnation of the emperor's coterie smacked of the values of an outraged bourgeoisie: "religion, morality, and *das deutsche Gemuth* [the German soul or temperament]."[83] The varying reactions to the Eulenburg Affair by *Mother Earth* and *Wilshire's* illustrate the important differences between the sexual politics of the socialists and the anarchists.

The anarchists may also have been more reluctant to use the Eulenburg Affair because they were aware that moral outrage of the sort that swirled around the emperor could be dangerous. Since anarchists were identified with sex radicalism any political critique that prioritized normative moral standards—particularly those involving sexual conduct—could prove dangerous. In such a climate the anarchists themselves were liable to become targets of censors and purity crusaders. And in fact, *Mother Earth* notes that one of the "first practical steps" taken by authorities eager to "restore the weakening faith" of the emperor's subjects was to initiate "a campaign of persecution against the Berlin anarchists."[84] The German government deflected attention away from its own supposed immorality by attacking the anarchists, the quintessential immoralists of the age.

Anarchists had not always discussed homosexuality in so favorable a manner as they did in the late 1890s and beyond. While their views were nowhere near as caustic as the socialist critics of Eulenburg, the first generation of anarchist sex radicals did not view homosexuality with tolerant eyes. Centered largely in the Midwest, the first wave of English-language anarchists were active in the three decades following the Civil War. Though there were not many discussions of same-sex love by anarchists in the 1870s, 1880s, and early 1890s, the mentions one can find are largely negative in tone. Like many of their non-anarchist contemporaries, these pioneering anarchists, as historian Hal Sears has pointed out, "considered homosexuality to be a physical disease or, at best, a psychic and moral perversion."[85] This was true even for those anarchists who kicked against the constraints of normative sexual ideas. In the course of her defense of free love, for example, anarchist Lois Waisbrooker condemned homosexuality. Though she praised the beauty of the ancient Greeks who, she believed, "followed the leadings of unperverted nature in their conjugal relationships," she lamented what she called "Grecian degeneracy"—that is, homosexuality. The homosexuality of the Greeks "was brought about not by following the leadings of nature but by departure therefrom." According to Waisbrooker, "artificial or anti-natural modes of living were substituted for the native simplicity of earlier times." Centuries of war, Waisbrooker wrote, "destroyed all the nobler, the better endowed specimens of Grecian masculinity, leaving only the...sordid, the craven, the malformed in mind in body" alive. "It is any wonder," she asked, "the Greeks degenerated?"[86] Interestingly, Waisbrooker's analysis upends the narrative that Greek degeneracy was caused by excess luxury and lassitude; war, she argues, was the seedbed of homosexuality.

Waisbrooker was not alone in making such arguments. In 1890, Moses Harman wrote that "abnormal sexuality," which for him included homosexuality, "is the result of the attempted enforcement of a false standard or morality, false from nature's standpoint."[87] Similarly, in 1885, C. L. James wrote, "vices are so largely the fruit of excessive wealth, abject poverty, overwork, oppression, and despair that with the removal of these causes they may be expected to become rare."[88] In other words, once the inequities of intolerance and economic disparity disappear "vice" will no longer flourish. The idea that homosexuality was a sign of corruption—an idea that motivated much of the socialists glee in covering the Eulenburg scandal—was quite widely held among a number of English-language anarchists in the 1870s, 1880s, and early 90s. It should be noted, however, that none of the anarchist sex radicals who discussed homosexuality argued that persons who engaged in same-sex behavior should be condemned or persecuted. The kind of vitriolic attacks made by the Socialist press against Eulenburg is absent from the few anarchist discussions of homosexuality written by the first wave of activists. The insistence on the rights of individuals to pursue their own desires was a paramount ideal, one that constrained and shaped anarchist sexual politics even though, as in the case of Waisbrooker, this principle was somewhat less than consistently applied.

By the late-nineteenth century, however, anarchist writing on homosexuality took a radical departure from the views expressed by Waisbrooker, Harman, and other members of the first wave. This transformation was visible in both quantitative and qualitative ways. First, the number of times that anarchist sex radicals discussed homosexuality increased markedly. Noted anarchists like Alexander Berkman and Emma Goldman regularly presented talks that explored the social, cultural, and ethical status of same sex love. Second, the tone of these presentations was quite different from the early, more sporadic mentions of homosexuality made by anarchist activists. While Waisbrooker believed homosexuality was a sign of decadence, anarchists like Tucker defended same-sex love as a rather pedestrian expression of human erotic variability. Beginning in the mid-1890s, leading anarchist sex radicals began to actively defend the rights of men and women to love members of their own sex. Homosexuality became one of the topics that the anarchist sex radicals devoted considerable attention to. No other Americans—outside of the medical, legal, and religious professions—devoted so much time and effort to exploring the social, moral, and ethical place of same-sex love. And neither did anyone else of the period develop a political understanding of the right of men and women to love whomsoever they wished, whenever and wherever they wished, in the manner of their choosing.

There are several reasons for the remarkable shift in attitude. The early-American anarchists had emerged largely from rural and small towns. In the 1870s and 1880s, some of the movement's leading papers, like *Lucifer the Light-Bearer*, were published in Kansas and other Midwestern, mostly rural states. By contrast, *Mother Earth* was published in Greenwich Village, a markedly different cultural and social environment than the world inhabited by Waisbrooker and her contemporaries. Tucker began publishing *Liberty* in Boston, but by the end of the century he moved to New York. There, he opened a bookstore on Sixth Avenue that, according to an account that appeared in the *New York Herald*, featured "more anarchist literature than…any other one place in the United States."[89] The more cosmopolitan anarchists of the new century were exposed to the more variegated sexual subcultures of the urban landscape. In New York City, as historian George Chauncey documented, homosexuality was unremarkable.

Members of the second wave of anarchist sex radicalism were also more familiar with the sexological literature on homosexuality that began to appear at the end of the nineteenth century. Much of this sexological literature—or at least the texts favored by the anarchists—were themselves products of nascent political efforts on the part of homosexual men and women, a theme that will be explored in greater depth below. For the time being, however, one example will suffice to illustrate this phenomenon: When John William Lloyd discussed homosexuality and Greece he did so influenced by the work of Edward Carpenter, whose studies of the sex life of the ancient Greeks were inspired by his desires to find historically validating examples of his own desires. Carpenter developed historical and psychological theories about same-sex desire because he wanted to promote a more liberal sexual culture than the one he lived in. The new sexological work being produced in Europe circulated widely among the anarchists, and Lloyd was hardly alone in his reading patterns. Emma Goldman, for example, read Carpenter, as well as Ellis, Hirschfeld, and other sexologists. The anarchist sex radicals examined in the pages below were consumers of the literature of the expanding science of desire, and their sexual politics were shaped by it.

But the most important reason for the shift in how American anarchist sex radicals viewed the issue of homosexuality, is that, by the end of the nineteenth

century, homosexuality had become a focus of surveillance and regulation by
police and other authorities. That homosexuality was given increased attention
is evident in the fact that, by the late-nineteenth century, convictions for the
crime of sodomy jumped and medical journals began to feature articles on
the subject. The level of police interest and the increase in medical literature
on the topic of same-sex love were directly related. To illustrate: in 1892, Dr.
Irving Rosse, a physician from Washington, D.C. read a paper at a meeting of
the Medical Society of Virginia that documented the extent of what he called
the "Perversion of the Genesic [procreative] Instinct" in the nation's capitol. It
also documents the degree to which homosexuality had become an issue of
concern for the police:

> From a judge of the District police court I learned that frequent delinquents
> of this kind have been taken by the police in the very commission of the
> crime, and that owing to defective penal legislation on the subject he is
> obliged to try such cases as assaults or indecent exposure. The lieutenant in
> charge of my district, calling on me a few weeks ago for medical information
> on this point, informs me that men of this class give him far more trouble
> than the prostitutes. Only of late the chief of police tells me that his men
> have made, under the very shadow of the White House, eighteen arrests in
> Lafayette Square alone (a place by the way frequented by Guiteau) in which
> the culprits were taken in flagrante delicto...[90]

Dr. Rosse's account is typical of the medical case studies and narratives that
began to appear in the United States at this time. In many of these texts, physicians document the degree to which police authorities had become interested
in these "crimes of sexuality" and indicate their willingness to assist in this
project.

In his description of the men who frequented Lafayette Park, Rosse links
homosexuality with Charles J. Guiteau, the disgruntled political aspirant who
assassinated President James Garfield in 1881. The trial that followed became an
important precedent in the judgment and treatment of the criminally insane.
This conflation of crime, insanity and homosexuality reflects the commonly
held belief that sexual attraction—much less activity—between members of
the same sex was a danger to the moral and social order. Because of this notion,
the police were increasingly vigilant in their pursuit of those who engaged in
homosexual acts. Dr. Rosse and other professionals often assisted the police in
their efforts to contain what was viewed as a growing moral and social problem.

It was not by accident, nor for idiosyncratic reasons then that the anarchist sex radicals began to struggle with the legal, social, and moral status of
same-sex love. At a time when few Americans cared to defend the rights of

men and women whose sexual and emotional life were made the target of arrest, moral censure, and social ridicule, the anarchists were not afraid to do so. Though the first generation of English-speaking anarchists in the United States had devoted relatively little attention to the issue of homosexuality, the second wave of American anarchist sex radicals adopted new views and they began to engage with the issue a great deal. Tucker, Goldman, Lloyd, Berkman, and other anarchists' level of interest mirrors the escalating attention that the police and other moral regulators were giving the subject. As the police began to step up their efforts to hunt down and arrest people like those poor souls caught "in flagrante delicto" in Lafayette Park, the anarchists began to step up their attacks on the police, their ideological allies, and assistants. The anarchist politics of homosexuality examined by this dissertation was created in the context of a dialectical contest between oppression and resistance, starkly illustrated by the Oscar Wilde trial of 1895. So it is to that trial, and the response that it prompted among the anarchists, that we now turn.

Vol. XI.—No. 19.　　　NEW YORK, N. Y., JANUARY 25, 1896.　　　Whole No. 331.

CHAPTER TWO:

THE WILDE ONES: OSCAR WILDE AND ANARCHIST SEXUAL POLITICS

IN 1900, EMMA GOLDMAN and her friend Dr. Eugene Schmidt took a walk in Paris' beautiful Luxembourg Gardens. Among the subjects the two discussed was the fate of Oscar Wilde, the English writer sentenced to two years of hard labor in a spectacular show trial in 1895 for committing "acts of gross indecency with men." Wilde moved to France following his release from prison. Goldman, who was in Paris for an anarchist conference, was meant to meet Wilde the previous evening, but missed her opportunity. Dr. Schmidt and Goldman clashed over whether or not Wilde's imprisonment was justified. In her autobiography, *Living My Life*, Goldman paints a vivid description of her defense of Wilde and of the doctor's reaction:

> During our walk in the Luxembourg [Gardens], I told the doctor of the indignation I had felt at the conviction of Oscar Wilde. I had pleaded his case against the miserable hypocrites who had sent him to his doom. "You!" the doctor exclaimed in astonishment, "Why, you must have been a mere youngster then. How did you dare come out in public for Oscar Wilde in puritan America?" "Nonsense!" I replied; "no daring is required to protest against a great injustice." The doctor smiled dubiously. "Injustice?" he repeated; "It wasn't exactly that from the legal point of view, though it may have been from the psychological." The rest of the afternoon we were engaged in a battle royal about inversion, perversion, and the question of sex variation.[1]

Unfortunately, Goldman missed her chance to meet with Wilde. He never recovered from his prison sentence and died shortly after Goldman's trip to Paris. Wilde died in exile, having fled England under the darkest of clouds. Convicted before the bar and the court of public opinion, Wilde's reputation as a poet, playwright, and social critic was overshadowed by the turn of the century's most spectacular sex crime trial.

Goldman's heated exchange with Schmidt was not the only time that she defended Wilde against those who condemned him. Wilde served as a touchstone for her views on sexuality. He was a glaring example of the harm done when the state mobilized its tremendous powers in the pursuit of enforcing common prejudices. Many of Goldman's colleagues shared her outrage at Wilde's imprisonment. During the trial, and in the years immediately following it, the anarchists rose to Wilde's defense. They attacked his jailers and those who applauded his prosecution. The efforts of Goldman and other anarchists on Wilde's behalf constitute the first articulation of a politics of homosexuality in the United States. In lectures, in articles in movement journals like *Liberty*, *Lucifer the Light-Bearer*, and *Mother Earth*, and in confrontations like that which Goldman had with Dr. Schmidt, anarchist sex radicals rose to the defense of the disgraced writer. The Wilde case came to serve as a lens through which the anarchists understood the ethics of same-sex eroticism.

Wilde's conviction was a wake-up call for anarchists. The trial prompted the anarchists to engage in an examination of the social, moral, and legal place of same-sex desire. The raw use of judicial power to convict a man for pursuing his desires was a vivid illustration of the kind of abuse that the anarchists most ferociously opposed. Wilde's prosecution was illustrative of the growing state interest in the regulation of sex. Convictions for sodomy and other sex crimes increased markedly in the late-nineteenth century in the United States and abroad. Beginning in the 1870s, laws like the Comstock Act, which prohibited the transmission of birth control information through the mail, and the Labouchere Act, under which Wilde was convicted, began to crowd statute books in the United States and Western Europe. This expansion of state power was the source of conflict with the anarchists who viewed such developments with great wariness. As the state began to seek ever-greater control over the private lives of its subjects, the anarchists reacted to that exercise of power. Anarchist sex radicals were often alone in defending the rights of people to choose their own partners, free from state interference or social condemnation.

The anarchists had, of course, always been wary of state power—opposition to the state was a fundamental tenet of all anarchists. The French anarchist Pierre-Joseph Proudhon expressed this sentiment well:

To be governed is to be watched over, inspected, spied on, directed, legislated at, regulated, docketed, indoctrinated, preached at, controlled, assessed, weighed, censored, ordered about, by men who have neither the right nor the knowledge nor the virtue. To be governed means to be, at each operation, at each transaction, at each movement, noted, registered, controlled, stamped, measured, valued, assessed, patented, licensed, authorized, endorsed, admonished, hampered, reformed, rebuked, arrested. It is to be, on the pretext of the general interest, taxed, drilled, held for ransom, exploited, monopolized, exhorted, squeezed, tricked, robbed; than at the least resistance, at the first word of complaint, to be repressed, fined, abused, annoyed, followed, bullied, beaten, disarmed, strangled, imprisoned, machine gunned, judged, condemned, deported, whipped, sold, betrayed, and finally mocked, ridiculed, insulted, and dishonored.[2]

Proudhon's animus towards the state was precisely the kind of outrage that the American anarchist sex radicals felt at Wilde's conviction. The attack on Wilde was a stark example of the way that the police "spied on," "docketed," "abused," "bullied," imprisoned," "deported," and "ridiculed" people who violated laws that regulated sexual activity. Benjamin Tucker, who, in his youth, translated much of Proudhon's work, used language that reflected Proudhon's deep distrust of state power to denounce those who attacked Wilde. "Men who imprison a man who has committed no crime," Tucker proclaimed, "are themselves criminals."[3] The Wilde case was a perfect example of the nature of the quality of "justice" and "morality" pursued by the state in its enactment of new sex laws.

Wilde's trial was a critical turning point in the American anarchists' view of homosexuality. Up until the scandal, there was relatively little discussion of the moral and social place of homosexuality among anarchist sex radicals. The mentions of homosexuality that do appear in anarchist texts prior to the trial tended to be negative in tone. After Wilde's trial, however, the anarchist sex radicals addressed homosexuality with greater frequency and in a more favorable light. In many of the post-trial discussions, the scandal is referenced either implicitly or explicitly. This is not to say that the Wilde trial was the only cause of this shift. Certainly there were other events and forces that brought about this change, not least of which was the rising attention paid to the topic by medical and state authorities. Across the Western world same-sex relations were being named and judged with increasing frequency. The anarchists were responding to the policing of homosexuality because the issue was of rising concern to the society in which they lived. Oscar Wilde's case is merely the best known of a variety of different things that indicate the growing interest in the topic of homosexuality. The anarchist defense of Wilde was a part of a larger debate and discussion of homosexuality that took place at the turn of the century in the both the United States and Europe.

Wilde's trial was not the first time sexuality served as a source of conflict between the anarchists and state authorities. Anarchist sex radicals were quite familiar with the pernicious effects of sex-crime prosecution. In 1886, for example, Lillian Harman, the daughter of the anarchist sex radical Moses Harman, pledged her love for Edwin C. Walker in a free love ceremony that was condoned by neither church nor state. The town of Valley Falls, Kansas, where Harman and Walker lived, was outraged, and the morning after their ceremony the pair were served with arrest warrants for the crime of unsanctified, unsanctioned cohabitation. Walker was sentenced to seventy-five days in jail, Harman to forty-five days; the couple were not to be released until they covered court costs. They spent six months behind bars before agreeing to pay their fine and court costs.[4] Other anarchist sex radicals faced similar harassment from state authorities. Ezra Heywood, one of the leading native-born anarchist sex radicals of the late-nineteenth century, was jailed numerous times for offending public morals. Heywood was convicted for circulating information on birth control, for publishing "obscene" works—such as Walt Whitman's poetry—and for attacking the social, legal, and economic inequities of marriage. Heywood served a number of years in prison for his crimes.

Heywood was involved in one of few discussions of homosexuality among anarchists that occurred prior to Wilde's trial. In 1890, Heywood was sentenced to two years hard labor for, among other things, reprinting a letter from Dr. Richard O'Neill, a New York physician who sympathized with the anarchists. The letter, which was judged to be obscene, was originally printed in *Lucifer the Light-Bearer* on 14 February, 1890 (Moses Harman had already served eight months for its publication), and was largely concerned with sexual abuse of women within marriage, but it also discussed homosexuality. In his letter, O'Neill describes how a "Mr. P. C. of California wrote [to him] asking if I could cure him of an insatiable appetite for human semen." Mr. P. C. wished to stop "roaming all over the country trying to find men to allow him to 'suck them

Lucifer the Light-Bearer, August 2, 1906 (courtesy of the Kate Sharpley Library).

off,'" and hoped that Dr. O'Neill might have a "cure."[5] It should be noted that, though Heywood made it clear that he disapproved of Mr. P. C.'s behavior, he did not excoriate Mr. P. C., nor did he urge O'Neill to treat his patient harshly. Heywood believed Mr. P. C.'s behavior was the result of the ill organization of the society in which he lived. It was the social order, not Mr. P. C. that needed reformation. Unfortunately, Heywood had little opportunity to engage in any further discussion of homosexuality. Like Wilde, Heywood died shortly after his release from prison, most likely from the tuberculosis he contracted while behind bars. Cases like Heywood's created a precedent for the anarchist view of Wilde's trial.[6]

Wilde's ordeal was a familiar one to the anarchists, and their response—the determined opposition to the exercise of state power to regulate morals—was in keeping with the history of their sexual politics. In the aftermath of his arrest and imprisonment, Wilde became a totemic figure among the anarchists. They felt that the attack on him was an attack on many of the values they held most dear. In her lectures and writings on drama and art, Goldman held up the disgraced writer as an exemplary, engaged intellectual whose views she shared. In her essay "Anarchism: What it Really Stands For," Goldman cites Wilde approvingly a number of times. "Oscar Wilde," she writes, "defines a perfect personality as 'one who develops under perfect conditions, who is not wounded, maimed or in danger.'" Goldman interprets Wilde's words as an implied endorsement of anarchist economic and social arrangements. "A perfect personality," she continues, "then, is only possible in a state of society where man is free to choose the mode of work, the conditions of work, and the freedom to work."[7] In a 1907 lecture delivered to an audience in Portland, Oregon, Goldman called Wilde's play *Lady Windemere's Fan*, a work that expressed the "revolutionary spirit in modern drama."[8] In 1912, the *Denver Post* reported that, in the course of one of her talks, Goldman "glorified Wilde, and intimated that while society forgives the criminal, it never forgives the dreamer."[9] Goldman saw Wilde as an anarchist—in spirit, if nothing else: "Oscar Wilde like all true artists is terribly contradictory. He eulogizes Kropotkin and repudiates anarchism, yet his 'Soul of Man under Socialism' is pure anarchy."

Even before his trial, Wilde was connected with anarchism. Though he was not himself an anarchist, he did ally himself with movement causes at a number of points in his life. Following the Haymarket Tragedy of 1886, for example, he signed a petition seeking clemency for the condemned American anarchists. Wilde felt, as Alexander Berkman did, that the conviction of the defendants was obtained through "perjured evidence" and "bribed jurymen," and that it was motivated by "police revenge" and the desire on the part of "money interests of Chicago and of the State of Illinois" to "punish and terrorize labor by murdering their most devoted leaders."[11] The petition, which included signatures by Eleanor Marx, Edward Carpenter, William Rossetti, William Morris, George Bernard Shaw, Olive Schreiner, and Annie Besant, was sent to Richard J. Oglesby, the Governor of Illinois, who eventually commuted the death sentence of two of the condemned Chicago anarchists.[12] Given the high visibility of the Haymarket Tragedy in the anarchist movement—remembrances of those killed at the event and those condemned to death were annual events—it is not surprising that Wilde's actions were praised in the movement. Before the scandal that engulfed his life and memory, Wilde had a well-deserved reputation of being a cultural critic of decidedly progressive tendencies.

On at least one occasion Wilde, spoke of himself as an anarchist. In 1893 the French journal *L'Ermitage* conducted a poll of writers and artists asking them their political views. Wilde responded that he considered himself "an artist and an anarchist."[13] One year later, Wilde repeated his claim. "We are all of us more or less Socialists now-a-days," he said. "I think I am rather more...I am something of an Anarchist."[14] By asserting this, Wilde aligned himself with what he saw as the rebellious, individualistic tendencies of anarchism. He was not a member of any anarchist groups, nor did he provide material support for movement causes. For Wilde and those disaffected intellectuals like him, anarchism meant a spirit of discovery, a rejection of received ideas, and the desire to lead one's life free of social conventions. This is what he meant when he stated that he considered himself "an artist and an anarchist." In Wilde's mind the two ideas—art and anarchy—were related in as much as they both promised a way to refashion the self in new and unfettered ways. Wilde's mixture of artistic ferment and ideas inspired by and borrowed from anarchism was a fairly commonplace fixture of life in the bohemian circles of London, Paris, and other Western European cities.[15] One can find a similar conjunction of ideas and tendencies a little later in the United States in people like Margaret Anderson, Robert Henri, Sadakichi Hartmann, Floyd Dell, and James Gibbons Huneker.[16]

Wilde also drew on anarchist ideas and texts in the construction of his work. In his first play, *Vera; or The Nihilists*, for example, Wilde quotes *The Catechism of the Revolutionist*, a political tract written by anarchists Mikhail Bakunin and Sergei Nechaev.[17] Prior to his death in 1876, Bakunin was considered the leading anarchist of the era. A Russian who embodied almost every stereotype of that country's revolutionary tradition, Bakunin fought with Karl Marx for control of the socialist movement. Nechaev was a young protégé of Bakunin; the two met in Geneva in 1869, and within months of their meeting, they composed *The Catechism*. The rhetoric of defiance and social revolt found in its pages assured it a long and infamous history. Its language mirrors the revolutionary fervor that Bakunin and Nechaev fed upon as they wrote. According to *The Catechism*, the revolutionary "has broken every tie with the civil order and the entire cultured world, with all its laws, proprieties, social conventions and...ethical rules."[18] Once the revolutionist has taken this dramatic step, he must struggle ceaselessly to bring down the powers that be. It is not hard to understand why Wilde—a sharp critic of Victorian morality, whose personal desires made him an outsider—would be drawn to Bakunin and Nechaev's manifesto. Ironically, the London production of *Vera* was shut down following the assassination of Czar Alexander II; a case of life imitating art which might have pleased Wilde, except for the fact that his play was now seen as too controversial for the stage.

Wilde was clearly drawn to the revolutionary rhetoric of *The Catechism*, but the intense nature of the relationship between Bakunin and Nechaev—which was the subject of gossip and political slander—may also have piqued his interest. When Bakunin met Nechaev he was smitten; the two were inseparable. According to historian E. H. Carr, "[Bakunin] began to call young Nechaev by the tender nickname of 'boy'... [and] the most affectionate relations were established."[19] Almost immediately rumors about the nature of the two men's friendship began to circulate. Bakunin was said to have written a note to Nechaev promising total submission to the younger man's desires; it was signed with a woman's name "Matrena." To those who traded in this story, Bakunin's relationship with his protégé smacked of homosexuality. Though Carr does not believe that Bakunin and Nechaev were erotically involved, historian George Woodcock argues that there "seems to have been a touch of submerged homosexuality" running like a current between the two men.[20] Whatever the case, rumors of the two men's relationship, fed in large part by political rivals, circulated in the Left. Historian Hubert Kennedy argues that Marx used the accusation of homosexuality against Bakunin, his ideological foe, in his successful attempt to expel him from the First International in 1872.[21] What exactly Wilde knew of these rumors is unknown but had he heard of Bakunin's infatuation with Nechaev—a distinct possibility given the apparently broad circulation of the rumors—it doubtless would have intrigued him.

When he did write about politics, Wilde sounded many themes that anarchists espoused. Like Kropotkin and Tucker, his ideas were forged in "reaction against industrialization, urbanization, modernization—against what we can more precisely call the growth of bureaucratized corporate structure[s] in the context of capitalist social relations."[22] Critics of the late-nineteenth centuries economic, social, and political conditions, Wilde and the anarchists sought to beautify and dignify labor. They juxtaposed an ideal world of creativity and craftsman-like dedication and pleasure in work, onto the conditions found in modern industrial production. Wilde expressed this vision on his tour of the United States in the early 1880s. In Bangor, Maine the local paper reported that Wilde "thought a great mistake of the age is found in the unwillingness to honor the mechanic, the working man, and his pursuits as they should be honored."[23] Against the relentless pace of industrial manufacture, Wilde argued for a return to craftsman-like production on a local and human scale. This is what Goldman meant when, in her 1912 Denver lecture, she approvingly cited Wilde's contention that "the secret of life is in art." Wilde's discussion of aesthetics was intended as a critical discourse and not merely a list of suggestions on housekeeping, fashion, and visual and literary arts. He championed art for its ability "to disturb the monotony of type, the slavery of custom, the tyranny of habit, and the reduction of man to the level of machine."[24] These are all values that one can find expressed in any number of anarchist publications in the United States and England during this period.

Many contemporaries saw Wilde's best-known political text, *The Soul of Man under Socialism*, reprinted widely across Europe and popular in the United States, as an anarchist text.[25] George Woodcock argues that "the uncompromisingly libertarian attitude of [*The Soul of Man under Socialism*] has much…in common with the ideas of…Peter Kropotkin." Written in 1891, Wilde's essay "had to be published for a time as *The Soul of Man* in order to avoid objections from publishers and distributors."[26] Wilde's rhetoric and goals bore a striking resemblance to those espoused by anarchists. Though somewhat vague as to how the social transformation he seeks would be brought about, Wilde maintained that the implementation of his utopian ideas "will lead to Individualism." He rejected the idea of state ownership of the means of production and offered critiques of Marx that were very similar to those made by Bakunin. Wilde warned that "If the Socialism is Authoritarian; if there are governments armed with economic power as they are now with political power; if, in a word, we are to have Industrial Tyrannies, then the last state of man will be worse than the first."[27] This was a vision that Goldman and her comrades could embrace and is precisely the kind of passage she referred to when she called his essay "pure Anarchy."[28]

Despite his ideological affinities with libertarian socialism, Wilde did not receive unanimous praise from the anarchists. In 1891 Benjamin R. Tucker, angry that commentators spoke of Wilde as an anarchist, criticized him for his muddled thinking. "The newspaper paragraphers," Tucker wrote, "all discuss Oscar Wilde's article on 'The Soul of Man under Socialism' and talk of his conversion to Anarchism, thus again showing that they are hopelessly incapable of understanding either what Oscar Wilde says or what Anarchism means."[29] In Tucker's estimation, Wilde was not rigorous enough in his distinctions and was too given to the kind of fuzzy, utopian feelings that Tucker delighted in dissecting. In his review of *The Soul of Man under Socialism* Tucker quoted Terence V. Powderly's views of Wilde's brand of socialism. Powderly, the Grand Master of the Knights of Labor, was skeptical of Wilde's ideas writing that:

> Oscar Wilde declares that Socialism will simply lead to individualism. That is like saying that the way from St. Louis to New York is through San Francisco, or that the way to whitewash a wall is to paint it black. The man who says that Socialism will fail and then the people will try individualism—i.e., Anarchy— may be mistaken: the man who thinks they are one and the same thing is simply a fool.[30]

Though Tucker uses Powderly's words, this should not be taken as his endorsement of the Grand Master of the Knights of Labor. Powderly was a bitter opponent of the anarchists; he felt they had tainted the labor movement with the smell of dynamite and disorder.[31] Tucker reciprocated Powderly's disdain, and hardly approved of his views. But in Tucker's estimation, even a broken clock tells the right time at least twice a day. Despite Tucker's disagreements with Wilde, the fact that both he and Powderly felt compelled to respond to *The Soul of Man under Socialism* illustrates the extent to which Wilde was taken seriously as a social critic and political theorist, by his contemporaries. One of the tragedies of the Wilde trial is that his politics have been almost completely overshadowed by his role in the century's most scandalous sex trial.

Benjamin Tucker (courtesy of the Kate Sharpley Library).

It was not only *The Soul of Man under Socialism* that was critiqued by anarchists who were annoyed that the poet's reputation as an anarchist was off the mark. In 1885, Tucker's colleague, John William Lloyd, took Wilde to task in the pages of *Liberty* for having written a poem that he felt maligned anarchism. Wilde had written a "Sonnet to Liberty," which decries "anarchy" and praises the virtues of "order," and expresses Wilde's fear of "the mob." It is possible that Wilde's awareness of himself as a sexually dissident figure may have heightened his sense of the very real dangers of the tyranny of the majority; certainly the public reaction to his conviction in 1895 was an illustration of how "the mob" can act with great cruelty. Such a reading of Wilde's politics was lost on Lloyd, who took great umbrage at Wilde's use of the term anarchism to mean disorder. It is, in fact, somewhat amusing to read the heated responses that the (mis)use of the term "anarchy" would provoke in the anarchist press. An anthology of such ideological outrages could easily be compiled. In the case of Wilde's transgression, Lloyd literally rewrote "Sonnet to Liberty," changing its name to "The Sacred Thirst for Liberty." In his new and improved version, Lloyd lambasted Wilde as a "false-tongued poet," and defended anarchism.[32]

Despite their mixed view of Wilde, the anarchists rallied to his defense when, in 1895, he was swept up into the scandal that would end his career. Critical jabs at Wilde, like those of Tucker and Lloyd, largely disappear after his trial and conviction. Wilde was actually involved in a series of trials, all of which revolved around questions of his sexuality and public reputation. The first trial was prompted by Wilde's suit for defamation of character against the Marquess of Queensbury, the father of Wilde's lover, Lord Douglass. Queensbury left a note at a club accusing Wilde of being a sodomite. Wilde challenged the accusation feeling that to let it stand would be damning. In short order the case against Queensbury collapsed and Wilde was brought up on charges of having committed "acts of gross indecency." Lord Douglass, who enjoyed considerable protection as a member of the nobility, was not brought before the bar. In the trials that followed, Wilde's relations with a number of male prostitutes were divulged. Although the more salacious details of the evidence were largely kept out of the press, Wilde's relationship with the young men he spent time with was widely understood to be sexual. In addition to exposing his real life sexual relationships, the prosecution spent considerable time elucidating Wilde's texts, including *The Picture of Dorian Gray*, searching for further proof of his criminal nature.

Wilde was sentenced to two years of hard labor by a judge who could barely restrain his loathing. Like the judge, many of Wilde's contemporaries were deeply stirred by the revelation of the rather pedestrian fact that acts of male homosexuality were regularly practiced in London. The Wilde scandal was of international dimensions. The English press covered the trial's unfolding in fascinated detail, though the specific nature of the charges made against Wilde were not made public. In the United States, the press was even more studious in maintaining an embargo on what they viewed as the more sordid aspects of the trial, though hints and insinuations appeared almost everywhere and Wilde's ordeal was well known. Some of the American press, such as Salt Lake City's *The Desert News*, did cover the trial—eighteen front-page stories and two editorials—but, like their English counterparts, they kept the exact nature of the charge unspoken.[33] This censoring zeal was evident by the fact that in America—as was reported in the pages of Tucker's *Liberty*—Wilde's works were pulled from library shelves.[34] The entire country seemed caught between endlessly discussing Wilde's fate and desperately trying to avoid mention of the carnal reality of the acts for which he was being jailed. This resonant silence was typical of the treatment of homosexuality during this period.

Wilde's American reputation was savaged. An amateur archivist of the period documented more than 900 sermons preached between 1895 and 1900 on the subject of his sins. Other guardians of public morality joined in on the tirade from the pulpit. In 1896 the president of Princeton, concerned for the welfare of his charges, compared Wilde to Nero, the Roman emperor infamous for fiddling while Rome burned.[35] Wilde's plays *An Ideal Husband* and *The Importance of Being Earnest*, which were running in New York at the time of his trial, were closed and a proposed traveling production of *A Woman of No Importance* was canceled.[36] Wilde was reviled for years after his release from prison. "The worst of his writing," opined the *New York Times Saturday Review* in 1906, "is beneath contempt and some is revolting."[37] A 1907 piece by Elsa Barker—whose work, it should be noted, was considered an indication of a minor Wilde revival—described Wilde as a "laureate of corruption" comparable to Satan in his fall. "We loathe thee," wrote Barker, "with the sure, instinctive dread of young things for the graveyard and the scar."[38] From such revivals all writers should be protected. Once a widely read poet and essayist, Wilde, over the course of his trial, was transformed into a symbol of "corruption," a person who was "beneath contempt."

Wilde's trial brought the question of the ethical, social, and legal status of homosexuality in the United States into sharp focus. While there had been previous scandals involving same-sex behavior—for example the Alice Ward/ Freda Mitchell case of 1892—the attention paid to Wilde in the media was unprecedented.[39] Havelock Ellis, the English sexologist, received a number of letters from Americans about the trial and its impact. "The Oscar Wilde trial," according to Ellis, "with its wide publicity, and the fundamental nature of the questions it suggested, appears to have generally contributed to give definitiveness and self-consciousness to the manifestations of homosexuality, and to have aroused inverts to take up a definitive attitude."[40] The trial forced many people to confront the issue of same-sex desire. The press' discretion was ineffective in keeping the details of Wilde's ordeal out of public notice. Private correspondence of the period was less reticent in treating the details of the trial. M. Carey Thomas followed the unfolding scandal and sent press clippings of the coverage to her passionate friend Mary Garrett. "I have hopes," Thomas wrote Garrett, "he will get off." The intrepid shopper on American college campuses could purchase a set of photographs, bound in scarlet, entitled "The Sins of Oscar Wilde."[41] By the time he entered jail, Wilde had "been confirmed as *the* sexual deviant for the late-nineteenth century."[42]

Anarchists were among the few public defenders of Wilde during his trial and its aftermath. They intervened forcefully in the ongoing debate that the trials set off. In conversation and in print the anarchists, in Goldman's words, "pleaded his case against the miserable hypocrites who had sent him to his doom."[43] In a cutting rejoinder to the religious leaders who were denouncing Wilde's sins, Mr. J. T. Small, a contributor to *Liberty*, asked whether Tucker might offer "a 'sermon' on the cowardice and hypocrisy of society in the way they are hustling Wilde's books out of the public libraries."[44] Though no sermon was forthcoming, Tucker did reprint a condemnation of Wilde's "daily torture" in prison, written originally for a French journal, by Octave Mirabeau, an anarchist, whose works Tucker sometimes published.[45] Mirabeau's reaction was widely shared among French artists and bohemian anarchists. *La Revue Blanche* (The White Review), for example, ran an article by anarchist Paul Adam entitled "The Malicious Assault," which protested Wilde's arrest. And, in 1896, a group of anarchists sponsored performances of Wilde's play, *Salome*. The painter Henri de Toulouse-Lautrec provided an illustration for Adam's article and designed the poster for *Salome*.[46] The reprinting of Mirabeau's article in *Liberty* indicates the degree to which Tucker was aware of and influenced by the European discussion of the Wilde case.

Like their French comrades, American anarchists refused to allow Wilde's works to be censored. To express solidarity with Wilde and to protest the widespread suppression of his work, anarchist journal *Lucifer the Light-Bearer* reprinted selections of Wilde's writings during and after his trial. Excerpts of his work had already appeared in the magazine, but in the context of the trial they took on a new importance. During the trial, Wilde's novels, plays, and poems were cited by the prosecution and were condemned as obscene. These texts, the prosecution argued, expressed the corrupt nature of their creator; they were dangerously steeped in the lusts for which their author was condemned. Merely reading them, it was argued, was to risk being infected with Wilde's disease.

The anarchists dismissed the idea that reading works like *The Picture of Dorian Gray* could lead readers to emulate Oscar Wilde. In an editorial in *Lucifer the Light-Bearer*, Lillian Harman, though not endorsing Wilde's actions, ridiculed the notion that his texts could lead others to engage in homosexual acts, and like J. T. Small, she condemned the widespread suppression of Wilde's work.

C. L. James also defended Wilde in *Lucifer*. Though James believed that Wilde's actions could be classified as a vice, he rejected the idea that homosexuality was a mark of insanity or that it was unnatural. And he certainly refused to accept the idea that there existed a basis for state regulation of homosexual behavior. If homosexuality is a vice, he argued, it is a minor one, akin to taking snuff or gambling. And unlike taking snuff, homosexuality had, according to James, a respectable pedigree. In the style of a number of contemporary apologists for homosexuality, James pointed out that the Greeks had permitted and even encouraged same-sex relations. Wilde's behavior, in other words, was hardly unprecedented. Given the high regard for Classical Greece that existed at the time, James felt that the condemnation of Wilde by the learned classes of England and America was hypocritical.[47] James, like a number of his colleagues, was not ready to pen positive defenses of same-sex love, but he strongly rejected the idea that behavior like Wilde's was deserving of punishment.

Of all the anarchists writing in the immediate context of the trial, Tucker was the most ferocious in his defense of Wilde. "The imprisonment of Wilde," wrote Tucker, "is an outrage that shows how thoroughly the doctrine of liberty is misconceived."[48] Like Goldman, Tucker believed that those who hounded Wilde were "miserable hypocrites." His condemnation, for Tucker, was an indictment against the culture that charged him:

> A man who has done nothing in the least degree invasive of any one; a man whose entire life, so far as known or charged, has been one of strict conformity with the idea of equal liberty; a man whose sole offense is that he has done something which most of the rest of us (at least such is the presumption) prefer not to do—is condemned to spend two years in cruel imprisonment at hard labor. And the judge who condemned him made the assertion in court that this was the most heinous crime that had ever come before him. I never expected to hear the statement of the senior Henry James, uttered half in jest, that "it is more justifiable to hang a man for spitting in a street-car than for committing murder" substantially repeated in earnest (or else in hypocrisy) from an English bench.[49]

This passage is perhaps the best defense of Wilde written on either side of the Atlantic. It is also a fine example of Tucker's learned and caustic pen. He uses Wilde's conviction to charge and convict those who presume to stand as the moral arbiters of their society. Wilde's jailers, Tucker insists—not Wilde—are the criminals. This unequivocal response would come to dominate the anarchist sexual politics of homosexuality in the years following Wilde's conviction, which starkly illustrated, for the anarchists, the danger of allowing the state to regulate same-sex relations. And the critique of those who supported Wilde's imprisonment became a useful way for anarchists to illustrate how their politics applied to private life.

Interestingly, in his defense of Wilde, Tucker questions the presumption that Wilde's desires were not widely shared. He acknowledged that many men had sexual relations with other men and did so to no one's detriment. One can even read Tucker's words as implying that most men—"most of the rest of us"—might find themselves in Wilde's place if they acted on desires that were commonly held, despite the "presumptions" that they reside only in a distinct category of men. This was, according to George Chauncey, a fairly common contemporary understanding of the nature of male sexual behavior: a man might seek sexual release through any number of partners, the gender of the partner being of less importance than the fact that they played the role of the receptor.[50] Wilde's age and status—most of his partners were younger, lower-class youth—would have signaled to most persons that he was the "dominant" partner is his relationships. In this regard, Wilde was a "normal man," capable and willing to satisfy his desires in a number of different ways. What then, Tucker asked his readers, made Wilde such a monster? It was hypocritical in the extreme, Tucker implied, to jail a man for an act that was, in fact, common. The cynical explanation for the judge's harshness is that the court was fully aware of how common Wilde's actions were. It was precisely that which caused the court to react with so much fury. Wilde's conviction was part of a show trial meant to brightly illustrate the boundaries of acceptable behavior.

Tucker was especially sharp with those on the Left who joined in attacking Wilde. London's *Daily Chronicle*, a publication associated with the Fabian socialists, was lambasted for "outdoing" the "Philistine press in its brutal treatment of Oscar Wilde." Named after Fabius, the Roman general who fought a slow and cautious war against Hannibal, the Fabians rejected revolution, instead pursuing reform of the existing political and economic order. Tucker could not resist implying that the position of the *Daily Chronicle* was a natural result of the Fabians' "brutal political philosophy." Tucker did allow that some of those who were "in semi-bondage to the same brutal philosophy" did rise to the occasion, though they did so, he implied, against the dictates of their beliefs. The Rev. Stewart D. Headlam, the editor of the *Church Reformer*, was "led, by his natural love of liberty and sympathy with the persecuted, in the magnificent inconsistency of becoming Oscar Wilde's surety." Tucker also gave "heartiest thanks" to Selwyn Image, a contributor to the *Church Reformer*, who wrote that "whatever in past days may have been [Wilde's] weaknesses, follies or sins, he has behaved in the hour of trial with a manly courage and generosity of spirit which I fear few of us under similar circumstances would have been virile and self-sacrific-

ing enough to exhibit." It was most unusual for Tucker, whose disdain for religion was well established, to quote a minister. Given the almost universal condemnation of Wilde, Tucker was forced to seek out allies in strange places.[51]

Tucker's laudatory note of Selwyn Image's description of Wilde as behaving
"with a manly courage and generosity of spirit" was very much in keeping with
the general depiction of Wilde that one finds in almost all anarchist texts. In
keeping with the way that both defenders and critics of Wilde used gendered
imagery, the anarchist sex radicals much preferred the "serious" Wilde of *The
Soul of Man under Socialism*, while the decadent, languid, feminized depictions
of him were favored by the writer's critics. Though attacks on Wilde almost
never failed to illustrate his effeminacy—a representation that drew upon and
helped reinforce ideas of homosexuality being a product of gender inversion—
those who defended him either avoided any mention of his gender identity
or framed his actions as gender appropriate. The anarchist sex radicals who
defended Wilde invariably portrayed him as being noble, strong, and resolute
in facing his accusers. Although few of them used the overt "manly" language
employed above, the general tone of their representations were consonant with
Image's terms. The anarchist sex radicals who rose to his defense represented
Wilde as a "normal man," albeit one whose sexual tastes ran afoul of the law
and social opinion.

In addition to taking on Wilde's European critics, Tucker lashed out at some
of his American foes. The statements of Dr. E. B. Foote Jr.—a liberal physician
who, along with his father, helped fund free-love and free-speech efforts—particularly incensed Tucker. The Footes were noted opponents of the moral cru-
sader Anthony Comstock, and Foote Sr. had been arrested for violating the
Comstock laws prohibiting the distribution of contraceptive literature.[52] The
younger Foote gave generously to the anarchist press, including to *Lucifer the
Light-Bearer*, and in later years, to Goldman's *Mother Earth*. On the question of
Wilde, however, Foote Jr. found himself in agreement with the poet's jailers.
Foote argued that Tucker had let Wilde off easily. Wilde's crime, according to
Foote, was "seducing" the young and impressionable "to his evil ways," and
these were acts that could not easily be excused. In a letter sent to *Liberty*,
Foote elaborated on this theme:

> One who has any knowledge of the men of his class well knows that one
> of their worst points is the disposition to seek out and make new victims of
> promising youth. This is made evident in their own confessions as quoted in
> Krafft-Ebing's *Psychopathia Sexualis*... It can hardly justify the let-alone policy
> when they set up shop to increase the "cult" of this sort of aesthetic culture;
> for they are not at all satisfied to find each other out (among the perverts of
> the same taste), but they are "hell-bent" on discovering fresh, virile, healthy,

vigorous, and unsophisticated young men of whom to make victims for vampires. You may say that youth should be so instructed and trained as to be safe against the wily, seductive attractions of even such glittering genius as that of Wilde and so say I; but, if State interference is permissible anywhere, it is against the vicious invasion of the family, which lures to destruction the finest specimens of manhood... Men of the...Wilde type don't recognize any youthful age limit, and boys are their constant prey...They can't and won't keep to themselves, and so a few—too few—get their deserts.[53]

Foote framed his attack on Wilde as a protection of the family and as a condemnation of those who, like the English writer, supposedly preyed on the young and innocent. Given the danger that these men presented, state intervention in the form of policing and punishment was merited. Moral order must be maintained by force if necessary, and if that meant empowering the state to throw men like Wilde in jail, Foote was ready to go along. Only in this way, Foote implies, can the plague of sodomy—an infection similar to the curse of the vampire—be stopped. Foote finished his letter to *Liberty* by comparing Wilde to Jack the Ripper, a seducer of little girls, lamenting that fact that Wilde was sentenced to serve only two years at hard labor and not twenty.

Foote's condemnation of Wilde for his seduction of "young innocents" was in keeping with contemporary accounts that demonstrated, in the words of Ed Cohen, "an obsessive concern with the effects of Wilde's 'corrupting influences' on the younger men with whom he consorted."[54] Of course, Wilde did have sex with men younger then himself. He was convicted on evidence that he had casual sexual relations with male prostitutes whose ages ranged from late-teens to early-twenties. By suggesting that Wilde was seducing "innocent youth," rather than hiring male prostitutes, Foote was able to sharpen his attack. Wilde responded to just such accusations in court, where he defended the relations he had with the young men in question. When asked what was meant by "the love that dare not speak its name," a coded reference to homosexuality drawn from a poem by Lord Alfred Douglas, Wilde himself made reference to the disparity in age between himself and his partners: "The love that dare not speak its name," said Wilde, "in this century is such a *great affection of an elder for a younger man* as there was between David and Jonathan, such as Plato made the very basis of his philosophy, as such as you find in the sonnets of Michelangelo and Shakespeare."[55] These were carefully chosen references, linking Wilde to some of the most celebrated figures of Western history. But this illustrious genealogy did little to counter critics like Foote who argued that Wilde had corrupted the young men he had sex with. Foote mobilized all the powers of the medical profession—citing the authority of Krafft-Ebing, as well as undocumented anecdote—to make the case that homosexuality is intrinsically linked to the seduction of youth. Foote's rhetoric speaks of vampires, the "cult" of the Wilde type, "the invasion of the family," and paints an image of literary decadence run amok, threatening the hearth and home through the display of "glittering seductions." Against the threat to youth and the family posed by the blinding glamour of Wilde, Foote argued that the only real protection is the power of the state.

While Tucker did not depict Wilde's relations linked to the glories of Ancient Athens or Elizabethan England, he found Foote's characterizations of the relationships Wilde had with his sexual partners wildly off the mark. Foote stressed Wilde's diabolical, hypnotic powers, and Tucker totally rejected the idea that he had played the role of the seducer. The young men Wilde had relations with were, according to Tucker, responsible for their own behavior. They were willing participants in a commercial exchange, not innocents whose lives had been ruined this man. In fact, there was no crime committed, since the behavior now being policed was engaged in by two consenting individuals. If Wilde were tried in the "court of equal liberty instead of ordinary law," Tucker wrote, the charges against him "would have been promptly dismissed on the ground that the alleged victims (not only Lord Douglas, but the others) were themselves mature and responsible persons and, as such, incapable of any seduction of which justice can properly take cognizance."[56] Wilde's partners may have been young, in other words, but they were hardly naïve. It was dangerous, Tucker maintained, to argue otherwise. The charge of seduction was an amorphous and problematic one. To argue that Wilde's sexual partners needed the protection of the state would be to legitimize external authority and begin down a slippery slope of increased moral vigilance on the part of the police. Tucker, always wary of the state, argued forcefully that people should be allowed to make their own choices, even at the risk of making mistakes they might later regret. As long as people were willing to bear the cost of their behaviors, no one had a right to limit those actions. In the words of one of his colleagues, "a bestowal of the liberty to do wrong is an indispensable condition of the acquisition of the liberty to do right."[57]

The Wilde case was not the first time that Tucker that dealt with the issue of sexuality and the age of consent. In 1886, for example, he protested attempts to raise the age of consent—the age at which a person might freely enter into sexual intercourse. The campaign to raise the age of consent—specifically for young women—swept the nation in the late-nineteenth and early-twentieth centuries, fed by lurid tales of child prostitution and anxiety over the sexualized culture of urban leisure. "The argument for raising the age of consent," according to historian Robert Riegel, "was that a man would be much less likely to seduce a young girl [into prostitution] if he realized that the law would classify the act as rape."[58] In Tucker's mind, the problem with this logic was that it interfered with liberty by bringing the state into the bedroom. It also flew in the face of the fact that adolescent girls regularly married older men with the blessing of parents, church, and state. Tucker argued that if the passions of a "girl of seventeen…of mature and sane mind, whom even the law recognizes as a fit person to be married…[should] find sexual expression outside of the 'forms of law' made and provided by our stupid legislatures" it was of no interest to anyone, but the girl and her lover. The campaign to raise the age of consent, Tucker argued, "belongs to that class of measures which especially allure stiff-necked moralists, pious prudes, 'respectable' radicals." He rejected the notion that raising the age of consent was necessary to protect the "honor" of young women, arguing that one could not more "dishonor a woman already several years past the age at which Nature provided her with the power of motherhood than by telling her that she hasn't brains enough to decide whether and in what way she will become a mother!"[59] Other anarchist sex radicals, like Lillian Harman who herself entered into a free-love relationship with a thirty-seven-year-old man at the age of sixteen, agreed with Tucker.[60] Unsparingly logical in his arguments, Tucker applied the same principles he articulated in the case of young women to Wilde and the young men he had sex with.

Given his views regarding state regulation of sexuality, it is not surprising to learn that Tucker characterized Foote's letter as "the most intolerant, fanatical, and altogether barbarous utterance that has come from a professed ultraliberal since I have been engaged in reform work." He reminded the younger Foote that his father had also been sentenced to jail on charges of immorality, as defined by the Comstock law. Foote Jr.'s intemperate words, Tucker stated, "justify me in reminding Dr. Foote Jr., that, in the eyes of the public, to be convicted by Comstock is scarcely a less disgrace than that which has fallen upon Oscar Wilde." Tucker lashed out at Foote, taking him to task for misrepresentation and for "betray[ing]…the fanatic's hatred of sin rather than the sane man's desire to protect against crime." Tucker refused to even consider the question of Wilde's sanity since "all noninvasive persons are entitled to be let alone, sane or insane." Tucker defended Wilde's work, stating that "his writings are a permanent addition to the world's literature" and arguing that "even [Wilde's] enemies admit that he has been perhaps the most influential factor in the achievement of that immense advance in decorative art which England and America have witnessed in the last decade."[61] Other anarchist papers picked up Tucker's defense of Wilde and his condemnation of Foote's response. *The Firebrand* very nearly repeated Tucker's own words: "Certain people who thought they knew as much as Dr. Foote thinks he knows would have sentenced E. B. Foote Sr. to twenty years imprisonment for his writings, and yet strange to say, the junior Foote does not seem to comprehend that he is in exactly the same frame of mind they were in."[62]

Four years after his heated exchange with Foote, Tucker was presented with the opportunity to help Wilde contribute yet another "addition to the world's literature." Tucker, who maintained his own press, was the first American publisher of one of Wilde's last major work of art, *The Ballad of Reading Gaol*, a powerful depiction of the cruelty of crime and punishment. The narrative poem describes the hanging of C. T. Woolridge, a man convicted of murdering his wife. The reader is left with the distinct impression that the punishment inflicted on Woolridge is no less a crime than the original murder that sealed his fate. "The poem," in the words of Richard Ellman, "had a divided theme: the cruelty of the doomed murderer's crime; the insistence that such cruelty is pervasive; and the greater cruelty of his punishment by a guilty society."[63] *The Ballad of Reading Gaol* is a bleak condemnation of mankind's capability for violence; in the words of Wilde's poem "each man kills the thing he loves."[64] In words that echo the title of Wilde's *The Soul of Man under Socialism*, Tucker wrote that in Wilde's prison poem "we get a terrific portrayal of the soul of man under Archism."[65] It is, of course, possible to interpret Wilde's poem as an attack on his own treatment by a "guilty society." Tucker certainly thought so. In his endorsement of the poem he wrote, "I especially commend its perusal to Dr. E. B. Foote Jr., who thinks that Wilde should have been imprisoned for twenty years."[66] Given the inevitable associations attached to Wilde's name, publishing the poem was as much an act of sexual radicalism as it was an effort to awaken public opinion against the terrors of the judicial system.

Though the ballad was brought to press in England in 1898, Wilde was unable to find an American publisher. Not even "the most revolting New York paper," he wrote his friend Reginald Turner, would touch his work.[67] In other words, not even the sensational press—whose coverage of crime and punishment was legendary—would print *The Ballad of Reading Gaol*. Tucker, who publicly defended the fallen poet during his trial, was more than willing to publish his poem. He set aside a number of other printing jobs and produced two editions: a handsomely bound book that sold for a dollar and an inexpensive pamphlet available for ten cents. Tucker encouraged his readers to "purchase a bound copy for his own library, and one or more copies of the pamphlet to give away." He also asked that his supporters "help this book to a wide circulation by asking for it at bookstores and news stands in his vicinity."[68]

Tucker was right in thinking that the notoriety of Wilde's work would attract readers and help his propaganda efforts. In May 1899, he wrote a friend, "The Wilde book has already brought me many queries from strangers regarding my other publications, and has given our work much publicity."[69]

Tucker's edition of *The Ballad of Reading Gaol* was widely reviewed in the mainstream press. This was most likely due to Wilde's perpetually scandalous reputation, his name continuing to sell tabloids even after his release from prison. Many of the reviewers confirmed Wilde's estimation of how Americans perceived him. *The Literary World*, like most publications, identified Wilde as the poem's author even though the author was identified only as C.3.3 (Wilde's cell number). They found that the poem "expresses a sickening sympathy for the criminal." That reviewer gave Tucker's edition a backhanded compliment playing on Wilde's tainted identity by noting that the poem's "publication in this present dainty form seems due…to the morbid attraction of its author's name."[70] Given the author's damaged reputation *The Philadelphia Inquirer* thought it "surprising that there should be any demand for what Wilde may write." Other papers were not so harsh. *The Albany Press* said of the ballad "it is horrible, gruesome, uncanny, and yet most fascinating and highly ethical." *The New York Sun* thought it "a pathetic example of genius gone to the dogs," but allowed "those who love the queer in literature will make a place for it on their bookshelves." *The Portland Oregonian* held a higher view of Wilde's poem, but reproached the author for "much unnecessary gloating over 'great gouts of blood.'" And in a review that must surely have warmed Tucker's heart, the *Pittsburgh Press* wrote, "B. R. Tucker, of New York, has just published one of the most remarkable poems of recent times… Those who are craving for a sensation…will do well to make themselves the possessors of this weird and pathetic ballad of a jailed one."[71]

It is unclear whether those who read reviews of *The Ballad of Reading Gaol* would have understood the reviewers' frequent characterizations of the work as "queer" or "weird" to imply sexual deviance. Such words did not necessarily convey any notion of erotic deviation. Though George Chauncey argues that the word "queer" was used at the turn of the century by men who "identified themselves as different from other men primarily on the basis of their homosexual interest," it was not synonymous with homosexuality.[72] However, given the reputation that Wilde had acquired since his imprisonment, any text associated with him would have some homosexual connotation. Certainly the use of the terms "morbid," "sickening sympathy," "gruesome," and "criminal" by the reviewers all served to remind readers of the recent trials and scandal. The mixture of words drawn from medical, moral, and legal categories indicate the various and complex ways in which these discourses formed the matrix within which same-sex relations were viewed. By refusing to allow themselves to be governed by the injunctions implicit in the condemnation of Wilde's work as "morbid" or "queer" the anarchists were contesting the dominant view of Wilde and those like him.

Tucker's reaction to the Wilde case was typical of the response that the anarchists had to the conviction. There are, for example, some striking similarities between Goldman's defense of Wilde against her friend Dr. Schmidt in 1901 and Tucker's critique of Foote six years earlier. In both cases, the anarchists were willing to contest the power of medical authorities to define the boundaries of acceptable behavior. Goldman's characterization of Wilde's conviction as a "great injustice" also parallels Tucker's view of the courts actions. And like Tucker, Goldman published and helped circulate some of Wilde's work. In one of the first editions of *Mother Earth*, Goldman published an excerpt from Wilde's essay *De Profundis*. Written while still in prison, this essay describes Wilde's struggle to make sense of his fate. Like *The Ballad of Reading Gaol*, *De Profundis* contains passages that are sharply critical of state power and the abuses of prison life. "Society," writes Wilde, "takes upon itself the right to inflict appalling punishment on the individual, but it also has the supreme vice of shallowness, and fails to realize what it has done."[73] A number of Wilde's works, including *The Soul of Man under Socialism* and *The Ballad of Reading Gaol* were advertised in the pages of *Mother Earth*, and bookstores and individual readers could order them through the Mother Earth Publishing Association.

Wilde became a powerful symbol within anarchist political discourse. In a letter to the German sexologist and homosexual rights activist Magnus Hirschfeld, Goldman explicitly linked her defense of Wilde to her anarchist politics. "As an anarchist," she wrote, "my place has always been on the side of the persecuted." Wilde, hounded by moralists and driven to an early grave, was an object lesson in the way that outsiders were treated. "The entire persecution and sentencing of Wilde," Goldman wrote, "struck me as *an act of cruel injustice and repulsive hypocrisy* on the part of the society which condemned this man." In protesting the treatment of Wilde, Goldman was also protesting the way in which all "the persecuted" were treated.[74] She even used a stanza from Wilde's *Ballad of Reading Gaol* as preface to an article she wrote about Leon Czolgosz, the young man who assassinated President McKinley in 1901. In condoning Czolgosz's actions she argued that he was a tragic product of a social order ruled by violence and coercion. Goldman compared Czolgosz to the prisoners that Wilde describes in his poem. That "inmates" go mad and strike out at their jailers is, as Goldman saw it, a "tragedy," but it is hardly unexpected.[75]

Other anarchists drew on Wilde's texts in the years following his imprisonment. John William Lloyd chose an excerpt from Wilde's essay, *The Soul of Man under Socialism* as a preface to his utopian novel, *The Dwellers in the Vale Sunrise*. In the passage Lloyd excerpted, Wilde looks forward to the day when "the true personality of man...will grow naturally and simply." In that future world, "man" will "not be always meddling with others or asking them to be like itself. It will love them because they will be different."[76] Wilde's text could signify libertarian social and cultural politics outside the realm of sexuality per se. *Dwellers in the Vale Sunrise* has a strong message of racial egalitarianism. Published in 1904, the novel portrays the life of a utopian community that models itself after those of "Indians, Eskimos, and other savages." Though the term "savage" has a jarring quality for contemporary readers, Lloyd used it in an ironic sense. This group of men and women, whose neighbors call them The Tribe, believe that these non-Western people's "social relations...are superior to the white man's." Sometimes called "white Indians" by their neighbors, The Tribe is a multiracial community that includes "some real Indians...and people of all colors, even one Chinaman."[77] Lloyd's representation of a racially and ethnically diverse social group living in harmony, though marred somewhat by a paternalistic tone, is a literary rebuke to the rising tide of Jim Crow and other forms of institutionalized racism that characterized turn-of-the-century America. Wilde's text, which champions a tolerant attitude towards human diversity, was a perfect accompaniment to Lloyd's vision of a racially harmonious utopia.

Within his novel, Lloyd cites Wilde as a political authority, at several points staging debates about economic or social questions between representative figures such as an urban socialist, a "natural man," a wise elder. These discussions serve as a way to explore the variety of possible solutions available to the pressing problems of the day. At one point, James Harvard, the urban socialist whose very name bespeaks learning, defends the use of machinery against those who feel that industrial development and modernity are inherently oppressive. "There is nothing abnormal about machinery," Harvard tells his listeners. "Kropotkin is right when he says our present killing servitude to the machine 'is a matter of bad organizations, purely, and has nothing to do with the machine itself,' and Oscar Wilde is right when he claims that the machine is the helot on which our future civilization shall rise."[78] Following Wilde and Kropotkin, Harvard argues that machines will free humanity from the need to perform tasks that sap the soul and body. Instead, people could devote themselves to cultivating their higher faculties. Lloyd's use of Wilde as a political thinker was very much in keeping with way in which *The Soul of Man under Socialism* and other texts were referenced by anarchists and others on the Left.

Lloyd's decision to use Wilde's text as a preface to his work illustrates how the disgraced writer's work functioned as a powerful and polyvalent resource for the anarchists. It was not just the content—the literal meaning of the words—that functioned in this way. Lloyd knew that by using the writing of a man who was tried and convicted for living his life as he chose, it would be part of the anarchist challenge to the powerful forces of moral opprobrium and social hierarchy. The passage from Wilde's essay advocates a liberal attitude toward social regulation and a celebration of variety in human expression. The economic principles of Wilde's variant of socialism had obvious appeals to the anarchists. His vision of a world where difference is tolerated, and even celebrated, fits well with Lloyd's politics.

But in the wake of his trial, using Wilde's writing was also a strategic signifier of Lloyd's sexual politics. Lloyd's attempt to grapple with the moral and social place of same-sex love is explored in greater detail below, but the fact that he himself may have been erotically drawn to men colors any interpretation of his choice of Wilde as textual frame for his novel. Though Lloyd's novels are little known among those who study homosexuality in American literature, *The Dwellers in the Vale Sunrise* is strongly marked by homoerotic desires. The main character, Forrest Westwood, reflects what historian Laurence Veysey characterizes as "the author's bisexual imagination."[79] Westwood, who reads Greek and Latin and wears nothing but a pair of knee-length trousers, is a combination of the Native American and Classical literary signifiers of same-sex desire.[80] The novel is replete with passages where Westwood's body is lovingly described. Westwood, though a member of The Tribe, is a singularly independent figure. He exists outside of the bonds of social convention and heterosexual pairing, living his life on the social and erotic margins of respectability. *The Dwellers in the Vale Sunrise* belongs to genre of homoerotic writing that literary historian James Gifford has identified as the "natural model" of homoerotic representation, which celebrates "the homosocial dream of the Bachelor and the Brotherhood, nearly always idealized to some degree, often featuring an Edenic landscape of freedom away from the pressures of the civilized world, where men could live with men and be free of constraints."[81] The citation of Wilde's most famous political text would quite usefully frame Lloyd's homoerotic literary utopia.

In addition to excerpts of Wilde's poetry and prose, articles on Wilde were featured in anarchist publications. The first issue of *The Free Spirit*, for example, featured a story by Rose Florence Freeman entitled "Oscar Wilde," which describes her experience of encountering Wilde's work as a young girl. Wilde's work and personal history deeply shaped Freeman's views of sexuality and moral boundaries. After reading one of his stories, Freeman approached a librarian to find out more about the author. Unwilling to spread the contagion of Wilde's decadence, the librarian was not forthcoming. "She told me the skeleton facts," Freeman noted, "and in her eyes I read evasion." When Freeman "asked what he had done that they sent him to prison," the librarian gave an "equivocal reply." Eventually, "and by persistent effort I discovered Oscar Wilde was sent to prison for a sin which was called unnatural." Freeman rejects this condemnation, seeing in Wilde a spirit "utterly free and Pagan." She "conceded to every being the right of sexual expression in whatever mode best enhanced his dream or fulfilled his desire." Despite the best efforts of those who condemned and continued to silence him, Wilde's voice emerged triumphant. "Those who have strutted before you," Freeman concludes, "mouthing their little morals and chuckling at your downfall have themselves been consigned to that oblivion toward which they so anxiously and with such foolish futility endeavored to turn you, their superior."[82] This vision of a triumphant Wilde was an apt symbol and reflection of Rose's own rejection of the values of the society in which she lived.

In several texts, anarchists identified themselves with Wilde. In 1916, Ben Reitman, Goldman's lover and lecture tour organizer, published a poem entitled "Vengeance" in *Mother Earth*. Reitman wrote the poem while imprisoned for the distribution of birth control information. Though it does not rise to the level of *The Ballad of Reading Gaol* or *De Profundis*, the poem contains many of the same themes as Wilde's prison texts. The fact that Reitman was jailed for a sex crime makes the comparison with Wilde's ordeal all the more compelling. "Vengeance" denounces those who put him behind "cruel steel walls" and denounces the "District Attorney [who] can send 100,000 to prison" and the "Judge who can take the light and liberty from 10,000 people."[83] These agents of the state are complicit in an unjust and oppressive system.

Reitman makes the comparison between his own imprisonment for a sex crime and Wilde's by explicitly referencing Wilde throughout his poem. In one passage Reitman tells his reader "I have been reading…Wilde," and in direct emulation of Wilde, he signs his poem using only his cell number, "Cell 424." The anarchist publication *Free Society* illustrated this when it printed an excerpt from *Ballad of Reading Gaol* under the new title, "The Prisoners,"[84] in August 1901. In Reitman's poem and other anarchist texts, Wilde functioned as a powerful symbol with which to express the way that the state worked to enforce sexual norms through imprisonment, censorship, and harassment.

One of the most striking uses of Wilde in anarchist work appears in Alexander Berkman's journal, *The Blast*. In January 1917, Berkman placed an excerpt of *The Ballad of Reading Gaol* on the cover. One of the most quoted passages from the poem, it reads: "But this I know, that every law that men have made for man, since first man took his brother's life, And the sad world began, but straws the wheat and saves the chaff with a most evil fan." The excerpt is laid over an illustration by Robert Minor, depicting a lynch mob chasing a lone man who is running for his life. In the background of this portrayal of mob violence, a scaffolds looms after.

This cover image is a complex one with multiple meanings and symbology. First, the image represents Tom Mooney, who was on trial for his alleged involvement with a bombing that took place at a Preparedness Day event in San Francisco in July 1916; Berkman certainly felt that Mooney was being hounded by a lynch mob and he defended him vociferously. The depiction of a lone man running from a mob was very much in keeping with how the anarchists portrayed Wilde's treatment by his tormentors. Whatever its interpreted meaning, the image was prescient. *The Blast* was shut down by the authorities shortly after the issue appeared. Wilde, here signified by the quotation of his text, had become a powerful symbol to the anarchists. He was a tragic figure with whom the anarchists could identify, and on whose behalf the anarchists made their case.

Even before the trial and imprisonment that martyred him in their eyes, Wilde appealed to the anarchists. The libertarian tone and content of Wilde's political writing and his occasional ideological self-identifications with anarchism were well known among his anarchist readers, but his imprisonment cemented the political bond. The defense of homosexuality became a way to expose the workings of "the miserable hypocrites" who acted through the state in the name of morality, justice, and the defense of order. Wilde's ideas about the value of individualism and the injustice of society echoed many of their own. With his conviction, imprisonment, and early death, Wilde rose to the level of a martyr. He came to signify something more than the prejudice against what Goldman called "inversion, perversion, and the question of sex variation;" Wilde became a symbol of the anarchist struggle to transform society. Sexual freedom, personal liberty, the freedom from coercion by the state, and the ideals expressed in *The Soul of Man under Socialism,* all came together in Wilde. By defending Wilde's right to love whomever he wished, the anarchist sex radicals were making a larger claim about the quality of the just society. From 1895 on, the defense of homosexuality was a persistent topic of discussion. No other political movement of the period engaged in a similar attempt to deal with the legal, moral, and social place of same-sex desire.

CHAPTER THREE:

FREE COMRADES: WHITMAN AND THE SHIFTING GROUNDS OF THE POLITICS OF HOMOSEXUALITY

IN 1905, EMMA GOLDMAN and her comrades gathered at her New York apartment to plan the launch of her new journal, *The Open Road*. The title was inspired by the work of Walt Whitman, a celebrated figure among many anarchists who saw a lyrical validation of their own beliefs in his work. Goldman felt that Whitman was "the most universal, cosmopolitan, and human of the American writers."[1] Her associate Leonard Abbott claimed that "The central motive of Whitman's best-known and most characteristic poetry is revolutionary."[2] Unfortunately, the name *The Open Road* was already taken and Goldman was forced to choose a new title: *Mother Earth*, but Goldman continued to champion Whitman. In an early article in *Mother Earth* titled, "On the Road," she urged her readers to follow Whitman on the "open road, strong limbed, careless, child-like, full of the joy of life, carrying the message of liberty, the gladness of human comradeship." This bracing message of adventure, exploration, and solidarity reflected Goldman's understanding of Whitman as a herald of a new world. Whitman's poetic voice depicted "wonderful vistas," which pointed to a way out of the crabbed society against which the anarchists struggled.[3]

Among the destinations that Whitman's "open road" suggested to his anarchist readers was sexual freedom. Whitman's work, Leonard Abbott declared, constituted "a direct assault upon Puritanism" and "called for a complete revision of sex-values."[4] In both form and content the writings of the "Good Gray Poet," as Whitman was sometimes called, presented a challenge to what the anarchists saw as the genteel tradition of Victorian reticence. "No one can read *Leaves of Grass*," wrote a contributor to the anarchist journal *Free Society* "without feeling that sex is sacred to Whitman in a way almost new to the unilluminated world."[5] In an essay entitled "Walt Whitman: Poet of the Human Whole," William Thurston Brown declared that, "If Whitman had done nothing else than sing the sacredness of the body and declare that the body is just as divine, just as clean, just as holy, just as sacred as ever the soul has been thought to be, he would have earned the never-dying gratitude of all the unborn myriads of human beings that are to come into this human world."[6] Whitman challenged the "distinction between sexual (bad) and spiritual (good)" hierarchy of values that, according to Jonathan Ned Katz "haunted" American culture.[7]

The anarchists were not alone in seeing in Whitman's work a message of sexual liberation. Among Whitman's most passionate admirers were readers who saw him as a defender of homoerotic desire. According to Leonard Abbott, "Homosexuals all over the world have looked toward Whitman as toward a leader."[8] Whitman's work provided these readers a language to discuss same-sex love free of the taint of sin, crime, degeneration, and insanity. English critic, John Addington Symonds wrote of Whitman that "no man in the modern world has expressed so strong a conviction that 'manly attachments,' 'athletic love,' [and] 'the high towering love of comrades,' is a main factor of human life, a virtue upon which society will have to rest, and a passion equal in its permanence and intensity to sexual affection."[9]

Symonds and other readers were especially responsive to Whitman's "Calamus" poems that described love between men as "the dear love of comrades." Edward Carpenter, for example, first encountered Whitman's work at the age of twenty-five. "What made me cling to [Whitman] from the beginning," he later recalled, "was largely the poems which celebrate comradeship. That thought so near and dear and personal to me, I had never before seen or heard fairly expressed; even in Plato and the Greek authors there have been something wanting (so I thought)."[10] Carpenter was profoundly shaped by his encounter with Whitman's work. In addition to writing essays on the subject of sexuality, including same-sex love, that made frequent reference to Whitman's work, Carpenter composed a collection of poems entitled *Towards Democracy*, which echoed the themes of *Leaves of Grass*.

Whitman's poetry and the homoerotic interpretations of his work, produced by critics like Carpenter, influenced a number of anarchist sex radicals. Whitman was a key figure through which a politics of homosexuality emerged in the anarchist movement. In the early part of twentieth century, the nature and quality of erotic desires represented in Whitman's work became the topic of conversation among a number of anarchist sex radicals. Unlike Wilde, Whitman was not involved in a dramatic scandal, trial, or a specific moment that brought the subject of homosexuality into sharp, public visibility. Whitman obscured his erotic attraction to men and, on at least one occasion, he explicitly rejected the suggestion that his work represented same-sex desire.[11] Not surprisingly, therefore, anarchist discussions of Whitman's work as it related to sexuality are uneven, complex, and shifted over time. While some saw in his celebration of comradeship a representation of same-sex desire, others read an affirmation of intense friendship and social bonds. In the nineteenth century the anarchists' discussions of Whitman's work and sexuality were largely concerned with the legitimate boundaries and expression of heterosexual desire. It is only in the twentieth century that discussions of Whitman's work and its relationship to homosexuality begin to appear with any frequency in the anarchist press. This shift mirrors the way that ideas about homosexuality evolved in the opening decades of the twentieth century. During this period, the meaning of Whitman's work and what it implied about its author and his admirers reflected the increased salience of the understanding of the homosexual as a distinct personality type, and of sexuality as a key to understanding human psychology.

By tracing the discussions of Whitman and of sexuality that were carried out by a number of anarchists—among them Benjamin Tucker, John William Lloyd, Leonard Abbott, and Emma Goldman—we can get some sense of the ways that shifting sexual norms and society's changing beliefs shaped the anarchists' politics of homosexuality. Lloyd, in particular, is an interesting figure in this study. In the early-twentieth century, he made a number of statements regarding the social and ethical status of homosexuality with specific reference to Walt Whitman. He also referenced Whitman's work in direct and indirect ways in his own sexual politics. Lloyd's relationship with Whitman was influenced by his reading of Edward Carpenter and other European critics, as well as sex radicals whose changing interpretation of Whitman's work brought the "Good Gray Poet's" erotic nature in to ever-sharper focus. But Lloyd had difficulty negotiating the rapidly changing sexual and political landscape of the early-twentieth century. He found the unstable

Leonard Abbott, circa 1905 (courtesy of the Kate Sharpley Library).

sexual terrain treacherous. Emma Goldman—in the years following her expulsion from the United States—also found her views of Whitman's sexuality and
the meaning of his work dramatically altered by her encounter with European
critics of his work. Just as was the case with Wilde, American anarchist sex radicals' understanding of Whitman's sexuality and the political implications of it
were profoundly shaped by European sex radicals.

In the nineteenth century, American critics and readers focused on poems
that represented relations between men and women when discussing the erotic
nature of his work. There were, for example, numerous attacks on Whitman's
poetry collection, "The Children of Adam," which contained poems such as "A
Woman Waits for Me." In this poem, Whitman declares that "all were lacking
if sex were lacking" and that "I pour the stuff to start sons and daughters fit for
these States, I press with slow rude muscle."[12] This kind of language did not go
unnoticed, and there were repercussions. In 1897, for example, the anarchist
journal, *The Firebrand*, was censored for reprinting "A Woman Waits for Me."
Until the twentieth century, though, Whitman's homoerotic texts, notably his
"Calamus" poems, which were beloved of readers such as Carpenter and Symonds, elicited little in the way of hostile commentary. This is not to say that
the homoerotic elements of Whitman's work went completely unnoticed: As
early as 1855, Rufus Griswold published one of the few nineteenth century
discussions of the homoerotic currents in Whitman's work. He condemned
Whitman as a "monster" of "vileness," and denounced his work for represent-
ing the *"Peccatum illud horrible, inter Christianos non nominandum,"* (the horrible
sin not to be named among Christians) a traditional legal and religious phrase
used to name same-sex acts.[13] But Griswold's attack, though ferocious, was
little commented upon; its indirect language reflected the contemporary difficulty of dealing with "sins" thought so "horrible" that they could "not be
named among Christians." That he used Latin rather than English in making
his charge made his accusation all the more obscure.

Anarchist discussions of Whitman and his work in the nineteenth century
reflected the prevailing erotic interpretations of Whitman's writing. The discussions and debates that did occur in the movement largely made reference to
illicit relations between men and women that figured in the work. In 1882,
for example, Benjamin Tucker engaged in a fight over an attempt to censor
Leaves of Grass on the grounds of obscenity. That spring, Oliver Stevens, the
district attorney of Suffolk County, Massachusetts moved to prevent Whitman's
publisher, James R. Osgood, from bringing out a second edition of the book,
and sought to ban its sale in the Boston area. Osgood buckled under the pressure, and Whitman was forced to find another publisher. Tucker responded to

the district attorney's attack by procuring a number of copies from Whitman's new publisher with the intention of distributing them. He later revealed that he "inserted an advertisement conspicuously in the daily papers of Boston, as well as [in his] own journal, offering the book for sale." Tucker refused to allow Whitman's work to be censored; he defied the actions of the district attorney through direct action. This bold move succeeded: Within the year, Tucker reported to *Liberty's* readers that "*Leaves of Grass* is now sold openly by nearly all the Boston booksellers. I have won my victory, and the guardians of Massachusetts morality have ignominiously retreated."[14]

Though Whitman's work was attacked because of its supposedly salacious nature, neither Stevens nor Tucker make any mention of the homoerotic elements throughout. To their eyes, as to most of their contemporaries, Whitman's defense of comradeship did not read as specifically homoerotic. Most nineteenth-century Americans did not equate closeness between men—even if expressed with kisses and hugs—with homosexuality. "Intense, even romantic man-to-man friendships," writes Jonathan Ned Katz, "were a world apart in the era's consciousness from the sensual universe of mutual masturbation and the legal universe of 'sodomy,' 'buggery,' and the 'crime against nature' (legally, men's anal intercourse with men, boys, women, and girls, and human's intercourse with beasts)."[15] Romantic friendships between members of the same sex were a respectable and valued element of middle-class social life. Homosexuality was identified with the sin of sodomy and dramatic inversion of gender roles, not with intense same-sex friendship. If same-sex relations were not tainted, as it were, by gender inversion and overt sexuality then they were considered noble and necessary. This meant that a wide range of same-sex intimacy was tolerated. "Romantic lovers and sodomites," writes Katz, "inhabited different spheres, leaving a great unmapped space between them."[16] In the nineteenth century, and even into the twentieth century, Whitman's depiction of "the manly love of comrades" was taken to be a commonplace, if somewhat excited, praise of friendship. It was only at the turn of the century that such close bonds began to be suspect.[17] Whitman, as Eve Kosofsky Sedgwick argues, straddles the homosocial world of the nineteenth century and the "homosexual/homophobic world" of the twentieth century.[18] The relative lack of attention paid to the homoerotic content in Whitman's work in the nineteenth century was a function of the fact that people were only identified as "homosexual" if they clearly expressed inappropriate gender behavior. Whitman did not fit this type. It was not until the 1900s that a more clearly defined notion of a "homosexual Whitman"—one premised primarily on a psychological category, rather than a gender identity—would emerge.

Though Tucker makes no mention of the homoerotic elements of Whitman's work, his defense of Whitman did contribute, indirectly, to Tucker's politics of homosexuality. The efforts to censor Whitman sharpened Tucker's critique of state regulation of public morals and personal behavior. Reflecting on his fight with Stevens over the merits of Whitman's work, Tucker mocked "the ever-watchful state" that rushes to protect "pure and innocent youth" from the harmful effects of thoughts and words. Tucker admitted that some might be offended by Whitman's frank discussion of the body, but argued that the costs of censorship are much higher. And though he hardly believed that reading Whitman would lead to illicit behavior, Tucker insisted that, even were this the case, the costs of suppressing sexuality were too great. "There is no desire, however low," Tucker insisted, "whose satisfaction is so fraught with evil consequences to mankind as the desire to rule, and its worst manifestation is seen when it is directed against the tongues and pens and thoughts of men and women." Tucker maintained that the state, and not works of literature, was the real threat to the health of society. "Abolish the State," he concluded, "and leave obscenity run its course."[19] Tucker's line of reasoning in his argument with Stevens was almost exactly the same as that which he employed in responding to what he called the "criminal jailers of Oscar Wilde" some thirteen years after his fight with "the guardians of Massachusetts morality." Some might find Wilde's behavior "low," but the State's actions were by far the greater evil.

Like Goldman's *Mother Earth*, Tucker's *Liberty* carried numerous discussions of Whitman's work and their relevance to anarchism. Their shared enthusiasm for Whitman was one of the few points of agreement between these two leading anarchists. "Walt Whitman," Tucker wrote in the early 1880s, "is an economist as well as a poet—and of the right and radical sort too."[20] *Liberty* reprinted critical articles on Whitman and offered readers the opportunity to order Whitman's work. Tucker was keen to remind his readership that he had stood by Whitman in his hour of need.

Liberty even reported on the lives of Whitman's associates: When William Douglass O'Conner, one of Whitman's earliest admirers, died in 1889, *Liberty* carried an extensive obituary written by Horace Traubel, Whitman's caretaker and one of his most devoted literary progeny. Whitman, who followed Tucker ever since being defended by him in 1882, wrote approvingly of the O'Conner obituary to friends.[21] It is clear from his conversations with Traubel and others that Whitman read *Liberty*. He was not an anarchist—despite the best efforts of some of his radical readers to make him so—but he did admire the anarchists' fire and passion. That Tucker and other anarchist sex radicals were among his defenders in the 1870s and 1880s, figured prominently in shaping his regard for them. "Tucker," Whitman told Traubel, "did brave things for *Leaves of Grass* when brave things were rare. I could not forget that."[22]

One of Whitman's most vocal advocates in *Liberty* was John William Lloyd. In a poem entitled "Mount Walt Whitman," written on the occasion of Whitman's death in 1891, Lloyd mourned the passing of the "great, gray rock." He declared that Whitman was the "poet of Nature, comrade of free men;" such a towering figure's passing was hard to believe. "Other poets have been Olympian," Lloyd wrote, "But you are Olympus itself."[23] Lloyd, a poet himself, admired Whitman's courage as a writer and an artist.

Lloyd's admiration was directly related to the poet's erotic sensibility. In an essay on Whitman's poetry published in an 1892 edition of *Liberty*, Lloyd praised his honest treatment of sexuality and the body. Whitman, Lloyd wrote, had "noble contempt for mealymouthedness which the great and the greatly-in-earnest have always shown, his words go to the birth of things, without shame or sham." He was the poet of "the rude, blunt man of simple ideas, direct action, and untamed loves and hates."[24] So passionate was Lloyd's advocacy of Whitman that their sexual politics were often compared. "Comrade Lloyd," wrote C. H. Cheyese, "is a passionate lover of freedom, and believing, like Whitman, that sex is the basis of all things, he unhesitatingly voices his thought on sexual relations."[25] Lloyd's feelings for Whitman were such that he became identified with the "Good Gray Poet" within the movement.

In October 1902, Lloyd returned to a discussion of Whitman and sexuality. No longer a contributor to *Liberty*, Lloyd published his piece on Whitman in *The Free Comrade*, a small journal he edited, whose very title echoes Whitman's rhetoric of the "manly love of comrades." Lloyd began his piece by resolutely affirming his attraction to the opposite sex. "The love of man for woman has been known to me, I can literally say, from my infancy. An aureola of beauty and divinity surrounded all women in my thoughts—a feeling that has rather grown with the years than lessened." But recently, Lloyd continued, he recognized that human desire and erotic attraction expanded to encompass men, as well as women, "so that now the whole human race, in general and particular" stood before him "in innate worshipfulness and lovableness." This statement, though indirect and cautious, is the strongest public declaration that Lloyd ever makes about the legitimacy and value of same-sex relations.[26]

In his essay Lloyd states that two men transformed his views on the subject of love and sex. "I owe much," he wrote, "to the teaching of [Walt] Whitman and [Edward] Carpenter." They were responsible for awakening in Lloyd an awareness of the erotic potential of "the whole human race"—that is, men as well as women—and giving him a vocabulary with which to express his feelings. Carpenter and Whitman's sexual ethics were refreshingly free of traditional injunctions against sexual pleasure. "Whitman and Carpenter rejoice in the fleshly-body of the human soul, which to them continually smiles from every crevice." According to Lloyd the two poets moved beyond the "abominable asceticism which grew like a fungus on early Christianity" and which holds "all normal human joys and functions as the baits on Hell's trap." Their post-Christian ethics allowed for an open defense of the body, an ethics of life rooted firmly in the natural expression of human desire. By arguing that these men's work could serve as a basis for a sex-positive outlook, Lloyd avoided directly discussing the sin of sodomy, and therefore, sidestepped the Christian injunction against homosexuality.[27]

Though Lloyd was particularly effusive in regards to Carpenter's work, he recognized the Englishman's debt to Whitman's writings. "Carpenter is to Whitman," Lloyd wrote, "as Elisha to Elijah, as John to Jesus, as Plato to Socrates."[28] Carpenter himself was the first to acknowledge this debt in an essay that appeared the same year as Lloyd's. He wrote that "Whitman by his great power, originality, and initiative, as well as by his deep insight and wide vision, is in many ways the inaugurator of a new era of mankind; and it is especially interesting to find that this idea of comradeship, and of its establishment as a *social institution*, plays so important a part with him."[29] Compared to "Whitman's full-blooded, copious, rank, masculine style," Carpenter felt that his own was "milder...as of the moon compared with the sun."[30] A number of critics echoed Carpenter's remarks. Havelock Ellis' first impression of Carpenter's work was that it was "Whitman and water."[31] Lloyd was more kind: For him, Carpenter was "Whitman's truest comrade, understood him best, is his best interpreter."[32]

John William Lloyd's poetry collection, *Songs of the Unblind Cupid*, 1899 (courtesy of the Kate Sharpley Library).

In this 1902 article, Lloyd focused on Carpenter's work rather than Whitman's because he, unlike Whitman, dealt explicitly with same-sex desire in his writing. Carpenter began writing about the topic of same-sex love in the waning years of the nineteenth century. At first, these essays were circulated amongst private contacts, but in the mid-1890s, the Manchester Labour Press published a number of pamphlets, notably *Homogenic Love, and Its Place in a Free Society* and *An Unknown People*, in which Carpenter explored what he called "homogenic love." "Homogenic," like "Uranian" and the "Intermediate Sex" were terms Carpenter used to discuss same-sex erotic relationships. Initially his works, which did not have broad distribution, circulated through private networks, particularly those in progressive and radical circles. That Lloyd was familiar with these works indicates though, that Carpenter's early writings on homosexuality did travel across the Atlantic. Carpenter also produced work that hinted at, but did not explicitly deal with, the topic of homosexuality. These texts were published by mainstream printers and had a broad circulation in both England and the United States. For example, in the same year that Lloyd wrote *The Free Comrade* essay, Carpenter published *Ioläus: An Anthology of Friendship*, which gathered together historical and literary examples of intense same-sex friendships. According to Jonathan Ned Katz, *Ioläus* was "one of the first collections of homosexually relevant documents of male-male intimacy."[33] Its title refers to demigod Hercules' love for the young, male mortal, Ioläus. Hercules was, of course, a paragon of masculine strength and nobility and so served as an impeccable touchstone for a treatment of same-sex love. Though Carpenter devotes much of his book to a study of Greek texts, he dedicated an entire chapter of *Ioläus* to Whitman's poetry of "comradeship."

Carpenter's writings on same-sex love were critical in the development of Lloyd's sexual politics. In his 1902 *Free Comrade* article Lloyd makes specific reference to a number of Carpenter's works that dealt explicitly with homosexuality. He is clear about the extent of the English sex radical's influence on his thinking:

> I think most of the moderns feel as I felt—that the love of man for man, and woman for woman was an abnormal if not a sinister thing, if at all intense or inspired by physical beauty. And perhaps it is well for Carpenter in his little books on "Homogenic Love," "An Unknown People," and in the recent "Ioläus," to remind us that friendship between those of the same sex is a spontaneous and inborn passion—in every way equal in intensity and tragedy to that between the sexes—to a multitude of human beings in our midst, and that among the ancient Greeks it was not only a respectable love, but the love, about which all the honor and joy and pride of the people centered.[34]

Lloyd responded to Carpenter's representation of homosexuality as a deep and warm friendship. In *Ioläus*, homosexuality resembled the masculine love that supposedly flourished among Greek warriors, rather than the illicit, degenerate, and sinful lust that consumed effeminate sodomites. The marshalling of Greek texts was important since, as Lloyd points out, same-sex relationships had a "respectable" place in that society. And, of course, Classical Antiquity held a very high place of honor in Anglo-American culture, recognized as it was as the

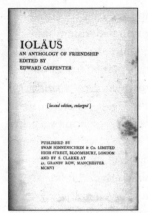

IOLÄUS
AN ANTHOLOGY OF FRIENDSHIP
EDITED BY
EDWARD CARPENTER

[Second edition, enlarged]

PUBLISHED BY
SWAN SONNENSCHEIN & Co. LIMITED
HIGH STREET, BLOOMSBURY, LONDON
AND BY S. CLARKE AT
41, GRANBY ROW, MANCHESTER
MCMVI

Ioläus, by Edward Carpenter (courtesy of the Kate Sharpley Library).

birthplace of democracy. Lloyd was drawn by Carpenter's claim that Whitman's work would usher in a new Greek age. His work suggested to both men that the "social institution" of comradeship, which is too often "socially denied and ignored," will "arise again, and become a recognized factor of modern life."[35]

By accumulating examples of same-sex friendship, Carpenter sought to develop a respectable genealogy for homogenic love. He hoped to show, in Lloyd's words, that "the love of a man for his comrade was a passion pure and divine." Seen in the light of thousands of years of "passion pure and divine," homosexuality was hardly "abnormal" or "sinister." On the contrary, it was—according to Lloyd—"utterly altruistic, faithful unto death," equal in quality and kind to the love "common between men and women of our day."[36] Both Lloyd and Carpenter responded strongly and favorably to Whitman's skillful use of the notion of comradeship as a covering frame for homosexuality. The language and terms associated with friendship could describe passionate attachment between members of the same sex without using the language of sin, crime, or pathology.

Perhaps the most appealing aspect of Whitman and Carpenter's work for Lloyd was that both men implicitly refuted the notion that male homosexuality was effeminate. "It would be easy to show," Lloyd wrote, "that in almost every instance such homogenic love takes place where national ideas are military and masculine."[37] By insisting on the masculine nature of male-same-sex love Lloyd was distancing the "manly love of comrades" from the figure of the "fairy," a man who signaled his erotic attraction to other men through his inversion of the masculine conventions of gait, dress, and mannerisms. Gender inversion was the key framework within which Americans and Europeans understood homosexuality. The fairy and his female counterpart, the "manly woman," were instantly recognizable personas.

Because of their transgression of gender and sexual norms, "fairies" were subject to acts of ferocious violence. Earl Lind, a self-described "fairy" and the author of the 1918 memoir *The Autobiography of an Androgyne*, tells of being thrown off an army base by a soldier named Murphy. According to Lind, Murphy toyed with him by lifting him by his hair, carrying him to the gate of the base, and throwing him on the road, kicking him and "crying out for me to get along home, while I was screaming in fright."[38] This was not unusual treatment. In fact soldiers, according to Lind, were "the easiest of conquests;" those outside the armed services were less likely to treat him well.[39] In addition to enduring near constant acts of violence, Lind was subject to verbal attacks and blackmail, behavior that accompanied almost all of his sexual and social relations. Given the violence and social ostracism "fairies" faced, it is not surprising that Lloyd, like Carpenter, John Addington Symonds, and others influenced by Whitman, argued that "same-sex passion is quintessentially manly."[40] These men gravitated to Whitman's figure of the comrade to represent homosexuality, in part, because it stood in sharp contrast to the much-derided fairy.

Lloyd concluded his discussion of Carpenter's sexual politics by asking his readers to open themselves up to variety in loves. His call for tolerance places homosexuality within a broad spectrum of loving and noble human relations:

> When we once enlarge ourselves on this matter of love, draw a free breath, so to speak, and take a really brave look around, we shall find that nothing but our superstitions on one hand and our selfish meanness on the other has kept us from a whole world of love and lovers always ready and waiting for us. There is no reason why every kind of love that has ever been known to man should not be accepted, purified, understood, embraced, and wisely made to yield its joy and service to the life of every one of us. Larger! Larger!—Let us be more! Let us give and accept more.[41]

"Larger" was a key term in Lloyd's political rhetoric, and it was one also employed by Carpenter, who described his politics as the "Larger Socialism."[42] In both men's lexicon, "larger" carries the connotation of the moral high ground, as well as an implicit endorsement of the diversity of sexual desire and activity. In this passage above, Lloyd implies that to restrict one's inclinations, or those of others, bespeaks a limited understanding of the multiplicity of human desire. This paean to sexual tolerance is very much in keeping with anarchist arguments regarding the expression of desire free of external authority.

Lloyd presents same-sex eroticism as being squarely within the range of a "larger love"—it is neither deviant nor marked as sharply distinct from heterosexual desire. This was a very frequent theme in his writing on sex. "If you have the Larger Love," Lloyd wrote in 1901, "every woman will be to you as lover, mother, sister, or daughter, and every man will be to you a lover, father, brother, or son."[43] This eroticized human family is, at the very least, open to the possibility of same-sex relations. Every person, regardless of gender, presents the possibility of friendship or sex—the two not being mutually exclusive. Elsewhere Lloyd would go further, stating in a 1902 essay that, "Our Hero must be that man or woman who can love the most men and women in the most beautiful, large, tender, and fearless way."[44] In a poem published that same year, "Not the Lover Who Loves But Me," Lloyd used the language of comradeship and "largeness" to represent an eros which allows a reader multiple interpretations of the gender, number, and nature of the lovers described within. "I love liberty more than all," wrote Lloyd. "My lover must love immensity/And all the great things more than me.../the comrade-touch is the closest kiss."[45] These are not unequivocal defenses of homosexual desire, but that is precisely the political effect that Lloyd sought through the concept of the "larger love." Like Whitman and Carpenter, Lloyd used "evasion and indirection [as] strategies to encode homoerotic content."[46] He worked hard to blur the conceptual distinction between "homosexual" and "heterosexual," framing desire within the idea of "larger love." The inclusiveness of the larger love allows for a wide range of desires, and situates them within a spectrum of respectable relationships.

Lloyd read Carpenter and Whitman as political, as well as poetic, masters. This is not surprising given that both men's essays and poetry directly addressed political questions. Carpenter, who Lloyd felt was "the greatest man of Modern England," was widely known among socialists for his poetry anthology entitled *Towards Democracy*.[47] The "democracy" that Carpenter urged his readers to seek was an individual, psychological, and social liberation, as well as an economic and political one. "*Towards Democracy*," writes Stanley Pierson, "foretold of the liberation of man's natural desires or instincts from the repressions of civilization."[48] Lloyd clearly appreciated the political implications of *Towards Democracy*, and in 1902, he wrote that Carpenter's anthology was "one of the great books of the world...a book full to bursting with human love, tender, insistent, compassionate, comprehending, cheering, consoling, exalting, a book manly and virile, breathing man's and Nature's ozone from every sentence." Comparing Carpenter directly to political figures he admired, Lloyd wrote that "the 'Democracy' of which [Carpenter] prophecies and chants is the 'Anarchy' of Kropotkin, the 'institution of the dear love of comrades' of Whitman, the 'fellowship' which is the 'life' of [William] Morris—the world of emancipated men, free and loving."[49] This mixture of social critics, literary figures, and revolutionaries was reflective of Lloyd's eclectic politics.

Reading Whitman and Carpenter as political texts was not an idiosyncratic act on Lloyd's part. "The poet of comradeship," writes Whitman-scholar Charles B. Willard, "gather[ed] about him a comitatus of devoted adherents."[50] A member in good standing of this group, Lloyd employed the term used by the most devoted followers of Whitman to describe themselves: "Whitmanites."[51] In Canada, England, and the United States, Whitmanite Societies formed, sponsoring journals, lectures, and providing forums for the discussion of literature and politics.[52] William James, a skeptical observer of this phenomenon, wrote that Whitmanites were "infected...with [Whitman's] love of comrades," and were eager to form societies, publish journals, and write, "hymns modeled on Whitman's 'peculiar prosody.'"[53] In his book, *The Changing Order: A Study of Democracy*, Oscar Lovell Trigg, one of the best known of the American Whitmanites, argued, "Whitman is the first great prophet of cosmic democracy... The entire volume of 'Leaves of Grass' is dedicated to the cause of unity—unity in oneself, unity with others in love and comradeship, unity of states in nationalism, unity of mankind in a spiritual identification." Like Lloyd, Trigg was drawn to Carpenter's work, which seemed to spell out in greater detail the political implications of Whitman's own more evasive voice. Trigg prefaced *The Changing Order* with an excerpt from Carpenter's *Towards Democracy*.[54]

Lloyd did not abandon his anarchism when he threw his hat in with the Whitmanites (which was not a formal movement, but a cultural sensibility). He continued to be active in the anarchist movement, though, in an act that illustrates his complex—not to say confused—political affinities, he also became a member of the newly launched Socialist Party. Lloyd advocated what he called "free socialism," a mixture of libertarian and communitarian impulses. Socialism was, for Lloyd, a moral impulse toward community, while anarchism was a set of ideas with which to throw off the dead weight of traditional morals. Both freedom and community, Lloyd argued, were necessary elements of the good life. Leonard Abbott, one of Lloyd's closest colleagues expressed the idea thusly: "To those who have lived selfishly and for themselves only, Socialism will come as a gospel summoning them to thought and activity on behalf of large social ends. To those who have been repressed by social custom and habit, who need, above all, self-realization and a clearer vision of their own powers, Anarchism will seem the indispensable message."[55] Anarchism, which was especially useful in rethinking social and sexual codes, persisted as a strong element of Lloyd's thinking.

Of course, not every single Whitman enthusiast was engaged in a defense of homoeroticism. Some of Whitman's fans were shocked to learn what their peers saw between the lines. One American who read John Addington Symonds' study of Whitman acknowledged that, "a part of it reaches the high water mark of criticism," but he recoiled at Symonds' erotic reading of the Calamus poems. "It seems that 'Calamus' suggests sodomy to him...I think that much learning, or too much study of Greek manners and customs, hath made this Englishman mad."[56] Most of Whitman's readers interpreted the bonds of "manly comradeship" as signifying platonic intensity of feeling between and among men—including friendship and class solidarity. Such intense feelings were widely celebrated on the Left. Nick Salvatore's biographical study of Eugene V. Debs, the leader of the Socialist Party, identifies the central place that "manliness" and "brotherly love" held in Debs' ethical vision. Debs was given to rapturous exhortations on behalf of "the ties and bonds and obligations [that] large souled and large hearted men recognize as essential to human happiness."[57] Such statements are nearly interchangeable with Lloyd and Carpenter's apologies for homoerotic love. It was the imprecision of the boundaries between deviant and respectable desires and relationships that made Whitman's work so attractive to Carpenter and Lloyd. Whitman's rhetoric of comradeship was multivalent and could speak to a specific idealization of same-sex desire, as well as to a set of powerful political and social values.

John William Lloyd's affinity with Edward Carpenter extended beyond ideology—the two men even looked alike. Both sported beards and wore the clothes of a workingman or hardy farmer. Both men represented themselves in publications and photos in relaxed poses wearing broad hats and collarless shirts. This was, of course, the very style of dress that Whitman, who thought of himself as "one of the roughs," favored.[58] But the connections between Lloyd and his English counterpart were more than sartorial: in *The Free Comrade* and elsewhere, Lloyd promoted Carpenter's work and compared it to his own. Both men were reformers, sex radicals, and champions of Walt Whitman. Carpenter's politics, like Lloyd's, was "in harmony with the main tenets of anarchist thought."[59] They embraced a non-sectarian socialism, arguing (in the Carpenter's words) that, "We are all traveling along the same road."[60]

Lloyd's ideological kinship with Carpenter was well known among his contemporaries. In a tribute published in England two years after Carpenter's death in 1929, Lloyd was described as "Carpenter's most devoted American disciple…who did more than any other follower in the United States…to familiarize [Americans] with his doctrines."[61] According to a 1902 profile by Leonard Abbott, which appeared in *The Comrade*—a publication aligned with the Socialist Party that published a wide array of Whitmanite poetry and essays—Lloyd "inherited Whitman's breadth," but he was "in a special sense the brother of Edward Carpenter."[62]

It is possible that Abbott, who moved to the United States from England in the late 1890s, introduced Lloyd to Carpenter's writings on same-sex love. Abbott met Carpenter "at a Socialist meeting in Liverpool, England" in 1895, where Carpenter "spoke on 'Shelley and the Modern Democratic Movement.'" Following his talk, Carpenter led the assembly in a chorus of "his Socialist hymn, 'England Arise,'" a poem from his collection *Towards Democracy*.[63] Abbott was deeply affected by meeting Carpenter, who he wrote had "been a living influence in my life during all this time."[64] Carpenter was especially important in shaping Abbott's sexual politics; according the historian Paul Avrich, Abbott "specifically linked his admiration for Whitman, Carpenter, and Wilde with his interest in homosexuality." Abbott called Carpenter a "homosexual saint" and his *Love's Coming of Age*, a "modern classic."[65] He may also have passed on copies of Carpenter's unpublished writings on "homogenic" love to Lloyd shortly after the two met in the early 1900s.

By 1910, Abbott joined Lloyd in editing and writing *The Free Comrade*. Their collaboration was a natural one as Abbott shared many of Lloyd's interests and enthusiasms. Like Lloyd, Abbott embraced both the Socialist Party and anarchism, seeing the two as complementary, rather than contradictory. Abbott also shared his coeditor's high regard for Whitman and Carpenter. In his introduction to the journal's readership, Abbott wrote, "the prophets of the gospel we preach are such as Shelley, William Morris, Walt Whitman, [and] Edward Carpenter." Whitman's *Leaves of Grass* and Carpenter's *Towards Democracy*, he added, "are the scriptures of our movement." Both men shared a belief in the importance of sexual politics. Abbott believed "that much of the storm and conflict of life during the next fifty years—perhaps the next five hundred years—will center about the problems of sex." In the first issue of *The Free Comrade* that the two worked on together, Abbott and Lloyd pledged to dedicate themselves to creating a world where sexual diversity was valued. In their magazine, the two men advocated a social order where "those who love many as spontaneously as others love one," as well as people with "homogenic" feelings, could freely express their desires.[66]

In addition to his essays in *The Free Comrade*, Lloyd addressed same-sex eroticism in the pages of other Whitmanite journals: In 1909, for example, Lloyd broached one of his favorite subjects—sex and social change—in the pages of *Ariel*. In his essay, Lloyd linked contemporary sexual mores with the economic and political rules of the day. "More than economics, more than religion," Lloyd proclaimed, "the sex question will be the battle ground for those who stand for or against Socialism....For a very little thought and watching must show any open mind that our present sex-relations are absolutely part and parcel of our present system—nay are fundamental and typical."[67] In order to enact change on the factory floor, Lloyd implied, that sexual relations must be revolutionized. Marriage, in particular, needed to be dismantled—it was the nexus wherein gender and class oppression were fostered and maintained. Men and women in marriage became either "a parasite" or "a spiritless, dog-like slave."[68]

Lloyd proposed alternatives to these deadening "sex-relations" that went far beyond abolishing marriage. Rather than prescribe a single ideal relationship, Lloyd envisioned a complex array of sexual combinations. "I believe," he wrote, "that for a long, long time, and perhaps forever, all sex-relations will be experimented with and tried—all that ever have been and others as yet undreamed of." The landscape would not be totally unfamiliar. In the future some "couples...will...cling together...a monogamy perfect because natural, spontaneous, unforced, and irrepressible." This is, of course, a fairly traditional description of free love unions; two people bound together by their wills alone, free of any external authority. Lloyd preferred the option of what he called "varietism" in which "demi-god men...will draw and hold the hearts of many women" and "queenly and goddess women" will compel the "worship" of "many men."[69] Varietism was a key element in Lloyd's notion of the "larger love." Margaret Marsh argues that varietism held particular appeal to anarchist women, who responded to its "implicit denial of emotional possession."[70] This vision of an array of alternatives to marriage very much reflects the anarchist alternatives to traditional sexual relations with which Lloyd was intimately familiar.

Lloyd included same-sex sexual relations in the utopian future he sketched out in his *Ariel* article. Among the cast of characters included in Lloyd's sexual taxonomy, are those attracted to members of their own sex. According to Lloyd, in addition to those who "will come near to loving the entire opposite sex...there will be those strange ones who, on whatever plane, high or low, can love only those of their own sex." Lloyd is careful in this article not to identify himself with the "strange ones" he describes. In fact by describing same-sex love as "strange" Lloyd is distancing himself from those who "can love only those of their own sex." While certainly more ambivalent than his support for Carpenter's ideas on "homogenic love" in *The Free Comrade* in 1902, Lloyd's discussion of an alternative sexual ethics is nonetheless significant. His vision of a future where "there will be strange love-groups and anomalous families different from any now seen or deemed possible" is remarkable for its break with contemporary mores.[71]

But Lloyd's ambivalence is nevertheless important. Though at times strikingly radical in his critique of sexual mores, Lloyd's sexual politics and his willingness to articulate them were fragile. He confined his discussion of same-sex sexuality to his own published journal and the pages of other small journals situated on the fringes of the utopian Left. Outside the protective penumbra of the Whitmanite movement, Lloyd felt vulnerable; he was unwilling to be identified as a "strange one." The shifting ideas about homosexuality, increasingly being discussed in the larger society also made Lloyd's particular sexual politics—which very much relied on a blurry distinction between "comrade-ship" and "homogenic" love—increasingly problematic.

By the first decade of the twentieth century, the "manly love of comrades" was no longer viewed as entirely innocent of erotic desire. The carefully policed distinction between the fairy and the comrade were breaking down, and Whitman was at the heart of his process. He served as an example of a man whose erotic interest in other men was not necessarily betrayed by an overt gender inversion. In this changing context, Lloyd's sexual politics and sense of security could be easily shattered. This is precisely what happened in 1911. In that year, Lloyd turned again to the subject of homoeroticism in *The Free Comrade*, and as in 1902, the discussion of same-sex attraction centered on Whitman. This time, though, Lloyd denied any association with the man he had, nine years earlier, cited as one of his greatest influences. He explicitly distanced himself from Whitman in order to prevent being identified as an overly enthusiastic advocate of "comrade love."

Though Lloyd had praised Whitman as a "prophet" in 1902, and a model in 1911, he now renounced him. "I am in no sense that I can see a disciple of Whitman," declared Lloyd. "I never particularly admired Walt's prose and certainly never followed it." This is an explicit rejection of his 1902 statement. Lloyd admitted that he found the "music" of Whitman's words pleasing, but not "the content of his words." The man who Lloyd had once praised as the "Mount Olympus" of poetry had fallen dramatically in his estimation. At the heart of Lloyd's dismissal was the dangerous subject of Whitman's sexuality. Lloyd announced that Whitman's works were suspicious in a specific sense: they reeked of homosexuality. "The 'sexual motive' of Whitman," Lloyd now wrote, "presented itself to me, rightly or wrongly, as largely a homosexual mo-tive, and homosexuality was something from which I always shrank, for me the hardest thing in life to understand."[72] Lloyd's rejection of Whitman amounted to a denunciation of "homosexuality;" this was both an act of literary criticism and sexual politics. Lloyd put distance between his literary work and Whitman's in order to avoid the charge of being too similar in his personal life.

Lloyd's statement can only be read as a moment of literary, political, and sexual panic. He spurned not just the assertion that Whitman had influenced his work, but the thought that his actions might resemble the poet's "manly love of comrades." In his renunciation, Lloyd jettisons language he had previ-ously employed, including Carpenter's term "homogenic love" and Whitman's "comrade," in favor of the more clinical term "homosexuality." This too was an act of distancing. Lloyd could not use the term comradeship, since to do so would betray his own familiarity with Whitman's work and reference the very terms that betrayed Whitman's "homosexual motive." Instead, Lloyd spoke as a detached sexologist, using the more clinical, expert term "homosexual." Just as the language of comradeship had served to place homoerotic relations within the broader realm of same-sex friendship celebrated within Whitmanite texts, now the use of the word homosexuality positioned Lloyd outside that world as a dispassionate observer. Lloyd was negotiating his own relationship to the "homosexual motive" through his use of language.

In order to understand the reasons for Lloyd's behavior, it is important to reconstruct the context in which it occurred. Doing so will allow us to isolate and make visible the larger social and cultural transformations—including understandings of same-sex love—that were sweeping through American society. The immediate cause of Lloyd's renunciation of Whitman was a speech that George Sylvester Viereck gave in the fall of 1911 at the University of Berlin. A transcript of the talk was published in the American journal, *Current Literature*, coedited by Viereck, and was reported on in at least one anarchist journal other than *The Free Comrade*.[73] Viereck's talk, like an agent in a chemical reaction, brought to a head a series of developments which lay at the heart of Lloyd's identification with Whitman. Lloyd's radically different public statements— the first articulated in 1902, the second responding to a broader audience in 1911—regarding his relationship to Whitman's work reveals the complex shift in the way that it was being reinterpreted as ideas about sexuality changed. Lloyd was negotiating an evolving social, literary, and political landscape, and was doing so in different cultural contexts. As the context changed, so too did Lloyd's ability and willingness to identify himself with Whitman.

In his Berlin lecture, Viereck divided American poetry into four schools, the first of which includes those "poets, who like Whitman…sing the song of comradeship" and advocate a "far-reaching democracy." Viereck included Lloyd in this group. Viereck was quick to "find an erotic note" in Whitman's work, arguing that they could be read, "as studies in the psychology of sex." He argued that, in Lloyd's writing, this sexual subtext is brought to the fore and even exaggerated, saying, "J. William Lloyd over-emphasizes the sex motive of Whitman." Viereck reduced Lloyd's "creed" to "sex worship," which he said was inspired by the poet of comradeship.[74] This juxtaposition of psychology, sexuality, and poetic interpretation was apparently the trigger that set off Lloyd's panicked response. It should be noted that Viereck nowhere uses the term "homosexuality" in his talk. Nonetheless, Lloyd interpreted his being linked to Whitman as an imputation of homosexuality. Whitman had become a charged symbol of the "homosexual motive."[75]

That it was Vireck who delivered the lecture is of key importance in understanding Lloyd's response. George Vireck was known as a decadent, libidinous poet—the very antithesis of the manly Whitmanite. Where Whitman and his admirers masked homoerotic desire within the penumbra of comradeship, Vireck amplified his dissident persona. According to Vireck's friend, Elmer Gertz, "The esoteric in love fascinated [him] because it afforded new whips with which to scourge the Philistines."[76] Vireck delighted in letting his friends know that at age sixteen he wrote a novel titled *Elinor, The Autobiography of a Degenerate*. The novel's protagonist passes "through every imaginable phase of sex experience," reflecting the author's "knowledge of Casanova, Krafft-Ebing, the Marquis de Sade, and Zola's 'Nana.'"[77] Though the novel, "a veritable catalog of lust," was never published "it was talked about in the Vireck circle."[78] Though less explicit than *Elinor*, Vireck's published work also featured strong homoerotic themes. One of his first collections of poetry, *Nineveh: and Other Poems*, includes poems that depict the Roman emperor Hadrian's love for the beautiful youth, Antinous, and one on the subject of Mr. W. H., the young man said to have inspired some of Shakespeare's love sonnets. Lloyd was familiar with Vireck's poetry, having reviewed it favorably.

It is also significant that Vireck gave his address in Berlin. At the turn of the century, Germany had the most visible homosexual rights movement. In 1897, Magnus Hirschfeld, the famous German sexologist and activist, established the Scientific-Humanitarian Committee in Berlin. Hirschfeld was only one of several influential sexologists, including Krafft-Ebing, Albert Moll, and Ulrichs, whose work was first published in Germany.[79] Hirschfeld was particularly important in this group because Vireck knew him personally. Vireck's father, Louis, a socialist who spent time in prison for his politics before moving to America, sponsored Hirschfeld's first lecture in Germany. The two continued to keep in contact after the Vierecks' move to the United States. According to Gertz, "George...succeeded his father in the line of friendship." Hirschfeld's ideas about the origin and nature of homosexuality differed sharply from Lloyd's. Hirschfeld maintained that male homosexuals constituted a "third sex," a sexological version of the fairy and a strikingly different gendered construction than the Whitmanite comrade. The connection with Hirschfeld and Germany would have made Vireck's speech seem all the more fraught with meaning to Lloyd.

Lloyd's reaction to the assertions of Vireck's talk was further colored by the fact that Leonard Abbott, his friend and colleague, worked alongside Vireck at *Current Literature*. Historian Laurence Veysey states that Abbott and Vireck were lovers.[80] Though the sources Veysey cites in his study are no longer available, there is evidence to support the claim that these two were romantically linked. Elmer Gertz, who knew both men, wrote that they "took to each other at once" and shared an intense relationship. Part of what drew them together was their mutual interest in homoerotic desire, an interest that was, in part, articulated through Whitman. According to Gertz, the two men "admired Walt Whitman and had a fascinated intellectual curiosity about the variation of the sex instinct."

Viereck and Abbott were not discrete about their relationship. According to Gertz, Viereck once entertained Abbott by singing "A Little Maid of Sappho" to him by moonlight, in Harvard Stadium.[81] Viereck betrayed his affections in print as well, dedicating the poem "The Ballad of the Golden Boy," a homoerotic retelling of Robert Le Gallienne's ode to a "Golden Girl," to Abbott. Viereck's poem describes Leonardo Da Vinci gilding the naked body of a beautiful "lad whose lips were like two crimson spots." The act is fatal, but the youth dies happy knowing that he has been transformed from lowly apprentice into "Great Leonardo's Golden Boy."[82]

One of the more interesting aspects of Lloyd's response to Viereck's Berlin speech is the complete absence of any mention of Carpenter. In his rejection of Viereck's assertion that he is a Whitmanite, Lloyd lists intellectuals and anarchists like Ralph Waldo Emerson, Josiah Warren, William Morris, and Henry David Thoreau as critical influences on his thought. These thinkers, not Whitman, Lloyd insisted are the ones to whom he was intellectually and politically indebted. Poor Carpenter—who in 1902 had merited the title of "the greatest man of modern England"—is completely absent in this list of worthies. Like Whitman, Carpenter disappeared from Lloyd's list.

Again, Lloyd's problem with Carpenter, as it was with Whitman, was that he latter had become an identifiable marker for homosexuality. By 1911, Edward Carpenter's work on same-sex love had reached a far broader audience than it had prior to Lloyd's 1902 writing about him. Carpenter's pamphlets, published by the Manchester Labour Press, had circulated in relatively small circles, but by 1911 he had begun to address homosexuality in texts published and distributed by more mainstream publishers. The 1906 edition of Carpenter's *Love's Coming of Age*, his most widely read book, for example, discussed "homogenic love," whereas previous editions had not. In 1908, Carpenter republished his Manchester Labour Press pamphlets in his book, *The Intermediate Sex*—the first of his major publications to deal exclusively with same-sex love. By 1911, therefore, it was no longer wise for Lloyd to have cited Carpenter in his denunciation of Viereck's speech. A panicking Lloyd could not possibly benefit from being associated with the quintessential "homogenic" Whitmanite.

Lloyd's reluctance to identify himself with Carpenter reflected the fact that the latter's increasingly open treatment of same-sex love led to public attacks on his sexual politics. In 1909, for example, M. D. O'Brien, an ardent Catholic and member of the antisocialist Liberty and Property Defense League, published "Socialism and Infamy: The Homogenic or Comrade Love Exposed: An Open Letter in Plain Words for a Socialist Prophet." The title of O'Brien's essay refers to the dual nature of the term comrade in Carpenter's political discourse, bringing to light the way that "comrade" signified both male lover and working class solidarity. Though O'Brien was no fan of socialism he felt even more strongly about "homosexual lusts" which he believed ought "to be treated in a lunatic asylum, or in a lethal chamber." O'Brien accused Carpenter of seeking to destroy the moral fiber of the working class by turning them away "from their wives to the male 'comrades,' who are more capable of satisfying their unnatural appetites." Apparently, O'Brien feared that the male members of the British working class were on the verge of being lured from their marriage beds by the siren-like lure of Carpenter and his fellow "comrades." The notion of innocence seduced by the call of decadence mirrors the kinds of claims made by Foote in his attacks on Wilde. In concluding his attack, O'Brien called upon Carpenter's readers to reject the call of comradeship. "Angels and ministers of grace defend us," he proclaimed, "[against] the comrade love's effect upon the comrades!"[83]

Similar attacks were made on Carpenter in the United States. One in particular, which appeared in *Socialism: The Nation of Fatherless Children*, a Catholic anti-socialist tract, is of special interest because it links Leonard Abbott, Lloyd's associate, to deviant sexuality. In it, the authors, David Goldstein and Martha Moore Avery, identify Abbott as "a leading socialist of New York," who wrote approvingly of Carpenter in *The Comrade*. They cite Abbott's review of Carpenter's *Love's Coming of Age*—where he proclaimed "as suggestive and notable a treatment of this subject, from the socialist point of view, as has yet appeared in the English language"—as a sign of Abbott's degenerate morals. "Yes," Goldstein and Avery mock, *Love's Coming of Age* "is indeed suggestive," not of a utopian future, but "of the period of Sodom and Gomorrah, in the days before God commanded these vile spots to be wiped from off the face of the earth."[84] In other words, Carpenter was a siren of sodomy luring men to their doom, and Abbott, a willing accomplice in his evil plot. Like their British counterpart, M. D. O'Brien, Goldstein and Avery made explicit what was largely implicit in Carpenter's work. In doing so they linked Abbott and the Whitmanite defense of the "manly love of comrades" to the sin of sodomy. It is not clear whether Lloyd was aware of Goldstein and Avery's attack on Abbott and Carpenter, but the fact that such attacks were being written on both sides of the Atlantic is an indication of the mounting risks of claiming kinship with Whitman and his most ardent admirers. Given this turn, it is not surprising that Lloyd omitted Carpenter from his retort to Viereck.

At the heart of Lloyd's reaction to Viereck's speech, however, is the shifting and increased identification of Whitman with homosexuality. There had been a low murmur of suspicion regarding the sexual nature of Whitman's work, and beginning in the 1870s, "scattered gay readings" of his work were published.[85] For example, in 1887, Cuban revolutionary José Martí, who greatly admired Whitman's work, felt it necessary to rebuke those "imbeciles" who, "with a prudishness worthy of school boys…believed they found in 'Calamus'…a return to Virgil's vile desire for Cebetes or Horace's for Gyges and Lyciscus."[86] Just as Carpenter used the relationship between Ioläus and Hercules, Martí made reference to Greek mythology to name homosexual desire. Of course, in Martí's case he did so with disgust, while Carpenter was attempting to uplift same-sex relations. All in all, Martí's was a rare reference to a queer reading of Whitman at the time.

As the century closed, however, the number of queer readings of the poet's work increased. By the 1890s, Whitman's critics began to refer to the emergent medical discourse on homosexuality in their discussion of his work. In 1898, for example, a review of an edited collection of Whitman's letters, appearing in *The Chap Book* noted that the poet was a figure of interest among "sexual psychopathists."[87] The phrase used by the reviewer is strikingly similar to the title of Krafft-Ebing's *Psychopathia Sexualis*, the most famous sexological text of the late-nineteenth century. By the early 1900s, increasing numbers of readers (Lloyd and Carpenter among them) were seeing in Whitman's "manly love of comrades" something more than a defense of same-sex friendship. These sexualized interpretations of Whitman cast suspicion on those who championed the his verse. One early-twentieth-century German critic went so far as to "suggest there might be a homosexual conspiracy designed to 'sell' Whitman's 'homosexual ideas' to the world in the guise of 'healthy' poetry."[88] Similarly, in his earlier talk in Berlin, Viereck was essentially identifying Lloyd as a member of this "homosexual conspiracy."

Viereck was responsible for very publicly exposing Whitman as a homosexual. In an article that appeared in *Current Literature* in 1906, he reported on the work of a "German medical writer" named Eduard Bertz, who, in 1905, had written a study of Whitman for Magnus Hirschfeld's journal of sexology, *Jahrbuche fur sexuelle Zwischenstufen* (The Yearbook for Intermediate Sexual Types). "Dr Bertz," wrote Viereck, "speaks of Whitman as a 'homosexual.'" In his essay, Bertz cited the work of John Addington Symonds, Marc Andre Raffalovich, Edward Carpenter, and Max Nordau. "Dr. Bertz," Viereck tells his readers, "comments of the strange mixture in Whitman of sensuous elements and religious frenzy, and on his exaggerated feminine compassion and love for humanity." What some had championed as the "manly love of comrades" was, according to Bertz, really an "exaggerated feminine" trait. The comrade exposed as a fairy in drag! Viereck finished his essay by noting that some of Whitman's German fans had taken sharp issue with Bertz's work, insisting that Whitman was "the prophet of a new world and a new race" and not an apologist for homosexuality.[89] Viereck made clear that he believed Bertz to be the better judge of Whitman's character and work.

Lloyd's response has to be understood in the context of these multiple layers of signification and association. Viereck's speech brought into focus the erotic elements of Lloyd's association with Whitman in a way that Lloyd found deeply disturbing. The mounting awareness of what Lloyd called "the homosexual motive" in Whitman's work proved troublesome. By the second decade of the twentieth century an increasing number of public discussions of homosexuality were being produced and read by medical authorities, moral arbiters, jurists, journalists, and other social commentators. The boundaries between homosocial and homosexual relations were being policed with greater severity. Whitman was one of the figures used to illustrate and examine this process. Articles like the one on Bertz in *Current Literature* were examples of the way that the conversation was being carried out. Here and elsewhere, Whitman was increasingly being identified as an exemplary "homosexual." In 1911, Lloyd was caught in the middle of this sharp and contested conversation about sexual identity, feeling exposed in a way he had not in 1902.

This does not mean that Whitman's sexuality ceased to be of interest to the anarchists. Nor does it mean that Whitman was no longer useful as a way to discuss homosexual desire and its social, ethical, and cultural place in society. Following her deportation from the United States for anti-conscription activity during the First World War, for example, Goldman developed a lecture on Walt Whitman that had a special focus on his homosexuality. However, Lloyd and Goldman treated Whitman and homosexuality very differently. Goldman did not adopt Whitman's language of comradeship rather she read it symptomatically as an indication that Whitman was a homosexual. This act of translation—which Lloyd found so very threatening—was, to Goldman, the key to understanding Whitman's work and personality.

Goldman, who was a great fan of the "Good Gray Poet," seems not to have addressed Whitman's relationship to homosexuality before the 1920s, though she certainly spoke of Whitman as an erotic figure. For example, in 1917 she delivered a lecture entitled "Walt Whitman, The Liberator of Sex," but made no mention of the homoerotic aspect of Whitman's work. And though Goldman delivered lectures on homosexuality before her exile, she did not, as far as we know, refer to Whitman in them. This indicates the uneven and complex nature of the ways in which Whitman's relationship to homosexuality emerged as a topic of discussion among anarchists—and Americans more broadly—in the first decades of the twentieth century. Prior to her years of exile, Goldman continued to view Whitman much as Tucker had in the early 1880s—as a sexual rebel, but one whose erotic rebellion did not extend beyond the boundaries of heterosexuality. It is only after the World War I, and during her exile in Europe, that Goldman began to reexamine her understanding of Whitman and the meaning of his work.

Though Goldman knew them both, there is no evidence that Abbott or Lloyd shared their views on the homoerotic aspects of Whitman's work with her. Both men were careful to compartmentalize their discussions of Whitman, feeling implicated in any discussion of the topic of same-sex love in a way that Goldman did not. Both felt vulnerable to being marked as sexual deviants, even by friends and comrades whose sexual politics quite explicitly included a defense of same-sex love. As we have seen, Lloyd distanced himself from Whitman when he felt it necessary. This was not unusual for public intellectuals grappling with the deeply personal and volatile issue of homosexuality at the time. Carpenter responded in much the same way at several points in his life. In 1909, for example, a reviewer for the *British Medical Journal* (*BMJ*) published a particularly hostile review of *The Intermediate Sex*, and Carpenter responded by writing a letter to the *BMJ* in which he maintained "there is not a single passage in the book where I advocate sexual intercourse of any kind between those of the same sex." He insisted that he was merely advocating "sincere attachment and warm friendship."[90] Carpenter may have been particularly anxious to respond to the *BMJ* since it was a voice of medical authority, and an increasingly important regulatory voice in sexuality. In judging the actions of Carpenter, Lloyd, and Abbott it is important to keep in mind the social context in which they operated. All three men articulated their politics in what historian Jeffrey Weeks poignantly describes as, "the shadowy area between honesty and public scandal."[91]

Like Lloyd, Goldman came to think of Whitman as, what she off-handedly referred to as a "pronounced Homo" by reading the work being produced by literary critics and others who explored the meaning of Whitman's text and life. As she was preparing her lectures on Whitman's sexuality in 1927, Goldman wrote her friend Ben Capes, that she was "gorging myself on everything pertaining to Walt Whitman, [including] biographies, commentators, and his own writing."[92] Much of the new Whitman scholarship reflected the rising influence of psychological explanations of sexuality. In Europe, where Goldman lived following her deportation, this type of study was fairly advanced. Bertz, for example, had expanded his thinking on the subject considerably since the early 1900s, publishing a series of articles on Whitman and same-sex love. But even in the United States, interpretations of Whitman as a "homosexual" were increasingly visible. In 1922, Earl Lind wrote that Whitman "stands foremost among American androgynes...many passages of *Leaves of Grass* and *Drumtaps* exist as proof."[93] Androgyne was Lind's term for what might be best understood as a "masculine fairy." Even the mainstream press began to reflect this emerging discussion of Whitman as the classic "American androgyne." For example, *Harper's Magazine*, in the late 1920s, published an article by Harvey O'Higgins, which argued that the "sexual expression" in Whitman's poetry "is dangerously near the homosexual level." Influenced by the popular Freudian theories of the day, O'Higgins commented that Whitman's condition was "to be expected" since the poet's "sexual impulse is anchored by a mother-fixation and [was] unable to achieve a heterosexual goal." Neatly reversing Lloyd's admiration of Whitman's masculinist representation of homosexuality, O'Higgins maintained that Whitman's defense of "the manly love of comrades" was proof of his psychological condition: "like many another case of arrested development he was always 'a man's man.'"[94]

Emma Goldman's interpretation of Whitman was also informed by the idea that his work expressed his essential psychological nature. Always an eager reader of sexologists and psychologists, Goldman was an early advocate of the theory that homosexuality was an innate drive that permeated the entirety of a person's life, work, and spirit. Her willingness to identify Whitman as a homosexual reflects her own belief, expressed on numerous occasions, that sex—conceived of as a fundamental drive or motivating urge—was a key to understanding human psychology. In order to understand Whitman then, it was essential to deal honestly with the root of his personality. Goldman was convinced that Whitman's "whole reaction to life and to the complexities of the human spirit can be traced to his own complex sexual nature."[95]

Goldman believed that Whitman had deliberately obscured the themes of his work and personality, in order to protect himself against homophobic attacks. She recognized this because she herself felt the attraction of secrecy when speaking about sex, politics, and revolution. Goldman began preparing her lecture on Whitman and homosexuality just as she started work on her autobiography and wrote a friend that she felt that she faced problems similar to Whitman's struggle with disclosure and secrecy. "I feel," Goldman wrote, "that it will be extremely difficult to write a frank autobiography." Her effort to be truthful echoed his; Whitman "began his career by flinging the red rag in the face of the Puritan Bull, and then spent the rest of his life in trying to explain what he meant by some of this ideas on sex and love." She also faced the same need for discretion because of the difficulty of writing a personal narrative that preserved the privacy of friends and family. Goldman thought Whitman was more interested in protecting his own reputation than in revealing the truth about himself. Though "his 'Calamus' poems are as homosexual as anything ever written…he absolutely denied it, and even advanced the story, whether true or not has never been proven, that he was the father of six children."[96] Goldman was intent on exposing Whitman's true nature in her lectures.

Goldman acknowledged that Whitman's need to obfuscate was due to the homophobia of the culture in which he lived. "I am inclined to think," she wrote, "that even his most devoted friends, with the exception of Horace Traubel, would have dropped him like a shot if he had openly owned up to his leanings." The fear of the taint of homosexuality was precisely what led Lloyd to act as he did in 1911. By denying Whitman, Lloyd was moving quickly to avoid guilt by association. Goldman lamented the fact that the truth about Whitman's sexuality was continuing to be denied. "This is best seen," she argued, "by the constant apologies that nearly all of his American and English biographers and commentators are making." In Goldman's opinion, by denying this side of Whitman his critics were diminishing the stature of their subject. "The fools do not seem to realize that Walt Whitman's greatness as a rebel and poet may have been conditioned in his sexual differentiation, and that he could not be otherwise than what he was."[97] In her lectures Goldman challenged "the fools" who continued to deny the fact of Whitman's "sexual differentiation."

Goldman saw it as her mission—and as a progressive step in her sexual politics—to clearly identify Whitman as a homosexual. This strategy did not work for Lloyd, whose sexual politics were, paradoxically, dependent on obfuscating the very thing that it named. Lloyd fled "the homosexual motive" in Whitman's work, while Goldman sought to bring it into sharper view. Though Lloyd advocated for the right of people to love members of their own sex, his politics of homosexuality was dependent on plausible deniability. As long as "the manly love of comrades" could remain unmarked in the larger social context of same-sex romantic friendship and homosocial bonds, Lloyd felt relatively safe. As the distinction between intense friendship and sexual interest between men collapsed, Lloyd's political language and his sense of safety followed. In 1911, when the cognitive dissonance between "the manly love of comrades" and "homosexuality" became too great, Lloyd retreated from his association with Whitman. For Goldman the reverse was true; as Whitman became increasingly identified as a homosexual, she was able to use him to discuss sexual ethics in a new way. She believed that by telling the truth about Whitman's nature she was opening up the subject for greater discussion, and clearing the way for social tolerance. What silenced Lloyd created the opportunity for Goldman to speak. Rather than following a pattern of increasing openness and disclosure we find that the changing social and sexual landscape within which they worked—as illustrated in the shifting views of Whitman—both inhibited and enabled different anarchist sex radicals to speak out on the moral, legal, and social status of same-sex love.

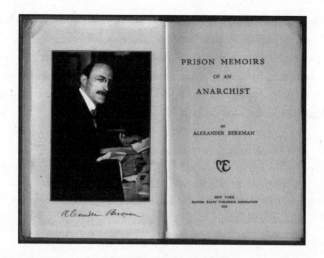

CHAPTER FOUR:

"LOVE'S DUNGEON FLOWER": PRISON AND THE POLITICS OF HOMOSEXUALITY

IN THE SUMMER OF 1916, Ben Reitman, Emma Goldman's lover, was released from New York's Queens County Jail. He had been imprisoned for distributing birth control information—an act of civil disobedience that was meant to highlight the injustice of state regulation of sexuality. Shortly after his release, Reitman addressed a gathering of supporters at New York City's Lenox Hall. "I was sent to jail," he told the crowd, "because I believe in happy, welcome babies and because I believe that motherhood should be voluntary, and also because Judges McInerny, Moss, and Russell decided that I had broken the law and must pay the penalty."[1] Reitman used his talk to condemn the penal system and the society that created it. "Jail, Judges, [and] Governments," he declared, "are all miserable failures. They are the greatest forces for evil, and they succeed in maintaining themselves only by ignorance and force."[2] This is a fair representation of the anarchist view of prisons and the judicial system. To Reitman and his colleagues, prisons were the concrete manifestation of turn-of-the-century America's hierarchical, undemocratic, and brutal social order. Speaking in the shadow of the war in Europe, Reitman told his audience that, "In a decent society we will need neither jails nor judges any more than we will need wars."[3]

To illustrate the absurdity of the prison system Reitman described the fate of a number of the men he met behind bars. He highlighted cases, dramatiz-

ing the deleterious consequences of New York's "repeat offender" laws, which
stipulated that repeat offenders receive lengthy and harsh sentences. Among
the cases that Reitman shared with his audience that day was a "young fellow...arrested on the charge of pederasty, a common form of homosexuality."[4]
Reitman presents the prisoner's story as clear evidence of the brutal and unen-
lightened nature of the judicial system:

> The Judge sentenced him to the penitentiary for fourteen years. As far as
> the Judges and the police are concerned, all the literature on that subject
> might never have been written. The Judges and the police and everybody
> else merely said that the boy was a degenerate and a dangerous criminal, and
> now for fourteen years he must languish in a hell all because God made him
> that way.[5]

It is unclear what Reitman means by "pederasty" in this instance. The term
was used to describe relations between an adult and a minor, but it could
also refer to relations between two adults. Reitman describes the prisoner as a
"young fellow" and a "boy" so it is possible that he was the younger partner.
More likely Reitman is using the term without specific reference to age-structured homosexual relations. We also don't know if aggravating circumstances
such as prostitution or public sex prompted the "young fellow's" arrest, nor is it
clear whether the prisoner's prior conviction, which doomed him to a lengthy
prison stay, was a sex crime or some other charge. Whatever the case, Reitman
dismissed the idea that the young man's actions rose to the level of criminal offense—he had done nothing for the court to concern itself with.

In his attack on the court's view of the "young fellow's" sexuality, Reitman castigated the court for its ignorance of "the literature on [the] subject."
The judges, in other words, were not versed in the new sexological discourse
on homosexuality that the anarchist sex radicals were familiar with. Since they
were unfamiliar with what Reitman saw as the enlightened, scientific perspective on such questions, they were merely acting out their bigotry and cruelty.
How else, Reitman implies, could one explain sentencing a "boy" to fourteen
years "all because God made him that way?" Reitman understood homosexuality as an existential condition not a sin or a crime, and he lashed out at what
he saw as the judge's ignorance. Reitman's colleagues might have flinched at his
mention of God—anarchists being overwhelmingly atheists—but they surely
agreed with Reitman's view that a sentence of fourteen years for "a common
form of homosexuality" was outrageous. Like Reitman, they saw the court's
actions as betraying a sad lack of knowledge, an ignorance that they might well
have expected from the bench, but that was lamentable nonetheless. And, of

course, the fact that judges and jailers should regulate sexuality was anathema to the anarchists.

That Reitman should discuss homosexuality in the context of a speech on the subject of prisons is unremarkable. Since the establishment of the modern American prison system in the early-nineteenth century, reformers, prison authorities, and former prisoners have written accounts of prison life that mention sex behind bars. As early as 1826, Louis Dwight, a prison reformer, wrote to inform government officials that in institutions "between Massachusetts and Georgia…the sin of Sodom is the vice of prisoners." Sex between prisoners was, in Dwight's words, a "dreadful degradation" that needed to be stamped out. Dwight hoped the authorities would take action. "*Nature and humanity,*" he wrote, "*cry aloud for redemption from this dreadful degradation.*"[6] In the decades that followed Dwight's report, many such pronouncements were made. In 1919, Kate Richard O'Hare, a member of the Socialist Party, lamented the "ugly fact that homosexuality exists in every prison and must ever be one of the sinister facts of our penal system."[7] Though writing nearly one hundred years after Dwight, O'Hare was in agreement with her predecessor that homosexuality was an ill disease bred in prison yards. By the early-twentieth century, there existed "a large literature on homosexuality among…prisoners."[8] This literature tended to reflect the view that sex in prison was an illicit, immoral, and criminal behavior—an evil weed that flourished in the hothouse environment of the nation's jails.

The views of American anarchist sex radicals who wrote on homosexuality and prison differed in crucial ways from other social critics and prison reformers. O'Hare's opinion stands in sharp contrast to those of Reitman and other anarchist sex radicals. When anarchists wrote about sex in prison, they did not approach the topic from a relentlessly negative perspective. O'Hare was, of course, a well known member of the Socialist Party, an organization whose sexual politics were strikingly different from the anarchists'. The contrast between their views is all the more striking when one realizes that O'Hare was actually imprisoned with Emma Goldman when she made her observations. O'Hare was in the Missouri State Prison for violating the Espionage Act, Goldman for conspiracy against the Selective Draft Law. While in jail, the two became friends, but O'Hare did not absorb Goldman's views on the question of homosexuality. Goldman knew about same-sex relations among prisoners, but nowhere does she denounce them in O'Hare's manner. In fact, in a letter to Magnus Hirschfeld, Goldman suggested that her politics around homosexuality was informed by the knowledge she gathered during her prison stays.[9] And while O'Hare denounced the homosexual relations she saw in the Missouri

State Prison, Goldman's memory of her prison stay was of the "warm heart beneath Kate's outer coolness."[10] Goldman was not a fan of the Missouri State Penitentiary but unlike O'Hare, she did not use prison homosexuality in her critique the prison system. She did not lash out at the relationships she and O'Hare witnessed.

The anarchists understood the phenomenon of homosexuality in prison through the prism of their larger sexual politics. Reitman, for example, presents the "young fellow" as a victim of injustice not a tragic product of a warped system. Reitman, of course, was not defending sexual exploitation and violence in prison. But that is exactly the point. Rather than critique prison life by exposing what O'Hare called "the sinister facts of our penal system," Reitman uses his discussion of prison to defend those who practice homosexual acts. The only "sinister fact" Reitman sought to expose was that someone who practiced a "common form of homosexuality" should be sentenced to jail—for fourteen years, no less. Other anarchists, including Alexander Berkman, condemned the sometimes brutal world of prison sex, but went further. Unlike O'Hare and those who shared her views, Berkman also wrote about consensual, loving relationships between prisoners. Like Reitman, Berkman's analysis of sex behind bars was informed by his larger political beliefs. The anarchist sex radicals used their attacks on prisons also as an opportunity to explore and defend the expression of same-sex desire.

Accounts of prison and prison life were a familiar genre of anarchist writing. A number of leading figures in the movement spent time in jail and later wrote about their experiences. These accounts were considered important political texts for the movement. Peter Kropotkin's account of his imprisonment and escape from the Czar's jails and his short imprisonment in France, published as *In Russian and French Prisons*, was well known among movement activists. "Here," wrote Leonard Abbott in a review of the book in *Mother Earth*, "are the very throb and passion and romance of the revolutionary struggle."[11] Goldman, Berkman, Reitman, and other anarchists also wrote about prisons, and like Kropotkin, their stories of imprisonment explored major themes in anarchist thought. The stark contrast between prison life and the ideals of anarchism made for tense and engaging reading.

In Russian and French Prisons only hinted at the existence of homosexual relations in prisons. In this, Kropotkin, whose radical views did not extend to questions of sexuality, was in full agreement with prison authorities. Of the existence of homosexuality, he wrote, "I shall say only what will be supported by all intelligent and frank governors of prisons, if I say that the prisons are the nurseries for the most revolting category of breaches of moral law."[12] Though he never specifically names the "breaches of moral law" he refers to, he does point the reader to other prison literature that is less reticent in dealing with the sex lives of prisoners.

Kropotkin's views do not reflect the sexual politics of some English-speaking American anarchists. It is in fact remarkable that, when it came to the question of homosexuality, Kropotkin found he shared the views of those who ran the prisons. Anarchists did not typically cite the views of "intelligent and frank governors of prisons" in their discussion of prisons. Kropotkin's views are in sharp contrast to those held by the American anarchist sex radicals. Reitman's defense of the "young fellow" is, clearly, quite different from Kropotkin's harsh condemnation of homosexuality. Reitman's more accepting attitude of the variation of sexual desire is far more representative of the sexual politics of the English-language anarchist movement. Even when discussing prison sexuality, the governing principles of free love that guided the anarchist sex radicals in their thinking remained paramount.

By far the most famous text written by an American anarchist that discusses the moral and social status of same-sex love in the context of prison is Alexander Berkman's *Prison Memoirs of an Anarchist*. Berkman's book is an account of the fourteen years he spent in Pennsylvania's Western Penitentiary following his conviction for a failed assassination of Henry Clay Frick, the manager of Andrew Carnegie's steel empire. Frick was in charge during the Homestead Steelmill Strike of 1892. The book, published in 1912, was widely reviewed inside and outside of anarchist circles. Some of his mainstream critics dismissed *Prison Memoirs* as the rationalization of a would-be killer, others saw more. A reviewer in the socialist journal, *The Coming Nation,* stated that Berkman's work "is a great human document, a remarkable presentation of prison conditions, and an intimate study of prison types."[13] Writing for *Mother Earth,* a young Bayard Boyesen said that "here, from an Anarchist, is a book of rare power and beauty, majestic in its structure, filled with the power of imagination and the truth of actuality, emphatic in its declarations and noble in its reach."[14] Boyesen's praise for Berkman's book mirrored that of anarchists and others sympathetic to their politics.

In order to ensure that his prison memoirs reached as broad an audience as possible, Berkman sought a noted writer to compose an introduction. He first approached Jack London, who had himself spent time in prison and had expressed some sympathy for anarchist ideas.[15] London's introduction proved too permeated by his political loyalties—he was a member of the Socialist Party—for Goldman and Berkman who ultimately declined to use it, partly because London criticized Berkman's attempt to kill Frick. Interestingly, Lon-

don's proposed introduction stated that, "It sickens one with its filth and degradation and cruelty, with its relentless narration of the evil men do. It smells
from the depths." To replace London, Berkman turned to Hutchins Hapgood.
Hapgood was wildly enthusiastic about the text and fascinated by anarchism.
His introduction was extremely complimentary. "I wish," Hapgood wrote, "that
everybody in the world would read this book...because the general and careful reading of it would definitely add to true civilization." Hapgood believed
that Berkman's book would help "do away with prisons" and he commended
Berkman's skill at illustrating the human relationships that structure prison life.
"[*Prison Memoirs*] shows, in picture after picture, sketch after sketch, not only
the obvious brutality, stupidity, [and] ugliness permeating the institution, but
very touchingly, it shows the good qualities and instincts of the human heart
perverted, demoralized, helplessly struggling for life; beautiful tendencies basely
expressing themselves."[16] Although Hapgood was clearly a partisan voice his
enthusiasm reflects that *Prison Memoirs* is one of the most important and widely
read texts to emerge from the turn-of-the-century anarchist movement.

Homosexual desire, in all its manifestations, is a key theme of *The Prison
Memoirs of an Anarchist*. It documents, not just the coercive sexual culture of
prisons—rape and prostitution—but also the consensual loves that exist behind
bars. It is this aspect of the work—its careful consideration of the possibility
of love between people of the same sex—that makes Berkman's text such a
rare document within the corpus of prison writing. Written from an insider's
perspective, his work is an astute sociological and psychological analysis of the
intimate life of prisoners. According to Berkman, prison life is, at times, deeply
marked by "the swelling undercurrent of frank irrepressible sex drive."[17] In
several lengthy passages, Berkman recounts the sexual and emotional brutality,
pleasures, and desires shared by his fellow prisoners. Towards the end, Berkman devotes an entire chapter to the moral, ethical, and social place of same-
sex desire. He presents love between inmates as a form of resistance to the
spirit-crushing environment of prison. The representations of homosexuality
in *Prison Memoirs* span the full range of human emotions and behavior. It contains one of the most sustained considerations of same-sex relations of any of
the published works produced by the turn-of-the-century anarchists. It is one
of the most important political texts dealing with homosexuality to have been
written by an American before the 1950s.

Berkman's text is not a simple defense of same-sex love, and the representations of homosexuality contained within are complex. In fact, Berkman
was quite critical of much that he witnessed in jail, which is especially obvious in the beginning of the book. Berkman's initial reactions to the existence

of prison homosexuality are shock and disgust. By the end of his narrative, however, he has considerably altered his view of homosexuality. In his memoirs, Berkman describes the evolution of his attitudes toward same-sex prison relationships and tells how his initially horrified response to homosexuality is replaced with understanding and even an appreciation for the erotic and loving relations between men. As one late-twentieth-century critic suggests, a reader could very easily find his or her "moral attitudes" regarding sex transformed by the vicarious experience of Berkman's own change of thought. Swept along by his revealing autobiographical work, the reader experiences the process by which the author "moves from a cold and abstract idealism to a warm and sympathetic identification, even to an unembarrassed and untroubled acceptance of the reality of homosexual love."[18] This analysis mirrors that made by Hutchins Hapgood, who wrote in his preface that reading *Prison Memoirs* "tends to complicate the present simplicity of our moral attitudes. It tends to make us more mature."[19]

Berkman and those who worked on *Mother Earth* were well aware of his memoir's importance as a work of sexual politics, and in their promotion, they presented Berkman's treatment of same-sex relations in prison as a major theme of the book. They sent letters to *Mother Earth*'s subscribers seeking prepublication orders for Berkman's book, and clearly indicated that the sex life of prisoners was among the topics that Berkman dealt with. Advertisements for *Prison Memoirs* in *Mother Earth* also highlighted the "homosexual" (the term used by the advertisements) content of the work. And following the book's publication, Berkman delivered lectures on homosexuality that drew upon the material in his memoirs. These lectures served to advertise the book and to elaborate on the sociological and political implications of the subject matter. Berkman's lectures both presented the erotic life of prisoners to a broad audience and contained a defense of the right of individuals to love whomever they wish. *Prison Memoirs* was marketed and presented as a significant contribution to the understanding of the social and moral place of same-sex desire in a number of different ways. In promoting the book, Berkman and his colleagues foregrounded its sexual politics.

Contemporary reviewers noted Berkman's "frankness of utterance" in regards to his treatment of homosexuality. "No detail of prison life is lost on Berkman's mind," a reviewer for *Current Literature* wrote in December 1912. "He dramatizes in particular, the abnormality of the prison situation. He shows us what happens when men are separated from women, when sex-instincts are repressed." The reviewers themselves, however, were less than "frank," choosing to omit any explicit discussion of homosexuality, all the while hinting at its presence. The reviewer for *The Coming Nation* told readers only that Berkman's book includes descriptions of "the hideous personal degradations fostered by the prison atmosphere."[20]

Prison Memoirs was also reviewed in periodicals outside the Left, including the *San Francisco Bulletin*, which played at the edges of what could and could not be named in public discourse:

> The book has one great fault which may go far to hurt its effect. True to his tenets, Berkman has excluded nothing from his account. There are things done in prisons which a writer must be content to pass over lightly; many which he must absolutely omit if his book is to be universally read. These things Berkman has told in detail.[21]

By not naming those "things done in prison which a writer must be content to pass over lightly" the *Bulletin*'s reviewer was carefully observing the rules of decorum to which Berkman refused to adhere. Of course, by indicating that the book was filled with these forbidden facts the reviewer was, if anything, heightening their salience. The unspoken jumps from the page. This is the same kind of resonant silence that commentators often used in treating the Oscar Wilde trial and other sexual scandals of the period.

A number of reviewers attacked Berkman's book because it dealt openly with homosexuality. Berkman, like many authors, keenly followed the critical readings of his work, and collected some of these negative reviews. Typical of these criticisms are the words of one reviewer, who categorized *Prison Memoirs* as "a book by a degenerate." This reviewer found Berkman's work to be "indecent…both a glorification of assassination and an apology, even justification, of unmentionable crimes." Shocked by the frank nature of Berkman's text, the reviewer declared, "Mr. Comstock had better look into this work." This critic, like others who wrote for what Berkman characterized as the "bourgeois press," was not explicit in his discussion of the sexual content of the book, but the words used to describe it—"unmentionable crime," "degenerate," "indecent"—more than hinted at why Anthony Comstock, the best-known sexual purity advocate of the period, should take interest in the book. Berkman characterized the negative reviews he collected as coming from the pens of "intellectual Mrs. Grundys," meaning that they were social purity activists.[22] With this implication, Berkman communicated that it was the sexual content of his work, not his role in one of the United State's most spectacular and well-known assassination attempts that was central to the negative reviews he received. His critics found the sexual politics of *Prison Memoirs* as objectionable as the book's anarchist politics. What the critics did not understand is that these two features of the book's politics were integrally related.

Though attacks on the sexual politics of Berkman's book were not uncommon, a number of readers appreciated the humanistic tolerance with which Berkman treated sexual relations between inmates. His depictions of same-sex relations in prison drew a particularly passionate response from homosexual readers. Among the most devoted champions of Berkman's work was Edward Carpenter. When Goldman visited Carpenter following her expulsion from the United States, she found that Carpenter and his lover George Merrill expressed a great deal of interest in Berkman's memoirs. Carpenter insisted that she tell him about Alexander Berkman. He felt, Goldman wrote in her autobiography, that the memoirs were "a profound study of man's inhumanity and prison psychology."[23] Carpenter bought the book shortly after its publication and "found it full of interest and suggestion," and not satisfied with a single reading, Carpenter "return[ed] to it again and again."[24] In a letter to Berkman, Goldman was rather blunt about why she believed Carpenter and Merrill showed such interest. "I am sure," she wrote to Berkman, "their interest is mainly because of the homo part in your book."[25] Though crudely put, Goldman's analysis was correct. Like a number of his readers, Carpenter was drawn to Berkman's politically charged examination of same-sex desires and behaviors among prisoners.

Given that reviews indicated sexuality had a central place in his narrative, Berkman's readers must have been surprised to learn how naïve the author was about homosexuality when he first entered prison. Berkman gives his readers the impression that he had never heard of or even imagined the possibility that members of the same sex could be erotically attracted to each other. The extent of Berkman's blindness regarding homosexuality is almost comical. In a chapter entitled "The Yegg," Berkman, who was twenty-one when he arrived in jail, describes an older man's attempt to convince him to become his "kid." This is the first time that Berkman is forced to confront what was, until then, a topic hidden in prison slang and innuendo opaque to him.[26] While working side-by-side in one of the prison's workshops, the older man, known as Boston Red or Red, regales Berkman with tales of his life on the road as a "yegg," or tramp. Part of that life was the sexual pleasure that tramps took in their "kids." Red, no stranger to prison walls, drops hints about his relationship with "kids," notably a teenager named Billie, in an attempt to seduce Berkman. Unfortunately for Red, Berkman had not the faintest clue that he was the object of Red's sexual interest.[27]

Growing frustrated with Berkman's naïveté, Red becomes increasingly direct. He tells Berkman that he intends to "assume benevolent guardianship over you; over you and your morals, yes sir, for you're my kid now, see?" Berkman's reaction—puzzlement over what Red means—spurs the "yegg" on. Red tries to "chaperone" Berkman in what he calls "moonology…the truly Christian science of loving your neighbor, provided that he be a nice little boy." Berkman still does not understand the drift of the conversation and replies by asking, "How can you love a boy?" Red, expanding a bit on the lingo of prison sex, at last comes to the point, stating, "A punk's a boy that'll…give himself to a man. Now we'se talkin' plain." A "punk," in other words, is the submissive sexual partner of an older tramp or a prison inmate.

Finally understanding, Berkman reacts violently, accusing Red of advocating "terrible practices." Even more maddening to the older man, Berkman says, "I don't really believe it, Red" and asks are there "no women on the road?" Red, shocked at Berkman's ignorance and moral outrage, accuses the anarchist of acting like a "holy sky-pilot," or a minister. Red insists that once the young man "delved into the esoteric mysteries of moonology" and "tasted the melliffluous fruit on the forbidden tree" he would change his opinions. When Berkman brushes him aside, Red, rejected, tells him that "you'll know better before your time's up, me virtuous sonny."[28] It is possible that Berkman portrayed himself as naïve in order to show the reader the emotional impact of his entrance into the sexual life of American prisons. By staging his encounter with homosexuality in prison as something abrupt that he had no previous knowledge of, Berkman communicates to his audience the experience of life behind bars in a way that mere sociological description could not achieve.

Berkman concludes his description of this exchange with Red by recounting his feelings of incredulity and shock at what he had been told:

> His cynical attitude toward women and sex morality has roused in me a spirit of antagonism. The panegyrics of boy-love are deeply offensive to my instincts. The very thought of the unnatural practices revolts and disgusts me. But I find solace in the reflection that "Red's" insinuations are pure fabrication; no credence is to be given them. Man, a reasonable being, could not fall to such depths; he could not be guilty of such unspeakably vicious practices. Even the lowest outcast must not be credited with such perversion, such depravity… [Red] is a queer fellow; he is merely teasing me. These things are not credible; indeed, I don't believe they are possible. And even if they were, no human being would be capable of such iniquity.[29]

At this point in his narrative Berkman sounds very much like Dwight, O'Hare, and other reformers, who condemned sexual relations among prisoners.

Though Berkman did not make the argument that the kinds of relationships pursued by men such as Red were a product of prison life, he nonetheless denounced them as being part of the hierarchical and brutal nature of the prison system. This is a result of Berkman being asked to play the role of a passive sexual partner to an older man, clearly this was not a role that Berkman was willing to entertain. The horror that he displays in his reaction to Red was likely heightened and fueled by the fear of domination that haunted him in prison. As a prisoner, Berkman was already rendered subject to the will of other men. Already seething with rage and overwhelming feelings of impotence at having failed in his attempt to kill Frick, the thought of being made a "kid" brought Berkman to the edge of violence.

Throughout his narrative Berkman condemns Red and other men who pursued relationships with younger, vulnerable partners. According to Berkman, some prisoners were so intent on their pursuit of sex that they were known as "kid men."[30] In addition to recounting his interaction with Red, for example, Berkman describes an inmate named "Wild Bill," a "self-confessed invert," who is well known for his pursuit of "kids."[31] Inasmuch as they aggressively pursue homosexual pleasure, Red and Wild Bill very much resemble the fairies described by Chauncey. Red, for example, tells Berkman that he prefers "kids" to women. "Women," Red states, "are no good. I wouldn't look at 'em when I can have my [kid]."[32] Wild Bill and Red actively pursue other inmates. A fellow prisoner recounts how Wild Bill "had been hanging around the kids from the stocking shop; he has been after 'Fatty Bobby' for quite a while, and he's forever pestering 'Lady Sally,' and Young Davis, too." At one point in *Prison Memoirs* Wild Bill is "caught in the act" behind a shed in the prison yard with Fatty Bobby.[33] It should be noted that "kids" were not necessarily as young as the term implies. A "Kid" was a passive sexual partner of an older prisoner who was often, though not always, an adolescent or a young boy. It is unclear how old Fatty Bobby and Lady Sally are, though we are told that Young Davis is nineteen years old.[34]

Berkman's anarchism played a role in how he viewed the sexual relationships of men in prison. As a result, he could not accept the subordinate, coerced status of "kid" for himself or for any other inmate, but this put him in conflict with the value system of many of his fellow prisoners. According to Chauncey, most inmates were indifferent to the behavior of men like Wild Bill. Having a kid was a sign of power. "The fact that a man engaged in sexual relations with another male" led him to lose little status among other prisoners; if anything, he gained stature in many men's eyes because of his ability to coerce or attract a punk.[35] Unlike the majority of his fellow prisoners, Berkman was not a product of the rough bachelor subcultures. The domination and hierarchy that characterized so much of prison life, including the relations between "kids" and "kid men," were anathema to Berkman's anarchist principles. This is not to say that Berkman condemned all age-structured same-sex relationships; at several points in his memoirs he offers positive examples of such pairs. What Berkman found so profoundly problematic about the behavior of men like Wild Bill and Boston Red was that they treated their "kids" as marked inferiors. It was not homosexual relations that he objected to, but sexual exploitation. And, it should be noted, he was particularly horrified when it was suggested that he should place himself in the role of a "kid."

The portrayal of "kid men" in *Prison Memoirs* significantly complicates our current understanding of how sexuality, gender, age, and identity interplayed at the turn of the century. The identity of the "kid man" indicates that the prison population recognized a social role for the "active homosexual." George Chauncey argues that such an identity did not exist; only passive partners were marked by sexual difference. "Most prisoners," he writes, "like the prison authorities, seem to have regarded the wolves as little different from other men; their sexual behavior may have represented a moral failure, but it did not distinguish them from other men as the fairy's gender status did."[36] But the notion of a "kid man" seems to contradict this. Like fairies, "kid men" were marked by their sexual desires; they were known for seeking out sex with other males. But neither Boston Red, nor Wild Bill—whose very name conjures up one of the great masculine icons of the period—are described as feminine. This is not to say that gender—which overlapped with, and was reinforced by, differences in age—was not a primary language through which prison sexual relations were symbolically organized. The youths Wild Bill and Red pursued, such as "Lady Sally," are clearly feminized. "Kid men," however, are presented as masculine and aggressive, and in this, do not differ from the stereotypical portrayal of manhood. They—the wolves—are identified by their erotic interest in other males, a difference that distinguishes them from other men. Chauncey may be right that "the line between the wolf and the normal man, like that between the culture of the prison and the culture of the streets, was a fine one," but it was a line that Berkman and the prisoners whose language he mirrored in his memoir found meaningful.[37]

Had Berkman gone no further in his investigation of the moral and social status of homosexuality in prison his writings would have been no different than Dwight or O'Hare's. But that he did go farther, differentiates Berkman's text from those of so many other writers. For, in addition to portraying the sexual brutalities of prison life, Berkman also explores the existence of loving, mutually supportive relationships among prisoners. He demonstrates the ways that prison love—what he, at one point in his narrative, calls "love's dungeon flower"—could feed the spirit and body of the men who lived inside. Erotic desire between men, in other words, is, at least in some of its manifestations, directly counterpoised to the values of the prison system that Berkman so powerfully condemns. It is these human portraits that transfixed readers like Carpenter and others who were hungry for positive public representations of their own private desires. In a culture that systematically denied the value of warm, loving, and empowering homosexual relationships, the representation of such relationships was a powerful act. Because of the importance that these relationships had for Berkman's reading public it is worth examining them in some detail.

By far the most remarkable account of love among prisoners provided by Berkman in his memoirs are those that describe his own affection for a number of young men. The first of Berkman's romantic friends is named Johnny Davis. Davis is a young man of noticeable physical beauty—Red comments on his attractiveness and Wild Bill "pestered" him constantly. Berkman too acknowledges Davis' beauty. Berkman titled the chapter where he describes his relationship with Davis, "Love's Dungeon Flower," a reference both to the nature of the two men's feelings for each other and to Davis' radiance compared to the drab interior of the prison.

Davis and Berkman met while they worked in the prison hosiery department, but the two men's relationship did not move beyond simple camaraderie until both men were locked up in adjoining cells in solitary confinement. Berkman was placed in solitary for allegedly "destroying State property, having possession of a knife, and uttering a threat against the Warden." Davis was there because he had stabbed a man named "Dutch Adams," who, like Wild Bill, was attempting to initiate a sexual relationship with him. Foiled in his efforts, Adams resorted to spreading rumors that he "used" Davis. Afraid that his "mother might hear about it," Davis, tells Berkman that "he couldn't stand it" and so stabbed Adams.[38] Davis' actions indicate the degree to which shame and dishonor could be attached to being a "kid." Confined to a lonely cell and unaware if Adams was alive or dead, Davis dwelt on the possibility of his being hanged for murder.

Berkman's attempt to calm Davis and reassure him that all was not lost is the means by which their relationship evolves and deepens. He tried to convince Davis that Adams might not die and argued that the circumstances of his case might work in the young man's favor. Berkman reminds Davis of "the Warden's aversion to giving publicity to the sex practices in the prison, and remind[s] the boy of the Captain's official denial of their existence." Davis is relieved by these words and responds to Berkman's kindness. As their conversation unfolds, Berkman notes "with a glow of pleasure," that there is a "note of tenderness in [Davis'] voice." The two grow closer. Davis is soon using Berkman's nickname "Sashenka"—an affectionate diminutive of Alexander—and convinces Berkman to call him "Felipe," the name of "a poor castaway Cuban youth," whom the young man had read about. Berkman, like so many other prisoners, is not immune to Davis' charms. As they drift off to sleep, Berkman pictures "the boy before me, with his delicate face, and sensitive, girlish lips." The feminization of Davis, the imagery of lips, and the focus on the young man's physical beauty signals Berkman's growing attraction to the youth and foreshadows what comes next in the narrative.

On the following day, the two begin speaking again, and the erotic element of their relationship "flowers." Davis asks Berkman whether he is in his thoughts and Berkman replies, "Yes, kiddie, you are." Davis reveals that he too has been thinking of him. After exacting a promise that Berkman won't laugh at him, he confesses the depth of his feelings. "I was thinking," Davis shyly admits, "I was thinking, Sashenka—if you were here with me—I would like to kiss you." Far from being horrified, Berkman responds with deep pleasure: "An unaccountable sense of joy," he writes, "glows in my heart, and I muse in silence." Davis, alarmed by his friend's quiet, asks, "What's the matter…are you angry with me?" Berkman reassures Davis that he is not angry—quite the contrary. "No Felipe, you foolish little boy," writes Berkman, "I feel just as you do." That very evening, Davis is taken from solitary, and as he passes Berkman's cell he whispers, "Hope I'll see you soon, Sashenka." Berkman, "lonesome at the boy's departure," sinks into sadness.[39]

Unfortunately, Berkman was never able to receive his kiss. Davis died shortly after his release from solitary. Berkman, unaware of his friend's death, fantasizes about helping to gain freedom for his Davis. Once out of the prison, mused Berkman, "I shall strain every effort for my little friend Felipe; I must secure his release. How happy the boy will be to join me in liberty!"[40] Berkman hoped to give Davis the gift of freedom, but death intervened. The resulting mixture of stillborn desire and loss haunts Berkman, and for some time, he obsesses about Davis. Although he corresponds regularly with several young female admirers, Berkman dwells on his dead friend. One correspondent sends him a picture of herself, but Berkman confesses to his readers that, her "roguish eyes and sweet lips exert but a passing impression upon me. My thoughts turn to Johnny, my young friend in the convict grave."[41] Though one of Berkman's fellow inmates with whom he shared his correspondence developed "a violent passion for the pretty face [of Berkman's female admirer]," Berkman ignores the lure of his admirer's image and nurses his feelings for Davis.

Berkman's relationship with Davis is difficult to evaluate as it falls somewhere along the spectrum of friendship and erotic relations. There was a strong emotional element to the pair's relationship, as well as a physical—if only imagined—component to the relationship. The extent of their intimacy is unclear, though I would argue on the basis of both historic and contemporary definitions, the two men's relationship had a strong element of homoeroticism. As far as we know, the two men did not have sex, but they did participate in an erotic fantasy. Berkman felt drawn to Davis' "delicate face, and sensitive, girlish lips" and he thrilled at the thought of kissing the youth. Davis, for his part, seemed all too aware of his own charms—physical and otherwise—and was quite willing to use them on Berkman. The language exchanged between the two is erotically charged. Berkman feminized Davis and referred to him as "kiddie," a word freighted with sexual connotations in their surroundings, and both Davis and Berkman used terms of endearment with each other. All of these elements—a kiss, terms of endearment, pining, and feelings of abandonment—are common enough in same-sex friendship of the period, but the intensity of feeling between the two men—of a sort usually missing in the cold cells of the prison—is depicted as uncommonly powerful. That element of passionate intensity gives the story of "Sashenka" and "Felipe" a powerful place within *Prison Memoirs*.[42]

Davis was not the only man that Berkman developed a strong attachment to while in prison. He also introduces his reader to an inmate he refers to as "my young friend Russell." Russell, who was "barely nineteen," possesses a "smiling face," "boundless self-assurance," and "indomitable will."[43] The description of the relationship between the two men is quite moving, and speaks to the intense feelings that Berkman had for some of his fellow prisoners. Contemporary readers were impressed with the depth of feeling that Berkman conveyed. To illustrate, in his piece on Berkman's memoirs, Bayard Boyesen wrote that "the incidents connected with the story of young Russell" are among the "most beautiful passages in the book."[44]

Similar to Davis, Berkman's relationship with Russell is ignited when the young man is put in solitary. The youth manages to communicate with Berkman through notes, but the strain of the separation and the harassment of the guards take its toll on Russell, who begins to "look pale and haggard." Berkman's anxieties grow, as does his fondness for the boy:

> With intense thankfulness I think of Russell…A strange longing for his companionship possesses me. In the gnawing loneliness, his face floats before

me, casting the spell of a friendly presence, his strong features softened by sorrow, his eyes grown large with the same sweet sadness of "Little Felipe." A peculiar tenderness steals into my thoughts of the boy; I look forward eagerly to his notes. Impatiently I scan the faces in the passing line, wistful for the sight of the youth, and my heart beats faster at his fleeting smile.[45]

Berkman comes to think of Russell in much the same way he did Davis. He feminizes Russell; his transformation into a second "Little Felipe" is accompanied by a "softening" of his features and his eyes grow large and luminous. Berkman's mood rises and falls at the sight of Russell. Just as with Davis, Berkman imagines the possibility of the two sharing freedom. His strongest feelings for his young friends are forged in the crucible of solitary. The "gnawing loneliness" of solitary added a special force to his feelings for Davis and Russell. That Berkman was physically separated from the young men may also have created a psychological space within which his homoerotic fantasies—free of the actual possibility of consummation—could develop.

Unfortunately, the parallels between Russell and Davis extend even to their early deaths. Russell, suffering from "a chill," is placed in the prison hospital. Desperate for news about his friend, Berkman feigns "severe pains in the bowels, to afford Frank, the doctor's assistant, an opportunity to pause at my cell." Berkman asks about Russell and is told that the youth is paralyzed, the victim of a mistake on the part of another of the doctor's assistants. Told that he will surely die, Russell bemoans his fate and sends Berkman piteous notes. Berkman purposefully wounds himself so that he will be sent to the infirmary. Once there, he steals to Russell's bedside. Unfortunately, little can be done. Russell falls asleep and Berkman "silently…touch[es] his dry lips" and departs. Whether this "touch" is a kiss or whether Berkman lightly stroked Russell's lips with his fingers we cannot know. Denied further visitation, Frank later tells Berkman of Russell's death. "His last thought," Frank reports, "was of you." Berkman adds a dramatic detail: Frank tells him that at the moment of his death, Russell cries out, "Good Bye, Aleck." Berkman's account of Russell's death, and the agonized portrayal of his reaction to the loss of his friend, bespeaks the strength and tenor of emotion that tied the two men together.[46]

Berkman struggled to depict and understand the nature of his relationships with Davis and Russell. He attempts to define and defend the possibility of mutual, freely-chosen, loving relations between men in an environment that was by its very nature, adverse to such relationships. Berkman clearly disapproved of the coercive nature of the "kid love" that everywhere flourished around him—his initial reaction to Red's overtures and his disapproving remarks about "kid men" and "kid business" illustrate this. But the friendships

Berkman developed were, in many ways, similar to those he was so critical of. He was clearly infatuated. Davis' offer of a kiss sent Berkman into rapture and there is a hint that Berkman kissed Russell as the young man lay dying. Elsewhere in his text however, Berkman denies that he felt any "physical passion" for his young friends, but this is true only if one accepts the most limited and arid definition of the term "physical passion." Berkman does, however, admit that he loved Russell "with all my heart" and his sadness at his death reflects a similar depth of feeling.[47] Berkman works hard to acknowledge the extent of his feelings for his passionate friends, while differentiating his relationship with Davis and Russell from those that "kid men" pursued.

Berkman resolves the emotional and definitional problems posed by his relationship with the two young men by introducing into his narrative a moral and ethical dialogue on the subject of homosexuality. In a chapter entitled "Passing the Love of Woman," he presents a discussion with a friend of his, George, on the subject of homosexuality. The title of the chapter references the relationship of Jonathan and David, two Biblical figures said to love each other with a love "passing the love of women." This relationship was a common reference point for nineteenth-century discussions of homosocial and homoerotic relations between men.[48] It's an odd choice of reference for an avowed atheist, but one that serves as a useful frame in which to explore same-sex relations. George is presented as an eminently knowledgeable, authoritative, respectable person with whom Berkman speaks about a subject that is omnipresent in prison. In this chapter, Berkman places the subject of homosexuality under explicit scrutiny. This is, in fact, the only chapter in which Berkman uses the word "homosexuality," as opposed to "kid love" or "kid business." "Passing the Love of Women" is Berkman's effort to settle the question of how the reader is supposed to understand and differentiate between the coercive homosexuality practiced by Wild Bill and the loving relationships that Berkman had with Russell and Davis. This chapter is a dramatic treatment of a topic that Berkman struggled with both in his literary art and in his life.

· While it is quite possible that Berkman had talks with his fellow inmates on the subject of homosexuality, it is likely that George is a literary creation. George is a rhetorical device created to put forth a reasoned discussion of sex in prison. Certain facts hint at this. For example, George is said to have been raised in the "Catholic tradition" and to have a great-grandfather who "was among the signers of the Declaration." This is an unlikely pedigree since only one Catholic was among the signers. George also happens to be a physician; he is first identified in *Prison Memoirs* by his nickname "Doctor George." That a descendant of an old American family, of wealth and professional standing, came to be locked up for "sixteen years for alleged complicity in... a bank rob-bery...during which [a] cashier was killed" is hard to believe.[49] George is a very unlikely inmate, but a very compatible foil for a dialogue on the ethical, social, and cultural status of same-sex love.

George's politics—sexual and otherwise—mirror Berkman's. Unlike nearly all of Berkman's other fellow inmates, George has considerable sympathy for anarchism. George can "pass the idle hours conversing over subjects of mu-tual interest, discussing social theories and problems of the day." Though he is not an anarchist, George is interested in the "American lecture tour of Peter Kropotkin" and considers himself a "Democrat of the Jeffersonian type," a de-scription that sounds remarkably like Benjamin Tucker's notion of anarchists as "unterrified Jeffersonians." George is also familiar with the discourse of sexol-ogy. Though prior to his imprisonment "he had not come in personal contact with cases of homosexuality," George's medical training allows him to speak with some authority on the subject. The use of the clinical term "homosexual-ity" signals George's knowledge and provides legitimacy to the discussion. A layperson would not be as useful a participant in a dialogue meant to establish the morality of a subject most often treated as a medical and psychological condition. In George, a liberal scientist, Berkman finds the perfect person with whom he can converse on a touchy subject.

In "Passing the Love of Women," George seeks Berkman's advice about his love for a young prisoner named "Floyd." He tells Berkman that he first noticed Floyd as he passed in a hallway. "He had been in only a short time," George recounts, "and he was rosy-cheeked, with a smooth face and sweet lips—he reminded me of a girl I used to court before I was married." Floyd, according to George was "small and couldn't defend himself," and found in George a protector and provider. George took particular interest in Floyd's health, assisting him with "stomach troubles" and securing for him "fruit and things," rare treats in prison.

The feelings the older man felt for the youth increased over time and be-came increasingly erotic in nature. "For two years," George tells Berkman, "I loved him without the least taint of sex desire." But over time, George's feelings deepened:

> by degrees the psychic stage began to manifest all the expressions of love
> between the opposite sexes. I remember the first time he kissed me... He put
> both hands between the bars, and pressed his lips to mine. Aleck, I tell you,
> never in my life had I experienced such bliss as at that moment... He told me
> he was very fond of me. From then on we became lovers. I used to neglect my
> work, and risk great danger to get a chance to kiss and embrace him. I grew

terribly jealous, too, though I had no cause. I passed through every phase of a passionate love.[50]

George's feelings for Floyd are very much like those of Berkman's for "Felipe" and Russell. In both cases, the friendship is structured by a significant age difference, the youth is feminized in the eyes of the older man, the older man is concerned with the general welfare of the beloved, and the attraction and emotional bond are mutual (or at least the older man experienced them as such). And in both cases the relationships between the younger and older prisoner are unsettling.

In telling George's story, Berkman is retelling his own. George is a literary device that allows Berkman to explore the nature of same-sex desire. Of course, the significant difference between George's relations with Floyd and Berkman's relationship with his young friends is that George admits that his love "manifest[ed] all the expressions of love between the opposite sexes." Berkman never reveals whether he had a physical relationship with another man while he was in prison.

George is unsure how to understand his experience of attraction to another male; he struggles with the meaning of his love for Floyd. George tells Berkman that he wants to "speak frankly" on a subject about which "very little is known...much less understood." The strain of the attempt is obvious. The "veins on [George's] forehead protrude, as if he is undergoing a severe mental struggle." George insists that he approached Floyd with pure intentions and wants Berkman to know he is different than the other inmates. "Don't misunderstand me," George tells Berkman, "it wasn't that I wanted a 'kid.' I swear to you, the other youths had no attraction for me whatsoever."[51] Floyd was a "bright and intelligent youth" of "fine character," and George's interest in him was, he insisted, not merely physical. He "got him interested in literature, and advised him what to read, for he didn't know what to do with his time." In other words, George is not a ruthless "kid man," like Red or Wild Bill. And George, unlike Red, does not explicitly prefer the company of "kids" to that of women—in fact, George is happily married. "Throughout [George's] long confinement," Berkman tells us, "his wife had faithfully stood by him, her unfailing courage and devotion sustaining him in the hours of darkness and despair."[52]

George insists that he was not merely interested in "sexual gratification," that his motivations were of a finer caliber. He carefully distinguishes his feelings for Floyd from the type of feelings that "kid men" had for their partners. George's animus, however, is directed against the youthful partners, not the

older men. Berkman relates that George was "very bitter against the prison element variously known as 'the girls,' 'Sallies,' and 'punks,' who for gain traffic in
sexual gratification." According to George, these youth "are worse than street
prostitutes." Though he described Floyd as looking like a girl, the contrast between the flagrant behaviors of the "Sallies" and Floyd's respectable demeanor
was a way to exorcise the taint of effeminacy from the two prisoner's love for
each other. Floyd may have been pretty enough to attract George's attention
but he was not a "street prostitute." The condemnation of this sort of language
functions as a way to distinguish what Floyd and George shared from effeminacy and prostitution. George needed to reassure himself that his relationship
with Floyd was something nobler than a sexual transaction, a trade of sex for
goods and protection. He wants to put considerable distance between himself
and the dangerous and devalued figures of the "sallies" and the "kid men."[53]

George was disturbed by the physical nature of his relationship with Floyd.
He tells Berkman that, despite the "passionate nature" of his love, he "felt a
touch of the old disgust at the thought of actual sex contact." Perhaps Red,
who expressed a rougher, working-class sexual ethos, was untroubled by sex
with his "kids," but George was of a different class and cast. Kissing and em-
braces were innocent enough, but genital contact, "seemed to me a desecration
of the boy." Even though Floyd "said he loved me enough to do even that for
me," George told Berkman, "I couldn't bring myself to do it; I loved the lad
too much for it." This was not mere lust, George insisted, "it was real, true love."
Despite Floyd's apparent willingness to have sex, George denies that he had
sexual intercourse with his beloved. The relationship ended when Floyd was
transferred to another cellblock. George was bereft: "I would be the happiest
man," he told Berkman, "if I could only touch his hand again, or get one more
kiss."

Berkman's presentation of George's relationship with Floyd as an intimate
one, yet limited in physical expression, echoes that of other sex radicals who
struggled to represent same-sex love free of reference to crime or sin. Like
George, men such as Edward Carpenter and John Addington Symonds insisted
that love between men was not merely sodomy, but an especially intense form
of friendship. Sex took second place in their descriptions of same-sex love. For
example, in one of his essays on "homogenic love," Carpenter downplayed the
sexual nature of same-sex love:

> Without denying that sexual intimacies do exist; and while freely admitting
> that in great cities, there are to be found associated with this form of
> attachment prostitution and other evils comparable with the evils associated
> with the ordinary sex-attachment; we may yet say that it would be a great

error to suppose that homogenic love takes as a rule the extreme form vulgarly supposed; and that it would also be a great error to overlook the fact that in a large number of instances the relation is not distinctly sexual at all, though it may be said to be physical in the sense of embrace and endearment.[54]

Carpenter's description of same-sex love was an artful attempt to get around the moral stigma that was attached to the genital expression of homosexual desire. Like George, who rails against the "sallies" and "girls" and the "punks," who trade sex for food and other favors, Carpenter distances his vision of same-sex love from prostitution and effeminacy. Playing down the sexual, Carpenter presented same-sex love as an intense spiritual and emotional bond, as a masculine friendship. Berkman's chapter describing his conversation with George functions in exactly the same way; he describes George's relationship with Floyd as something other than mere "kid business." Throughout his narrative, Berkman downplays the erotic element of those same-sex relationships—like those he had with Davis and Russell—which he would like to present as noble and good.

Having finished telling the story of his love for Floyd, George looks to Berkman for his opinion. It's a moment fraught with tension. "You—you're laughing," George exclaims. There is "a touch of anxiety in his voice," as he was concerned that Berkman would interpret his behavior as "viciousness." Most prisoners, George tells his friend, "take everything here in such a filthy sense." But Berkman reassures his friend that he understands perfectly and is more than sympathetic. "I think it is a wonderful thing; and George—I had felt the same horror and disgust at these things, as you did. But now I think quite differently about them." Like George, Berkman had come into prison with a strong distaste for homosexuality, but as Red had predicted, he had come to see things differently. The reason for this change of heart is that Berkman shared George's experience of love for a fellow prisoner. "I had a friend here," Berkman admits, "His name was Russell... I felt no physical passion toward him, but I think I loved him with all my heart." Berkman does not mention "Felipe," his first "kiddie," but the reader would, of course, know of this relationship. Berkman finishes his talk with George by telling him that his anxiety is misplaced. "George," Berkman reassures his friend and his readers, "I think it a very beautiful emotion. Just as beautiful as love for a woman."[55] This positive affirmation of George's relationship with Floyd concludes Berkman's chapter on the social and cultural value of homosexuality.

As his date of release approached Berkman turned away from the relationships he had formed in prison. He wrote that, "Thoughts of women eclipse the memory of the prison affections," but Berkman's interest in the nature and ethics of "prison affections" continued.[56] This was demonstrated in that his first act was to insist on depicting his prison experience of same-sex sexuality and affection in his memoirs. In Goldman's autobiography, she reports that one of the publishers who considered the manuscript "insisted on eliminating the chapters relating to homosexuality in prison," but Berkman refused to bowdlerize his text.[57] With the help of friends like Lincoln Steffens and others who provided financial support, the Mother Earth Publishing Association was able to bring out *Prison Memoirs*. Goldman solicited support in the form of advanced subscriptions and contributions from *Mother Earth* readers in a letter that highlighted the sexual content of Berkman's work, including the treatment of the "Physical, Mental, and Moral Effects" of life behind bars and "The Stress of Sex" and "Homosexuality." *Prison Memoirs,* Goldman wrote, "promises to be one the of the most valuable and original contributions to the psycho-revolutionary literature of the world."[58] The framing of *Prison Memoirs* as a "psychological" work—one advertisement in *Mother Earth* called it a "contribution to socio-psychological literature"—is key, given the central importance that Berkman gives medicine and psychology, as in the personification of George and his attempt to grapple with the ethics of homosexuality.[59]

Berkman further signals his interest in the politics of homosexuality by framing his text with Oscar Wilde's work. As a preface to his prison memoirs, Berkman chose an excerpt from Wilde's poem *The Ballad of Reading Gaol*. It is the perfect accompaniment for the book, since both works condemn the prison system. The Mother Earth Publishing Association also realized that the two men's work fit well together. In the back of the first edition of *Prison Memoirs*, Wilde's poem and his essay *The Soul of Man under Socialism* were offered for sale by mail order. Even before Berkman's prison memoirs were published, Wilde's prison writings were being touted in the pages of *Mother Earth*. An excerpt from Wilde's essay, *De Profundis*, which speaks to experience of imprisonment, appeared in one of the first issues of the journal. In *De Profundis*, Wilde expresses his hope that if he is able to make of his prison years "only one beautiful work of art I shall be able to rob malice of its venom, and cowardice of its sneer, and to pluck out the tongue of scorn by the roots."[60] *The Ballad of Reading Gaol* and Berkman's *Prison Memoirs* are just such works. Both texts transform the fate of the condemned into moving and politically radical works of art.

Berkman was not the only one who linked Wilde with the injustice of the prison system. In a letter to Hirschfeld, Emma Goldman condemned the cruel way that Wilde had been treated. She wrote, "[Wilde's sentencing] struck me as an act of cruel injustice and repulsive hypocrisy;" an unjust act by an unjust society. Goldman specifically linked Wilde's mistreatment with the oppression of homosexuals, and championed him, as she told Hirschfeld, because "As an anarchist my place has ever been with the persecuted."[61] Like Berkman, Goldman also used Wilde's work in her own writings on prison and the criminal justice system. In an essay attacking the prison system, Goldman cited a section of *The Ballad of Reading Gaol* which describes jails as sources of "poisonous air," which throttles those who were forced to breath it.[62]

Other anarchists also cited this particular poem when discussing prisons. When Marie Ganz was in Queens County Jail, for example, she read *The Ballad of Reading Gaol* to her fellow inmates. According to Ganz, the prisoners listened "intently to every word, until they burst into tears."[63] Wilde's witness was a powerful document that made its mark on anarchist prison writing.

In naming Wilde as a literary and political inspiration, however, Berkman was choosing sides in a debate over sexuality—a debate that was most clearly symbolized by Wilde's trial and imprisonment for a sex crime that linked imprisonment, homosexuality, and political dissidence. It did not escape Berkman that in writing *The Ballad of Reading Gaol*, Wilde was condemning the legal system that sent him to prison for homosexual acts. In *Prison Memoirs of an Anarchist,* Berkman frames Wilde's imprisonment as a political act. In the chapter "Passing the Love of Woman," he writes that George "speaks with profound sympathy of the brilliant English man-of-letters...driven to prison and to death because his sex life did not conform to the accepted standards." George exonerates Wilde of any wrongdoing, shifting the blame onto "the world of cant and stupidity."[64] This defense of Wilde, articulated within the chapter in his prison memoirs that is most concerned with exploring the ethics of same-sex love, makes explicit what is implied by Berkman's choosing *The Ballad of Reading Gaol* as a preface to his own work. That choice—aligning himself with Wilde as a literary companion—was a resonant act with a broad series of implications.

The clearest indication that Berkman continued his interest in the question of the moral and social status of homosexuality is the fact that he gave a series of lectures on the subject after *Prison Memoirs* was published. Berkman, like Goldman and other anarchists, made frequent use of lectures in their propaganda work. Berkman developed and delivered a talk called, "Homosexuality and Sex Life in Prison," which drew upon his observations and experience in prison. Unfortunately, there are no known surviving transcripts of this or any other of Berkman's public presentations on homosexuality, but two reports of such lectures appear in the pages of *Mother Earth*. This particular lecture was an appeal for tolerance and better understanding of the diverse expressions of erotic desire and was apparently a popular speech—a further example of the everyday observation that sex sells. In the words of Reb Raney, one of *Mother Earth*'s correspondents who heard Berkman speak in San Francisco in 1915, "the interest of the human family in the chief source of our earthly commotion seems never to recede from the boiling pitch."[65] No doubt the popularity of sex as a lecture topic was one of the reasons Berkman chose to speak on the subject of "prison affections." The money earned on one night could help underwrite weeks of more prosaic work. But that was not his reason—if fundraising had been the only consideration, Berkman could have chosen to speak on any aspect of sexuality. He spoke on same-sex eroticism.

Berkman's homosexual politics reflected his pragmatic view of the ethics of sexual desire. In his lectures he contended, "you can't suppress the unsuppressible," and that to make a crime out of erotic desire was—and he knew this from personal experience in prison—cruel and bound to fail. You cannot regulate the fundamental human need for emotional and physical affection. This position reflected basic anarchist doctrine, as well as Berkman's experience behind bars. He began his days in prison believing in the aberrant nature of homosexual sex, but by the end of his sentence, he had come to a less rigid view of human nature. According to one audience member, Berkman's "handling of the sex question exhibits a breadth and comprehension I have never seen surpassed." By insisting on the complexity of human sexual expression, Berkman "show[ed] that the better we understand a problem the less liable we are to tangle the skein by grasping at a single thread."[66] Just as he did in *Prison Memoirs*, in his lectures Berkman insisted on respecting the complexities of the human heart.

Berkman's treatment of the topic of homosexuality in his lectures reflected his political ideals. He advocated a tolerant disregard for the sexual habits of others, a position consistent with the principles of anarchism. He was apparently an effective speaker: Billie McCullough, who attended a series of Berkman's lectures in Los Angeles in 1915, was deeply influenced by what she heard. "He instinctively gives you credit for having common sense," McCullough wrote, "and therein is the effectiveness of his work." By framing radical notions in commonplace garb, Berkman succeeded in moving his audience members. McCullough, for example, found her views transformed by Berkman's presentation: "I've read Ellis and a few others along these lines," she reported, "but had remained a narrow-minded prude, classifying all Homosexualists as degenerates." But having heard Berkman speak on the subject McCullough declared that she now had a "clearer vision" of a subject she had previously considered as a psychological and moral disorder. So powerful was Berkman's argument in favor of sexual liberalism that she felt his "lecture should become a classic."[67]

Any possibility that "Homosexuality and Sex Life in Prison" would indeed become a classic was cut short by Berkman's imprisonment in 1918 on the charge of conspiring against the selective draft law following the United States' entry into World War I. Arrested in New York, Berkman was sentenced to two years in Atlanta Federal Prison. Though far shorter than his earlier imprisonment, Berkman's stay in Atlanta was harsh. He spent seven months in solitary for denouncing the beatings administered to his fellow inmates. Berkman was unbowed. As he had done in the Western Penitentiary of Pennsylvania, Berkman attempted to expose the rank and cruel conditions in Atlanta. After his release, Berkman published an open letter to the Atlanta prison warden, Mr. Zerbst, in which he protested the "criminal neglect of sick prisoners…the unwholesome food…the favoritism of men with 'pull,' the discrimination against political prisoners, the corrupt system of 'stool pigeons,' the fake trials at which the work of one drunken guard outweighs that of a dozen soldiers, political prisoners, and other inmates of character and integrity, whose sole crime consisted in the expression of an unpopular opinion during the war." Berkman even protested the low pay of the prison guards! "The struggle for existence," noted Berkman, denies the guards and their dependents a decent living and "makes the guards surly, cranky, and quarrelsome" and prone to "vent their misery and ill-humor upon the unfortunates in their power."

In Atlanta's prison, Berkman again confronted "kid business," and once again he railed against it. In his letter to the warden, Berkman warned, "I have not yet even hinted at the existence and the actual encouragement of homosexual practices.…I have not started yet, Mr. Zerbst, but I *will*, and that very soon."[68] [Italics in original.] Given his advocacy of sexual liberalism and his claims that love between men could be a "wonderful thing," it is somewhat jarring to note that, in the letter, Berkman described homosexuality as an "aberration." But Berkman was not referring to consensual relations between men; he was denouncing the sexual exploitation of inmates, a practice that was apparently tolerated and even encouraged by Zerbst and the prison guards. Berkman had made similar charges in *Prison Memoirs*. He always made quite clear distinctions between the ethical nature of sexual acts that were freely entered into and those that were coerced. Despite his threats, Berkman was unable to take on Zerbst and the federal prison system. Upon his release Berkman was deported, and he never returned to the United States.

But Berkman's departure from the US did not bring an end to his political activism, including his interest in sexual politics. In the mid-1920s, Berkman and Goldman sought to have *Prison Memoirs* reissued in England, and they approached Edward Carpenter and Havelock Ellis about writing a preface for the new British edition. The decision to potentially include Carpenter and Ellis was not casually arrived at. Both had written on the subject of prison reform, as Berkman and Goldman well knew. In one of her essays on prisons, Goldman cited works by both Ellis and Carpenter to support her contention that "nine crimes out of ten could be traced, directly or indirectly, to our economic and social inequities, to our system of remorseless exploitation and robbery."[69] Most importantly, the two men, and in particular Carpenter, had expressed sympathy for the anarchists. Carpenter had even played a role in assisting a number of English anarchists, known as the Walsall Anarchists, who were imprisoned in April 1892 for conspiracy to make a bomb.[70] But by the time the two men were approached with the idea of writing a preface for Berkman's book, the greatest claim to fame that either man had was their respective writing on sexuality. And more to the point, both men were associated with the scientific study of homosexuality and with efforts to ameliorate the lives of homosexuals. A preface by either Carpenter or Ellis would highlight those sections of the *Prison Memoirs* that dealt with sex behind bars.

Ellis declined the offer, but Carpenter—whose interest in Berkman's book was longstanding—readily accepted. By writing a preface to Berkman's memoirs, Carpenter could address a number of issues that he cared deeply about. His critique of prison and the legal system were quite similar to the anarchists'. He denounced prisons as "an epitome of folly and wickedness" in which "the state is seen, like an evil stepmother, beating its own children, whom it has reared in poverty and ignorance."[71] This is echoed in Berkman's writing that prisons were "but an intensified replica of the world beyond, the larger prison locked with the levers of Greed, guarded by the spawn of Hunger."[72] Of course, Carpenter was also intrigued by Berkman's politics of homosexuality.

Historian Jeffrey Weeks argues that Carpenter's interest in prisons and the politics of sexuality were connected. By writing about those who society scorns and punishes, Carpenter was protesting his own status as an outsider. "In the position of modern-day criminals," Weeks writes, "Carpenter saw a model for his own position as a homosexual, as an outlaw of society."[73] It is possible that this kind of metonymic equivalence of "the prisoner" with "the homosexual" was part of what motivated Berkman's relatively sympathetic treatment of same-sex relations behind bars. Since those who committed homosexual acts were by definition outlaws, and anarchists had a decided bias for those who stood outside the law, it follows that defending homosexuality was an act of defiance against the law and those who enforced it—the state.

While his own prison reformism was an important reason for Carpenter's decision to write a preface for *Prison Memoirs*, by the time he was asked to write it, he was much better known as a sex radical than a prison reformer. In the early years of the twentieth century, Carpenter had published a number of works, such as *Love's Coming of Age* and *Intermediate Types Among Primitive Folks*, which dealt explicitly with homosexuality. In 1914, he assisted in the founding of the British Society for the Study of Sex Psychology (later renamed the British Sexological Society, or BSS), becoming the group's first president. The BSS aimed to provide a forum "for the consideration of problems and questions connected with sexual psychology, from their medical, juridical, and sociological aspects." To that end, the group sponsored lectures and published pamphlets on same-sex desire. According to Weeks, "public education on homosexuality was a major theme from the beginnings of the society." Agreeing to write an introduction to Berkman's book fit in perfectly with Carpenter's work with the BSS and that group's stated desire to throw light on "sexual psychology, from their medical, juridical, and sociological aspects."[74]

Goldman convinced Carpenter to write a preface to *Prison Memoirs* by arguing that doing so would give him the opportunity to highlight the sexual politics of Berkman's book:

> I know of no one in England or A[merica] who is so fit to introduce Berkman's work on his prison experience and all that went with those dreadful fourteen years than you. You who have so ably pleaded against prisons, you who have understood the suffering and hopelessness of the victims of our cruel social fabric. And there is also your deep human understanding of the men and women who in their sex psychology divert from the so-called normal and who are branded by our social and ethical stupidity as degenerate. Indeed, there is no other great figure in this wide land who could and would do justice to the work of Alexander Berkman and the subjects he treats therein.[75]

Goldman's praise of Carpenter's reform work culminates with her lauding of his defense of those "men and women who in their sex psychology divert from the so-called normal." This is not an attempt at flattery, but it reflects the fact that, by the 1920s, Carpenter's reputation had been strongly colored by his writings on sex. Goldman and Berkman were quite aware of Carpenter's reputation and were willing to trade on the sexual aspect of *Prison Memoirs* in order to promote the book. Anarchist tracts may not have been good business in the 1920s, but books on sexuality were best sellers. As Goldman herself told Berkman, "Economic subjects do not draw, only current events...or sex."[76] But the decision to choose Carpenter was not entirely based on market considerations. *Prison Memoirs* was a significant work of sexual politics, and asking Carpenter to write a preface that highlighted an aspect of Berkman's book that many, Carpenter among them, found compelling was an important political decision.

Carpenter's preface, which appeared in 1926, was a modest contribution, hardly one page in length. He was older and had difficulty working at his former pace. Though he employed a less forceful voice than that of the young Hutchins Hapgood, who wrote the introduction for the first edition of *Prison Memoirs*, Carpenter shared Hapgood's enthusiasm for the value of the book. He did not expect every reader to "embrace Alexander Berkman's theories, nor yet to approve the act which brought upon him twenty-one years among the living dead," but Carpenter was sure that anyone who picked up *Prison Memoirs* would be impressed by the "deep psychological perceptions and the fine literary quality of the work." Carpenter makes no direct mention of the sexual content of Berkman's book, but hints at the range of human emotions and behaviors treated therein. "There are in the book," wrote Carpenter, "cameos describing how friendships may be and are formed and sustained even in the midst of the most depressing and dispiriting conditions." These gems cut from prison rock reveal, according to Carpenter, a beauty that one would not expect to find behind the walls of a jail. In addition to providing a "vivid picture of the sufferings of those detained in American prisons," Carpenter felt that Berkman "makes one realize how the human spirit—unquenchable in its search for love—is ever pressing outward and onward in a kind of creative activity." The creative activity extends to the inmates' struggles to find companionship behind bars. The English edition's dust jacket echoes Carpenter's coy language, promising readers that Berkman's book describes, "life as it is lived inside prisons...nothing is left out."[77]

As well as the addition of Carpenter's preface, Berkman once again included an excerpt of Oscar Wilde's *The Ballad of Reading Gaol*—the same one that appeared in the first American edition—to frame his work. Carpenter's oblique reference to the sexual content of *Prison Memoirs* was echoed and amplified by the inclusion of Wilde's poem on the page opposite. The two men represented different aspects of the social position of homosexuals within society: the victim and the rebel. Wilde was the symbol of the tragic consequences of state regulation of erotic desire and expression—the anarchist sex radicals had long used him as a key figure in the politics of homosexuality. Carpenter was a much less tragic figure. Oscar Wilde and Edward Carpenter's names would have brought to mind homosexual desire and the politics engendered by that desire.

The number of copies of the English edition of *Prison Memoirs* that circulated in the United States is unknown. There was a second American edition published in 1920, though it did not have Carpenter's preface. But a reader does not need Carpenter's guidance to understand that *Prison Memoirs* is one of the most important political texts of the early-twentieth century, which treats same-sex desire. Few other books of the period are as nuanced or sophisticated in their approach to the question of homosexuality. *Prison Memoirs of an Anarchist* is not an apologia for same-sex love. Berkman's text is a complex investigation of the question of same-sex love in a brutal environment. Unlike the majority of writing by prison reformers and those who have themselves spent time in prison, Berkman does not use homosexuality as a club with which to beat the prison system. While he does not hesitate to condemn the often brutal nature of prison's social and sexual relations, he does not stop there. In addition to acknowledging and condemning the exploitation of "kids" in prison, Berkman portrays consensual, supportive relationships between members of the same sex. These relationships included those Berkman had with other prisoners—relationships which helped Berkman survive his many years in jail. *Prison Memoirs* is a key political text in the body of works that the anarchists produced on the subject of prisons and on the ethical, social, and cultural place of same-sex desire in American society.

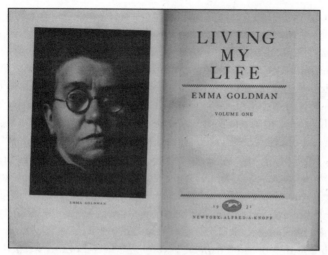

CHAPTER FIVE:

"'URNINGS,' 'LESBIANS,' AND OTHER STRANGE TOPICS'": SEXOLOGY AND THE POLITICS OF HOMOSEXUALITY

IN 1902, JOHN WILLIAM Lloyd expressed his hope that he would "live to see the day when we shall have an American (better still an International) Institute and Society of Sexology, composed of our greatest scientists, philosophers, physicians, and men and women of finest character studying sex as fearlessly as geology, discussing it as calmly as the 'Higher Criticism,' and publishing it far and wide in a paper which no Church nor State can gag."[1] Like geologists or readers of esoteric texts, this gathering of "men and women of finest character" would untangle the layers of desire and identity, providing a road map to the complicated inner world of sexual desires. Lloyd hoped his group of scientists, learned scholars, and doctors would study sex free from the threat of state censorship and theological injunction. Though produced by professionals, the knowledge emanating from this learned council would be provided to a broad audience in an easily available publication. The "International Institute and Society of Sex" would constitute a vital organ of a free society run in accordance with the principles of anarchism.[2]

Lloyd was not alone among the anarchists in wishing to see the topic of sex receive more "scientific" attention. Like the myriad psychiatrists, sociologists, doctors and others who contributed to the field of sexology, anarchist sex radicals published articles, delivered lectures, and distributed literature dealing with a broad variety of sexual topics. In doing so, they hoped to bring clarity to a subject they felt was too little understood.

Emma Goldman, one of the most famous—not to say infamous—sex radicals of the early-twentieth century, was particularly interested in sexology and the politics of sexuality. She was, however, seriously disappointed in the quality of most of the work she encountered. "Nowhere," she observed, "does one meet such density, such stupidity, as in the questions pertaining to love and sex." Goldman expended considerable time and resources fighting this "puritanical mock modesty."[3] She felt compelled to speak on the politics of personal life. "Nothing short of an open, frank, and intelligent discussion," she wrote, "will purify the air from the hysterical, sentimental rubbish that is shrouding these vital subjects, vital to individual as well as social well-being."[4] Many of Goldman's colleagues shared her view that the "puritanical mock modesty" of American culture could be dangerous. Hulda Potter-Loomis warned that "restrained or restricted sexual desire has been the cause of insanity in thousand of cases."[5] The anarchist sex radicals fought to counter what they felt were ill-conceived, uninformed, and dangerous ideas about the nature of sexual desire and its role in shaping individual psychology.

American anarchist sex radicals favored European sexologists over their local counterparts. To some extent this reflects the fact that European sexologists were far more productive than the Americans, as there was simply more and better-known work being written in Europe—especially in England and Germany.[6] But the anarchists' preference for European scholarship was also influenced by their political values. When it came to the question of sex, the anarchists felt that the United States was, as one contributor to *Mother Earth* wrote, "a provincial and hypocritical nation."[7] This was particularly true in regards to the question of homosexuality, and the anarchist sex radicals were deeply influenced by the work that European sexologists produced on the subject of same-sex love and desire. Goldman claimed, for example, that it was the "works of Havelock Ellis, Krafft-Ebing, Carpenter, and many others which made me see the crime against Oscar Wilde."[8] She and other anarchists drew on the work of European sexologists in their attempt to define the ethical, social, and cultural place of same-sex desire.

The connections between the anarchist sex radicals and European sexologists went beyond mere familiarity with published texts. Anarchists sought out and communicated with the scientists they admired. And a number of sexologists were interested in the work of the anarchist sex radicals. In 1913, for example, Lloyd visited England where he met Carpenter and Ellis. In a letter to a friend Lloyd told of his visit, which included a trip with Carpenter's lover,

George Merrill, "to the 'Pub.'"[9] Unfortunately, Lloyd offers little detail on the nature of his adventures with Carpenter and Merrill, but he was more forthcoming about his visit with Ellis. "I told him who I was," Lloyd later recalled, "and remarked that I did not suppose he remembered me, but I had once exchanged a letter with him, and that I came from America." Lloyd was flattered when Ellis proclaimed "Oh yes! I remember all about you," and quickly retrieved two of Lloyd's works from a bookshelf, as well as "some clippings about me." Though certainly pleased by Ellis' warmth, Lloyd claimed not to be surprised that the Englishman should give him such an enthusiastic welcome. Their friendship was "not so strange," Lloyd thought, "for we were both sexologists (I…an amateur, he…a master)."[10] In Lloyd's mind, he and his fellow anarchist sex radicals were members in good standing of the "International Institute of Society and Sexology." All were struggling to deal with the increasingly salient problems of sexuality and its place in modern life.

The anarchist sex radicals were drawn to those sexologists and psychologists whose work seemed to them to be useful correctives to contemporary prejudices and moral rules. When, for example, Goldman heard Sigmund Freud speak at Clark University in 1909, she felt that "his simplicity and earnestness and the brilliance of his mind combined to give one the feeling of being led out of a dark cellar into broad daylight. For the first time I grasped the full significance of sex repression and its effects on human thought and action."[11] The anarchist sex radicals read much of the sexological literature, as Goldman did Freud, as a roadmap out of "a dark cellar." Goldman told Magnus Hirschfeld that his works "have helped me much in shedding light on the very complex question of sex psychology, and in humanizing the attitude of people who came to hear me."[12] Lloyd praised Ellis' work in very similar terms. He thanked Ellis for "redeeming the study of sex from shame and reproach, and elevating it to its proper place as among the most fundamentally essential sciences."[13] Bolton Hall, a friend of Emma Goldman, echoed Lloyd's words, writing of Ellis that "when nobody else believed in telling the truth about sex, when it was as much to proclaim oneself an outcast to say that sex was clean and beautiful when rightly used, he dared to say and said it in such a way that he was heard and made it easy, at long last, for us to speak."[14] The anarchists read the sexologist's writings as useful analytic and political tools in their attempts to challenge society's sexual rules and regulations.

The anarchists' linkage of sexology and radical sexual politics may strike some as odd. Much has been written on the negative impact of sexology on the lives of those marked by sexual difference: its deforming and false claims of objectivity, its imposition of warped subjectivities on powerless people, and its complicity with the legal and cultural oppression of sexual difference. In her intellectual biography of Emma Goldman, for example, Bonnie Haaland is critical of Goldman for adopting the vocabulary of the sexologists, which contributed to the "pathologization of sexuality by classifying sexual behaviors as perversions, inversions, etc."[15] Haaland is not alone in seeing sexology as a tool of oppression. "The sexologists," according to Lillian Faderman and Brigitte Erikson, "emphasized…the unusual, i.e., abnormal nature" of same-sex love.[16] Jonathan Ned Katz is also strongly critical of the sexologists, particularly the medical establishment: "The treatment of Lesbians and Gays by psychiatrists and psychologists," he writes, "constitutes one of the more lethal forms of homosexual oppression."[17] How then to explain Lloyd's call for a sexological society run according to anarchist principles? It would seem impossible, to paraphrase Audre Lourde, that the anarchists could have used the master's tools to bring down the master's house.

The portrayal of sexology above, as presented by Haaland, Katz, and others is overly negative. Sexology was a complex set of texts, practices, and influences that was wielded by cultural and political players in contradictory ways. It was not a monolithic institution that spoke power to the powerless. The study of same-sex desire and behavior, writes Vernon Rosario, has been used "in order to legitimize opposing political aims: the normalization and defense of homosexuality, or its pathologization and condemnation."[18] The field of sexology—which was the purview of a broad array of scientific, humanistic, and literary scholars of both professional and amateur standing—was deeply contested. While some sexologists worked hand in hand with regulatory institutions, others worked to undermine the ideas that enabled and legitimated the policing of human desire. A number of leading sexologists, such as Karl Heinrich Ulrichs and Edward Carpenter, were themselves homosexuals whose scholarship was part of a larger political project. Readers of the works of Carpenter, Ulrichs, and their peers, as well as the hundreds of men and women who collaborated with the sexologists by submitting their life stories for study believed, in the words of Vernon Rosario, "that objective science would dispel centuries of moral and legal prejudice against homosexuals."[19] Though the critiques of sexology presented by Faderman and others have merit, they are one-sided and overly negative. Sexology was, in many instances, a powerful challenge to the crudest forms of social, cultural, and legal oppression. Anarchist sex radicals, though not uncritical of sexology, shared the vision of the practitioners of the new science of sex. Sexology was a multivalent discourse that can only be analyzed in light of how it was used, by whom, and to what end.

Anarchist sex radicals helped to circulate sexological texts in the United States. To illustrate: in the late 1880s and 1890s, Benjamin Tucker made available literature and social criticism that dealt with questions of sexuality through his publications and his New York City bookstore. This was, in part, because risqué literature sold well and helped underwrite the works on banking and land reform that Tucker so loved, but he also sought to make available knowledge about sex that he felt was in keeping with his basic political principles. In the early 1890s, Tucker created the "Sociological Index," a clipping service that featured "the most important articles…that appear in the periodical press of the world." The Index was advertised in *Liberty* and readers could order articles listed in the Index for a fee. One of the sections in the Sociological Index was "Sex." Here one could find articles entitled "Progress of National Divorce Reforms," "German Prudery," and "Girl Student Life in Zurich." Other sections of the index, such as "Ethics" and "Belles-Lettres," also carried articles on the subject of sexuality. Most were from English-language publications, but the contents of the foreign press were also made available. Tucker, a Francophile, was especially keen on making available the works of French authors.

In addition to providing the Sociological Index to its readers, *Liberty* also advertised books for sale that treated the topic of homosexuality. Interested readers now need not visit Tucker's bookstore in order to have access to what was often called "advanced" literature. Among the books Tucker made available was the first English edition of Krafft-Ebing's *Psychopathia Sexualis: With Especial Reference to Contrary Sexual Instinct.* This book, essentially a collection of annotated sexual biographies, played a critical role in the consolidation of medical discourse of sexuality and sexual identity. For many people whose erotic and emotional life focused on members of their own sex, Krafft-Ebing's book functioned as a mirror with which they could see themselves. The very logic of the work—which highlights variation and personal history—militates against the idea that sexual mores can conform to hard and fast rules. Though it has had quite a number of critics, *Psychopathia Sexualis* was, in its time, a reformist tract. According to historian Harry Oosterhuis, "some of [Krafft-Ebing's] colleagues suspected him of too much sympathy toward sexual deviants." Other critics charged him with disseminating "homosexual propaganda," and many believed that his pleas for decriminalization went way too far."[20] By making works such as this available to a broad audience, Tucker was deliberately helping to spread and reinforce new ways of thinking about sexual identity and behavior.

At times, Tucker's dissemination of sexological literature took an even more direct route. In 1889, *Liberty*, edited by Tucker, published an essay by Edward Carpenter entitled "Custom." This essay, which first appeared in the English journal, *Fortnightly Review* and was later collected in Carpenter's *Civilization: Its Causes and Cure*, is a critique of the role of "custom" in determining tastes, behaviors, and morals. In it, Carpenter employs a comparative analysis that demonstrates that social and cultural values are products of social forces and not ordained by divine rules or regulated by the laws of nature. Once we systematically examine the "customs in which we were bred," Carpenter argues, "they turn out to be only the practices of a small narrow class or caste; or they prove to be confined to a very limited locality, and must be left behind when we set out on our travels; or they belong to the tenets of a feeble religious sect; or they are just the products of one age in history and no other."[21] The seemingly timeless, ancient, and sanctified rules of culture are, Carpenter argues, historical constructs reflecting particular class, regional, or religious interests. They should not, therefore, carry the binding imperatives that we ascribe to them. In other words, the ideas and values of the world in which Carpenter lived were subject to revision.

Though "Custom" does not explicitly treat homosexuality, it foreshadows the arguments that Carpenter would make in his essays on "homogenic love" and "sexual inversion." "Custom" argues that beliefs about what is right and wrong in matters of sex are subject to geographical, temporal, and cultural variation. When we examine "the subject or morals," Carpenter notes, we find that they "also are customs—divergent to the last degree among different races, at different times, or in different localities; customs for which it is often difficult to find any ground in reason or the 'fitness of things.'" Though moral codes are arbitrary they are nonetheless vigilantly policed. "The severest penalties," Carpenter observes, "the most stringent public opinion, biting deep down into the individual conscience, enforce the various codes of various times and places; yet they all contradict each other." The enlightened person, Carpenter goes on to say, should seek to shrug off the dead weight of history. In order to be able to appreciate the fullness of life we must open ourselves to new habits, actions, and tastes. The liberated woman or man of the future will, "eat grain one day and beef then another...go with clothes or without clothes...inhabit a hut or a palace indifferently." And this embrace of difference will extend to sex. Carpenter hoped that in the future people "will use the various forms of sex-relationship without prejudice....And the inhabitants of one city or country will not be all alike."[22] Tucker found Carpenter's praise of diversity and tolerance to be an excellent addition to the valuable work on sexuality and psychology that he made available to his readers.

Though Tucker was familiar with the work of Carpenter, Krafft-Ebing, and Ellis, he himself did not employ sexological vocabulary. Nowhere in his writing on sex does he identify someone as a homosexual, invert, intermediate type, homogenic lover, or for that matter, a heterosexual. In his defense of Wilde, for example, Tucker never identifies him as a homosexual, nor does he speak of sexual identity or community. In great part this is due to Tucker's insistence on the primacy of the individual. In his political discourse, Tucker always spoke of the right of individuals to meet their needs and desires in free association with other individuals. He tended to use gender neutral, non-specific language when doing so. Tucker's sexual politics were couched in the language of choice, rights, and limits, a more abstract line of reasoning that was not rooted in identity. As long as a person was willing to bear the full weight of his or her actions, Tucker would defend their right to act as they wished. He defended those who engaged in "vice," for example, because people had a right to act according to their own dictates so long as they did not harm others. Tucker's political perspectives were informed by his wide reading in psychological and sociological discourse, but he did not adopt the language and rhetoric of sexologists when framing his sexual politics.

Among the anarchist sex radicals, Goldman was the most voracious consumer and distributor of sexology. She was an enthusiastic participant in debates over sex; read sexological literature; attended lectures by psychologists, sociologists, and other professionals; and befriended the spokespeople of the new science. This is not to say that Goldman always agreed with what she heard and read. She could be a sharp critic, and once wrote to Ben Reitman that Dr. Stanley Hall's 1912 lecture on "Moral Prophylaxis" was "awful." Hall was the leading American psychologist of the day, best known for his book *Adolescence: Its Psychology and Relations to Physiology, Anthropology, Sex, Crime, Religion and Education.* While she appreciated that Hall "emphasized the importance of sex," giving it "almost as much credence to it as I," she was troubled that the lecture was introduced by a minister, and that Hall argued, "We need sex instruction to preserve Christianity, morality, and religion."[23] This linking of religion, sexual morals and regulation was anathema to Goldman. She respected the work that Hall had done in the field of psychology, but she "felt sorry for the American people who were accepting such infantile stuff as authoritative information."[24] Unfortunately for Americans, Hall's presentation was representative of current sexual thinking among the country's professionals. Like her own colleagues, Goldman was rather disappointed in American sexologists, and rarely cited them, other than to refute their work.

Emma Goldman had a decided preference for European sexologists, particularly Carpenter, Ellis, and Magnus Hirschfeld, all of whom she viewed as social critics and dissidents. Goldman especially agreed with their liberal views on homosexuality. She wrote to Ellis that she acquired his book, *Sexual Inversion*, in 1899 shortly after its publication, and considered it one of her "greatest treasures." *Sexual Inversion* (actually coauthored by John Addington Symonds, whose name was removed after his death because his estate objected to his being associated with the work), was one of the first English-language publications to address same-sex relations. Ellis was notably more favorable towards the subjects of his study than many of his contemporaries, in the words of Vern Bullough, he "struggled to avoid any language of pathology" and "attempted to emphasize the achievement of homosexuals."[25] Goldman responded favorably to Ellis' approach. "I followed your work," she told him, "read nearly all I could get hold of and introduced them to the mass of people I was able to reach through my lecture work."[26] Goldman identified Ellis and his ideological kin as part of a larger movement for social justice, one with which she identified and helped foster. By helping to make *Sexual Inversion* better known Goldman felt that she was aiding in the amelioration of the social and ethical status of the men and women Ellis wrote about. Goldman may have been especially drawn to Ellis' work because his study on homosexuality was—indirectly—linked with anarchism.

When it first appeared in England, Ellis' *Sexual Inversion* was published by the same press as the one used by the Legitimation League, an anarchist sex reform group that advocated free love unions and ending the social ostracism of illegitimate children and their mothers. The Legitimation League operated a bookstore and published a journal titled, *The Adult*. The police, convinced that the Legitimation League was intent of destroying English morals, monitored the group's activities and the appearance of Ellis' work offered the police an opportunity to attack them. In 1898, an undercover police agent purchased a copy of *Sexual Inversion* from George Bedborough, the editor of *The Adult* who was working at the Legitimation League's bookstore. In Ellis' words, the police hoped to "crush the Legitimation League and *The Adult* by identifying them with my *Sexual Inversion*, obviously, from their point of view, an 'obscene' book."[27] Ellis learned of Bedborough's arrest on the charge of selling *Sexual Inversion*—which was described by the police as "a certain lewd, wicked, bawdy, and scandalous libel"—from a telegram sent by American anarchist, Lillian Harman, who had been elected president of the Legitimation League in 1897. Though the League was severely affected by the police actions, Ellis was undeterred and continued to conduct and publish his research. This complex intertwining of Ellis and the English anarchists may well have inclined Goldman to identify his views and politics with her own.[28]

Goldman saw the work of those she identified as progressive sexologists as blending seamlessly with the larger goals of anarchism. Like them, she believed that the scientific study of human nature was an indispensable step in the march towards freedom. Goldman went so far as to call Carpenter and Ellis anarchists. This was not a novel interpretation of Carpenter, whose name had been associated with anarchism by Lloyd and Tucker previously. Carpenter cultivated his kinship with the anarchists, assisting Peter Kropotkin with the research for his book, *Fields, Factories and Workshops* and contributing a very flattering greeting to a special issue of *Mother Earth*, celebrating the life and work of Kropotkin. Ellis, despite his tangled history with the Legitimation League, was less quick to ally himself with the anarchists. When told of Goldman's opinion of him, Ellis demurred. But his refusal of being labeled anarchist did not dissuade Goldman. "I am amused," she wrote her friend Joseph Ishill, "at Ellis's statement that he is not an Anarchist because he does not belong to an organization." Goldman praised Ellis' "philosophical outlook" which she believed was "infinitely bigger and more important than that of many people who go under the name of Anarchists."[29] Ellis was an anarchist in spirit, if not in name.

Through her interest in the work of sexologists, Goldman was exposed to contemporary medical and psychological ideas on homosexuality. In 1895, Goldman was in Vienna to pursue training as a nurse with a special emphasis on obstetrics and gynecology, when she heard a lecture on homosexuality. This lecture, delivered by "Professor Bruhl," made a significant impact on her, as it was apparently the first time that she had heard same-sex love being treated in a scientific manner. Initially, though, Goldman found the doctor's talk "mystifying." In his presentation, Bruhl "talked of 'Urnings,' 'Lesbians,' and other strange topics." This was Goldman's introduction to the emerging sexological terminology on homosexuality, and in the decades that followed, she would become quite familiar with these new terms. At the time, though, they were novel. The audience members, many of whom signified their sexual identity by their gender inversion, also fascinated Goldman. The audience members, Goldman recalled "were strange," consisting of "feminine-looking men with coquettish manners and women distinctly masculine, with deep voices." Bruhl's lecture introduced Goldman to the emergent and increasingly powerful medical and psychological language of sexual difference. By observing her fellow audience members, Goldman also learned about the semiotics of sexual identification that "urnings" and "lesbians" crafted for themselves.[30]

Sexological literature had a great impact on how Goldman conceptualized the politics of homosexuality. She absorbed the sexologist's worldview, speaking of homosexuals as a distinct category of humanity: an identity that had psychological, social, and cultural manifestations. She employed the language of sexology—"homosexuals," "inverts," "intermediate types," and "homo-sexualists"—in her writing and lectures. The use of inconsistent terms reflects the fact that there was no single dominant framework or set of ideas that Goldman embraced. When it came to the literature on sex, Goldman was a promiscuous reader. However, one cannot discount the importance of the larger political and social analysis that Goldman brought to any social question. The discourses that shaped Goldman's sense of sexuality reflected both the specialized medical and psychological discourse of sexology and the broader currents of thought and politics within which Goldman operated. Goldman was drawn to those sexologists whose work best fit in with her basic political ideals. She was accustomed to thinking of oppressed groups: the working-class, women, ethnic minorities. Hutchins Hapgood said of Goldman that she "always associated anybody in any way frowned upon by middle-class society, no matter whether they should be frowned upon or not, with the general victims of an unjust order."[31] Goldman, who was never so alive as when defending the downtrodden, was predisposed to see homosexuals as an oppressed social group; they were another set of "outcasts" that needed a champion.[32]

Like Tucker, Goldman and her associates helped circulate the sexological literature they admired in the United States. Goldman's own writings and lectures on love and sexuality make frequent references to the work of Edward Carpenter, Havelock Ellis, and Magnus Hirschfeld, helping to introduce this work to her audiences. Carpenter, Ellis, and other sexologists' books were sold on Goldman's lecture tours and were offered as premiums to those who subscribed to *Mother Earth*. In 1912, for example, subscribers who sent in $5.00 would receive "Berkman's 'Prison Memoirs,' Proudhon's 'What is Property,' Frank Harris' 'The Bomb,' Kropotkin's 'Russian Literature,' and Edward Carpenter's 'Love's Coming of Age.'"[33] Both Carpenter's book and Berkman's memoirs include substantial material on same-sex eroticism. Those who subscribed to *Mother Earth* would therefore be provided with a relatively rich library of literature treating homosexuality. In addition, many issues of *Mother Earth* carried advertisements that offered "important books on sex" and "anarchist and sex literature" for sale. Readers of the November 1915 issue of *Mother Earth* could order August Forel's book *The Sexual Question: A Scientific, Psychological, Hygienic and Sociological Study of the Sex Question*, a work that, according to the ad copy, addressed "Homosexuality...and other important phases of sex."[34] Goldman's journal and her lecture tours were important channels for the dissemination of sexological literature.

In addition to advertising the work of sexologists, Mother Earth published articles by sexologists and non-anarchist sex radicals. In 1907, the journal carried an article by Dr. Helene Stöcker entitled "The Newer Ethics." Stöcker was a German feminist who supported divorce law reform, the free circulation of information about contraception, and access to legal abortion, and she was also a member of Magnus Hirschfeld's Scientific-Humanitarian Committee, the German gay rights group. "The Newer Ethics" is an examination of the "sex question" in light of the work of the philosopher Friedrich Nietzsche. While Stöcker does not directly address the question of homosexuality in her essay, she argues—in a manner remarkably similar to Carpenter—that in matters of love people should "not bow slavishly to custom." According to Stöcker, Nietzsche's work "teaches the beauty and purity of love, which for hundreds of years has been branded as vicious by the unhealthy imagination of the church." People, Stöcker argued, should pursue their passions free of guilt. The new ethics, she wrote, "strikes at the root of the old and confused notions, which identify 'morality' with the fear of conventional standards, [and] 'virtue' with 'abstaining from sexual intercourse.'"[35] Though she did not identify as an anarchist herself, the views she expressed in "The Newer Ethics" were in concert with those of the anarchist sex radicals.

Several of Goldman's colleagues shared her interest in sexology, homosexuality, and the politics of sexuality. Ben Reitman, Goldman's lover during the years she was most actively interested in the politics of homosexuality, is especially important in this regard. According to Candace Falk, "Ben had always been fascinated with and sympathetic to homosexuality."[36] He was exposed to the phenomenon at a young age. When he was twelve, Reitman began to ride the railways, mixing with the men and boys who traveled from city to city, seeking employment. This largely male world was characterized by a rough sexual culture in which homosexual behavior was not uncommon.[37] This early experience of the sexual subculture of casual laborers, tramps, and hobos seemed to have marked Reitman; he retained a lifelong interest in the life he had as a youth. In the late 1930s, for example, Reitman published a book, *Sister of the Road: The Autobiography of Box-Car Bertha as Told to Ben Reitman*, which listed "well-marked homosexualists" as one of the categories of women who took to the road.[38] When Reitman became a physician, he continued to move in social worlds where homosexual behavior was common. He lived his life at the margins of respectable society. Reitman's biographer writes that "underworld types and down-and-outs gravitated to Ben's office, as did prostitutes, pimps, dope addicts, and sexual perverts."[39] Given their mutual interest in homosexuality and sexology, it is likely that Reitman shared his personal observations and knowledge with Goldman.

Goldman's most notable interventions in the politics of homosexuality were her lectures. Lectures were one of the key tools used by both anarchists and sexologists in their attempts to spread their ideas. Goldman was a powerful speaker whose stage presence, according to Christine Stansell, was "by all accounts mesmerizing."[40] Though portrayed as a rabble-rouser in the popular press, much of Goldman's power as a speaker resulted from her willingness to treat controversial subjects—like sex—dispassionately. This is not to say that she was not an entertaining speaker. When Goldman lectured on the subject of "Sex" at Harry Kemp's college in Kansas the "hall was jammed to the doors by a curiosity-moved crowd." Those who came for a show were no doubt disappointed, as she did not treat the subject of her talk in a sensational fashion. According to Kemp, Goldman "began by assuming that she was not talking to idiots and cretins, but to men and women of mature minds," but when one of the professors jumped to his feet to denounce Goldman's too frank manner of speech, she responded by poking fun at the outraged moral guardian. In a fit of temper the professor shouted at the top of his lungs: "Shame on you, woman! Have you no shame?" The professor's outraged outburst set off the gathered students who Kemp writes, "howled with indescribable joy." Goldman shared in their mirth and "laughed till the tears streamed down her face." According to Kemp, for "the four days she remained [on campus] her lectures were crowded."[41]

Goldman delivered most of her lectures on homosexuality in 1915 and 1916. There is no clear reason why these years should be the high water mark for her interest in the politics of homosexuality, but perhaps the heightened radicalism of the First World War-years created a context in which she felt she could speak out on controversial topics. Well before America entered the war in 1917, the political climate of the United States was inflamed by the conflagration consuming Europe. The nation was torn by debates over intervention, pacifism, and the politics of empire. In this hot house atmosphere Goldman addressed a wide variety of topics including homosexuality. One could draw an analogy with the late 1960s and early 1970s when the politics of the Vietnam War, the rise of the New Left, the turn towards Black Power and radical variants of Feminism, movements that were related in complex ways, created a cultural and political context in which gays and lesbians were radicalized.[42]

This was the height of her lecturing on same-sex love, but she certainly addressed the topic in lectures prior to 1915. In 1901, for example, the journal *Free Society* published a report of a lecture she gave in Chicago that touched on the moral and ethical place of same-sex love. In her talk, Goldman "contended that any act entered into by two individuals voluntarily was not vice. What is usually hastily condemned as vice by thoughtless individuals, such as homosexuality, masturbation, etc., should be considered from a scientific standpoint, and not in a moralizing way."[43] Goldman's argument in 1901—that consensual relations and behaviors that cause no harm to others should in no way be regulated—was the basic message of all her presentations on the subject of homosexuality. She thought of this analysis—informed as it was by her readings in sexology—as a scientific, rather than moralistic, viewpoint. By the second decade of the twentieth century, however, Goldman's lectures offered more than a simple defense of homosexuality. She began to speak as an authority on the subject; Goldman's lectures were exercises in sexological education. Her sociological and psychological perspectives on homosexuality were reflected in the content of her talks, and it was from this perspective that Goldman addressed the topic of homosexuality in her lectures in the years immediately before the war.

Like the sexologists she admired, Goldman derived much of her information on same-sex affection from her own observation and social analysis. She acknowledged that she learned much of what she knew about homosexuality from her friends and acquaintances. In 1915, she wrote a friend encouraging her to attend her lecture on the "Intermediate Sex...because I am speaking about it from entirely a different angle than Ellis, Forel, Carpenter and others, and that mainly because of the material I have gathered during the last half dozen years through my personal contact with the intermediate, which has lead me to gather the most interesting material."[44] Goldman's personal relations with "intermediate types"—a term Carpenter used to describe homosexuals— enriched her understanding of sexuality and may well have provided her with the impetus to expand upon a theme which previously had been one of several topics that she treated in her lectures.

Goldman's lectures were often the means by which she met the "intermediate types" she befriended. In 1914, Goldman met Margaret Anderson who had come to hear her speak. Sexual radicalism was a key element of Goldman's appeal to Anderson. Goldman, according to Anderson, "whose name was enough in those days to produce a shudder" was "considered a monster, an exponent of free love and bombs."[45] For Anderson, who had set herself on the path of bohemian rebellion, there was an aura of danger around Goldman that was part of her fascination. Anderson introduced Goldman to her lover, Harriet Dean, with whom she published *The Little Review*, a journal of art and culture. Goldman described the two as a classic butch-femme couple, though she did not use the term. According to Goldman, Dean "was athletic, masculine-looking, reserved, and self-conscious. Margaret, on the contrary, was feminine in the extreme, constantly bubbling over with enthusiasm."[46]

Dean and Anderson were drawn into Goldman's political efforts and the controversy that they produced. The two women helped arrange Goldman's lectures in Chicago, selling tickets for the lecture out of the offices of *The Little Review*. Dean's family, who lived in the city, was mortified. They offered to pay for the printing cost associated with Goldman's lectures if she would agree to refrain from speaking on free love. Anarchism, it would seem, was an acceptable topic of conversation, but free love was out of bounds. The Dean family seemed not to have appreciated the fact that free love and anarchism were, for many, the same thing. Surprisingly, it seems that the family did not object to Goldman's intention to lecture on the subject of the "Intermediate Sex." It is possible that they were unaware of the lecture or could not understand what the subject of the talk was from the title of the speech. Or perhaps they did not perceive Dean and Anderson's relationship to be sexual in nature, or perhaps saw it as a variant of the Boston Marriage that was quite common among professional women of the era. It is also possible, though unlikely given the horror with which they reacted to the idea of the family name being associated with free love, that they understood that Dean and Anderson were lovers, but were indifferent. Whatever the case, Goldman refused to change her lecture topics, and Dean and Anderson stood by her.

Anderson and Dean gravitated towards anarchism because it promised psychological, social, and sexual freedom. "Anarchism," exclaimed Anderson, "was the ideal expression for my ideas of freedom and justice." In short order, the pages of *The Little Review* were filled with praise of anarchism, and Goldman was invited to contribute. She returned the favor, advising the readers of *Mother Earth*, "to subscribe to Margaret C. Anderson's magazine." Goldman viewed Dean and Anderson as fellow radicals who were melding art and activism in an attempt to create new social relations. She praised *The Little Review* as a "magazine devoted to art, music, poetry, literature, and the drama," one which approached these subjects "not from the point of view of *l'art pour l'art,* but for the sake of sounding the keynote of rebellion in creative endeavor."[47] Anderson and Dean's unconventional sex life was part of their rebellion. "Strongly individualized," Goldman observed, "they had broken the shackles of their middle-class homes to find release from family bondage and bourgeois tradition."[48]

It is impossible to know how many of Goldman's admirers were gay men or lesbians, but Dean and Anderson were hardly the only homosexuals who were drawn to her. Emma Goldman also received support from a New Jersey man named Alden Freeman, a wealthy man who lived in East Orange, New Jersey. In 1909, he shocked his neighbors by offering his estate to Goldman when other lecture venues were closed to her. Goldman delivered her talk to a large and excited audience. For Freeman this was an act with deep personal resonance. According to Will Durant, at the time a friend of both Freeman and Goldman, "Freeman...signalized his freedom from tradition by having Emma Goldman lecture on the modern drama in the barn of his home." According to Durant, the reason for Freeman's surprising hospitality was that he was a "homosexual, ill at ease in the heterosexual society that gathered about him." As a homosexual, Freeman felt alienated so he "sympathized with...rebels and contributed to their projects."[49] There was an intimate relationship, Durant suggests, between Freeman's feelings of sexual difference and his interest and support of anarchism. Following Goldman's "barn" lecture Freeman provided financial support to Goldman and kept in touch with her even after her exile from the United States.

Others seemed to have felt as Freeman did. There is a fascinating story of the influence that Goldman's lectures had Alberta Lucille Hart. Though born a woman in 1892, Hart chose to live life as a man. Anarchism played a role in this dramatic process of personal transformation. Hart struggled with his identity and his relationships. In 1916, "[Hart] heard many lectures by Emma Goldman and became much interested in anarchism."[50] The lectures and subsequent investigations into anarchism gave added impetus for Hart's decision to live his life as he saw fit. He eventually moved to a new city where he married a woman and pursued a career as a physician. This was the kind of act of individualism that Goldman's ideas spoke to. Her unyielding defense of the right of the individual appealed to Hart at a critical point in his life. Because of her willingness to speak on behalf of homosexuals and others considered deviant, Goldman seemed to have held a special appeal to those men and women whose sexual desires or gender identity led them to feel "ill at ease" in the society they lived in.

The most interesting relationship between Goldman and one of her admirers is the case of Almeda Sperry. The two met after Goldman spoke on the politics of prostitution. A working-class woman who lived in the industrial town of New Kensington, Pennsylvania, Sperry had both male and female lovers, her politics as unconventional as her sex life. Inspired by Goldman, Sperry flung herself into the anarchist movement. For a number of years she worked tirelessly, helping Goldman in her efforts to broadcast anarchist ideas. In 1912, for example, she worked to secure a lecture hall for Goldman in New Kensington and wrote to her friend, "You've got to come, Emmy, for the people need you awfully."[51] Sperry enthusiastically distributed anarchist literature: "I am going to get a list of all the radical people in this valley," Sperry wrote Goldman, "and I mean to visit them all! I want to make my place the headquarters for Anarchist literature in the Allegheny Valley and I will."[52]

As her interest in anarchism grew, so too did Sperry's feelings for Goldman. This proved to be a point of conflict between the two women—Sperry wanted to move the relationship deeper while Goldman resisted. Sperry was as enthusiastic in her pursuit of Goldman as she was in distributing anarchist literature. In one particularly telling letter Sperry wrote that Goldman had appeared to her in a dream. The imagery of the dream is strongly erotic:

> You were a rose, a great yellow rose with a pink center—but the petals were folded one upon the other so tightly. I prayed to them to yield to me and held the rose close to my lips so that my warm breath might persuade them to open. Slowly, slowly they opened, revealing great beauty—but the pink virginal center of the flower would not unfold until the tears gushed from my eyes when it opened suddenly revealing in its center a crystal drop-dew. I sucked the dew and bit out the heart of the flower. The petals dropped to the ground one by one. I crushed them with my heel and their odor wafted after me as I walked away.

The violent eroticism of Sperry's dream—a mixture of desire and hostility—is characteristic of her exchanges with Goldman. Sperry seems to have been angry that Goldman did not share her passionate desire. This is not to say that Goldman was entirely cold to Sperry—she did hug and kiss her, but the meaning of her actions is unclear. While there is some indication that, in the words of Blanche Wiesen Cook, Goldman may have "experimented" with Sperry, most likely Goldman's understanding of the meaning of this physical contact was different from Sperry's.[53] As Jonathan Ned Katz writes, "the letters indicate that Goldman returned Sperry's affection, though with less passion and desperate need than Sperry felt."[54] The tone of the latter's letters—their insistent, baroque quality—bespeaks a good deal of erotic frustration. Sperry wanted to deepen her physical contact with Goldman but Goldman resisted. The tortured imagery of Sperry's dream reveals how she experienced Goldman's refusal of her advances.

In spite of her feelings of ambivalence toward her, Sperry fascinated Goldman. Goldman introduced her to her friends, including Hutchins Hapgood and Ben Reitman (who certainly interpreted Goldman's interest in Sperry as being sexual in nature). Reitman, whose sexual adventurism was infamous, proposed to Sperry that she join him and Hapgood in a threesome. Sperry, not a little bit disgusted by Reitman's proposal, refused. Alice Wexler argues that Reitman was motivated, at least in part, by his attraction to Hapgood, a strikingly hand-some man.[55] Wexler argues, that he was as interested in getting into bed with Hapgood as he was with Sperry. Goldman denied having a sexual attraction to Sperry, but she was clearly enthusiastic about her new friend, describing her to colleague Nunia Seldes as "the most interesting of American women I have met." Goldman even considered publishing Sperry's letters, which she found "wonderfully interesting" and "a great human document."[56] Sperry was well aware of the sociological nature of Goldman's interest in her. In a letter, she wrote of Goldman—using a third-person construction that matched form to content—"Perhaps she is just studying me—all my personalities for the good of her cause—studying this peculiar product of our civilization."[57] Sperry was quite perceptive. Goldman was studying her; Sperry was one of those "in-termediate types" who supplied Goldman with "interesting material" for her lectures.[58]

Goldman delivered her lectures on the topic of same-sex eroticism to a broad audience. Unlike most presentations by physicians and other profession-als, Goldman's talks were open to the public and held in accessible venues. Occasionally, there were other public lectures on homosexuality, such as those given by Edith Ellis, the wife of Havelock Ellis, who visited Chicago in 1915, but they were rare. Lecturers like Ellis usually spoke only in major cities, and their tours were limited in scope and reach. Goldman's lectures were advertised in *Mother Earth* and the non-anarchist press, and she spoke in large and small cities across the nation, addressing audiences in New York; Chicago; St. Louis, Washington, D.C.; Portland; Denver; Lincoln, Nebraska; Butte, Montana; San Francisco; San Diego; and others. She spoke in a wide variety of venues: from local labor halls to Carnegie Hall. Goldman estimated that 50,000 to 75,000 people a year heard her speak. Though not every listener came to her presen-tations on homosexuality, the numbers of people who heard Goldman speak on the topic of same-sex love were significantly higher than any other of her contemporaries.[59]

Goldman's lectures on homosexuality drew large and responsive crowds. On the night of a presentation in Chicago in 1915, Goldman feared the worst as the evening "was visited by a perfect cloudburst," an event known to ruin many a public gathering. Nonetheless, she has happy to report that "a large and representative audience braved the storm" to hear her speak.[60] In that same year, "Anna W." reported in *Mother Earth* on one of the Goldman's lectures on "homo-sexuality" that she gave in Washington, D.C. Goldman, writes Anna W., is a "sympathizer and true friend of the socially outcast," who "in the face of strenuous general opposition to the discussion of a subject long enshrouded in mystery and persistently tabooed by all other public speakers…delivered a most illuminating lecture on homo-sexuality." According to Anna W. a "dignified, tense, and eager audience crowded the hall to its fullest capacity." Consumed by curiosity audience members actively sought information from Goldman. "The frankness and celerity with which they questioned and discussed were evidences of the genuine and deep interest her treatment of the subject had aroused."[61] Goldman was clearly responding to a thirst for public discourse on the topic.

Goldman was more forceful than other speakers in her exploration of the social, ethical, and cultural place of same-sex desire. Margaret Anderson, for example, thought Edith Ellis paled as a speaker in comparison to Goldman. Ellis' speech did not go "quite the whole distance" and, comparing Ellis to Goldman, Anderson argued that Ellis' stage presence did not "loom as large as some of her more 'destructive' contemporaries." The reference to Goldman's "destructive" power is a playful jab at her unmerited reputation as a bomber, and her well-merited reputation as an "explosive" speaker. Ellis, on the other hand, failed to grasp the nettle. Though she cited Carpenter's work, Ellis did not discuss "Carpenter's social efforts in behalf of the homosexualist." Instead of engaging in a direct political confrontation, Ellis merely pointed to the fact that not all homosexuals were to be found in insane asylums; some occupied thrones or were famous artists. But Anderson was unimpressed, "It is not enough," she insisted, "to repeat that Shakespeare and Michael Angelo and Alexander the Great and Rosa Bonheur and Sappho were intermediaries." Ellis, unlike Goldman did not ask the key question: "how is the science of the future to meet this issues?" According to Anderson, Ellis underestimated her audience and failed to "talk plainly." Having heard Goldman speak on the subject, Anderson lamented that Ellis could not have emulated her more "destructive" contemporary. "I can't help comparing [Ellis]," Anderson wrote, "with another woman whose lecture on such a subject would be big, brave, beautiful…Emma Goldman could never fail in this way."[62] Goldman's political passions and her engagement with the "science of the future" led her to be more direct and confrontational in her discussion of matters others treated with kid gloves.

It is difficult to know what effect Goldman's words had on her audience members. How many came because they were searching for answers about their own feelings? Did they find those answers? The examples of Anderson, Sperry, Hart, and Freeman would seem to indicate that they did find Goldman's talks useful. But what of those who perhaps had not given homosexuality much thought prior to hearing Goldman speak? Did they attend the lectures for a lark? Were some of her audience members engaging in a form of sexual slumming? And what was the result of their having heard the lectures? Anna W. was convinced that the lectures were transformative. She wrote, "I do not hesitate to declare that every person who came to the lecture possessing contempt and disgust for homo-sexualists and who upheld the attitude of the authorities that those given to this particular form of sex expression should be hounded down and persecuted, went away with a broad and sympathetic understanding of the question and a conviction that in matters of personal life, freedom should reign."[63] It is easy to dismiss Anna W.'s enthusiasm as that of a partisan, but it is quite possible that for many, Goldman's lectures were important influences in shaping their opinions on matters of morals and social tolerance. For some, Goldman's lectures may well have been the first time that they heard a matter of visceral importance to their lives aired without reference to Sodom and Gomorrah, the insane asylum, or the legal code.

As in the case of Almeda Sperry and Margaret Anderson, audience members often sought out Goldman following her lectures. And she was receptive. In her biography, Goldman wrote of the "men and women who used to come to see me after my lectures on homosexuality…who confided in me their anguish and their isolation." Striking a somewhat dramatic and protective tone, Goldman noted that they "were often of finer grain than those who had cast them out." Her audience members seem to have taken an active role in seeking out information about themselves; this no doubt explained their presence at Goldman's lecture. "Most of them," according to Goldman, "had reached an adequate understanding of their differentiation only after years of struggle to stifle what they had considered a disease and a shameful affliction." Goldman felt that anarchism had a special message to those who spoke with her about their deep psychological struggles. "Anarchism," Goldman believed, "was not a mere theory for a distant future; it was a living influence to free us from inhibitions, internal no less than external."[64]

Goldman's message of tolerance and understanding was a perfect foil to the bitter denunciations of moralists. In her autobiography, Goldman recorded the impact her lecture had on one of her listeners: According to Goldman, the young woman who spoke with her at the end of the evening's discourse "was only one of the many who sought me out." The young woman shared with Goldman the story of her struggles:

> She confessed to me that in the twenty-five years of her life she had never known a day when the nearness of a man, her own father and brothers even, did not make her ill. The more she had tried to respond to sexual approach, the more repugnant men became to her. She had hated herself, she said, because she could not love her father and her brothers as she loved her mother. She suffered excruciating remorse but her revulsion only increased. At the point

of eighteen she had accepted an offer of marriage in the hope that a long engagement might help her grow accustomed to a man and cure her of her "disease." It turned out to be a ghastly failure that nearly drove her insane. She could not face the marriage and she dared not confide in her fiancé or friends. She had never met anyone, she told me, who suffered from a similar affliction, nor had she ever read books dealing with the subject. My lecture had set her free; I had given her back her self-respect.[65]

The young woman's inchoate understanding of homosexuality is striking. As a member of a respectable, middle-class family, which no doubt sheltered their children, Goldman's listener apparently was not familiar with women and men who lived queer lives. Nor had she come across sexological literature, news accounts, or fiction that described her "disease." The young woman had never met someone who openly deviated from the gender and sexual norms of her family's social milieu, but clearly medicine and psychological health—or "disease," in this case—was the framework through which she understood herself. How this young woman came to this understanding is unclear since, she told Goldman "she had never read books dealing with the subject." She may never have directly confronted texts that framed sexual desire as a question of "health" or "disease," but she adopted the perspective nonetheless. Goldman's use of sexological discourse may have been liberating to the young woman, as it offered an alternative, though still familiar way, of envisioning her desire free of negative bias.

Goldman did not encounter much official resistance to her presentations on homosexuality. There exists only one known attempt to censor her that was, at least in part, a result of the fact that she was speaking out on same-sex love. According to Goldman, her 1915 tour "met with no police interference until we reached Portland, Oregon, although the subjects I treated were anything but tame: anti-war topics, the fight for Caplan and Schmidt, freedom in love, birth-control, and the problem most tabooed in polite society, homosexuality."[66] The Portland police arrested Goldman as she was about to deliver a lecture on birth control, on the grounds that distributing information about contraceptives was illegal. Ben Reitman, who organized the tour, was also arrested. The judge who heard the case released the prisoners—since the lecture had been halted, no information had been distributed. This tactical error on the part of Portland's moral arbiters allowed the judiciary to extricate all involved from what might have proved to be a most sensitive public proceeding.

The evening prior to her arrest Goldman had delivered a talk on homosexuality, and that she was likely to deliver her talk again was, in part, responsible for her troubles. Though she was arrested before speaking on birth control, that fact that she had previously spoken on homosexuality was an important reason for her being censored. Goldman's arrest was precipitated by the actions of Josephine DeVore Johnson, the daughter of a local minister and the widow of a judge. Johnson wrote a letter to Portland's mayor in which she specifically mentions Goldman's lecture, "The Intermediate Sex (A Study in Homosexuality)," as part of the offense against public morality that threatened their fair city. Goldman's "advocacy," wrote Johnson, "is a new and startling note, and one that cannot be struck in this city without questions being asked as to how it is permitted." Johnson was particularly upset because admission to Goldman's lecture was open to the public. Portland's Collegiate Socialist Club was even promoting the lecture series and planned on providing "intellectual people" with complimentary tickets. Johnson was worried as "there are some young boys who attend Miss Goldman's lectures" and more might be expected to come and see her speak in the future. Johnson's portrayal of the lecture suggests that the audience was a dangerous mixture of intellectuals, anarchists, youth, and sexual deviants. Goldman's "unspeakable suggestions," pleaded Johnson, must not be allowed to sully the innocence of Portland's youth.[67] Her insistence that the mayor act to protect Portland is an illustration of the complex ways in which homosexuality was both silenced and made the subject of debate and discussion—in letters, official actions, and other sites—at the turn of the century.

It is not true, as Johnson claimed, that Goldman was striking "a new and startling note" to Portland's public life. Goldman's arrest was the final echo of one of the turn of the century's most notorious local sex scandals. The issue of homosexuality erupted into public light in Portland three years before Goldman came to town, when, in November 1912, the police raided the Portland YMCA and arrested more than twenty men on charges of sexual indecency. These men implicated others—eventually fifty men in all. A panic spread through the city as some men fled arrest and others were horrified to learn that a supposed bastion of good morals was a den of perversity. According to John Gustav-Wrathall, "this scandal not only implicated members of the YMCA's traditional constituency—middle-class, male Protestants of 'high moral standards'—but it vividly brought to public attention the existence of a lively cruising scene on YMCA premises, and the existence of a gay subculture not only in Portland but in virtually every major city in America."[68] Peter Boag writes that the 1912 Portland YMCA scandal was "the greatest of the era's and region's same-sex vice scandals."[69] The YMCA participated in the purge of its members by cooperating with the police, expelling suspect members, and holding a community meeting to address the public's concerns. While YMCA officials sought to contain the scandal, the *Portland News* "sarcastically characterized men involved in the scandal as 'nice, charitable, boy-loving men.'"[70] This was the context in which Johnson, Portland's mayor, and Goldman battled for the city's soul. Without the YMCA scandal, Portland's authorities may well have never acted to silence Goldman. The barely healed wounds of the 1912 scandal were inflamed by Goldman's open treatment of a subject that Johnson and the city's mayor wanted to return to obscurity.

Mother Earth wasted little time in publishing "A Portrait of Portland," a scathing exposé of Goldman's arrest. The essay's author, George Edwards, lampoons the false modesty of the town's moral custodians when it comes to the question of homosexuality. He also reminds his reader that the outrage Portland's leaders displayed was an act, a display of false modesty. "No thinking person," Edwards wrote, "minded very much the facts which came to light a year or two ago regarding the prevalence of homosexuality in that city. They knew that every city includes homosexuals in proportion to its size, and that their natural congregating places are the Y.M.C.A.'s." The author assumes that *Mother Earth's* readers are among those "thinking people" who are familiar with the sexual geography of America's cities. And like Goldman, Edwards assumes that there exists a distinct population—proportionate in size to the general population—that can be identified as homosexual. In other words, homosexuals live in cities and occupy an identifiable social space. This was, of course, the great "discovery" of the sexologists, a finding trumpeted in medical journals and psychological literature of the period. The readers of *Mother Earth* and those who attended lectures by Goldman and other anarchist sex radicals were kept abreast of these developments in the social and sexual sciences. The language and analysis employed by Edwards is indicative of the extent to which the terms and concepts of sexological discourse had permeated the anarchist movement.

In his attack on the Portland authorities, Edwards makes use of a gendered language of "prudery" and "modernity," coding the latter as male and the former as female. He contrasts Goldman's modern, sexological perspective to those of Portland's authorities who "like the old time 'ladies' were properly shocked when anybody mentioned their legs." Rather than face the facts, Portland's "old time 'ladies'…pretended that [they had] no such members." Those who came to Goldman's lecture expecting to hear of salacious goings-on at the local YMCA were disappointed. "The lecture," Edwards reported, "proved perfectly respectable, although requiring a little closer concentration to facts and logic than Madame Portland was used to bestowing on any discourse."[71] Goldman spoke in the measured voice of the expert on human sexual behavior, not at the hot pitch of the pornographer. Though anarchists were often portrayed as bomb-throwing lunatics in the popular press, they were, in fact, more often on stage than behind a barricade. Like the sexologists they admired, the anarchist sex radicals sought to bring what they thought of as the cold, rational light of science to bear on a topic that others preferred to keep hidden from view. In spite of the fact that she was fueled by her political passions, Goldman approached the subject of homosexuality from a dispassionate perspective. This is not to say that Goldman's lectures did not spark controversy, indeed, Mrs. Johnson's response is just one indicator of the extent to which talk about homosexuality, even of the most reserved sort, led to strong reactions among those who felt their most deeply held moral values to be at risk.

One of Goldman's last interventions in sexology and the politics of homosexuality occurred in the early years of her exile. In 1923, she wrote Magnus Hirschfeld to protest an article that appeared in his journal, *Jahrbuche fur sexuelle Zwischenstufen* (The Yearbook for Intermediate Sexual Types). The article, written by Dr. Karl von Levetzow, argues that Louise Michel, a hero of the Paris Commune and a well-known French anarchist, was a homosexual. Goldman, though careful to state that she had "no prejudice whatever, or the least antipathy to homosexuals," absolutely denied Levetzow's interpretation of Michel's life.[72] Hirschfeld, on the other hand, shared Levetzow's views. "I was shocked," Goldman wrote Havelock Ellis, "when I saw the photographs of that marvelous woman among the collection of homosexuals in Dr. Hirschfeld's house. I was shocked not because of any squeamishness on the subject, but because I knew Louise Michel to be far removed from the tendencies ascribed to her."[73] Goldman clung to the legend of Michel as the "Red Virgin." On its surface this nickname simply refers to the fact that Michel never married, but it also signals a narrative of self-refusal and enforced simplicity, the story of a woman who spent her life in struggle on behalf of the oppressed. In Goldman's eyes, Michel was a model of devotion who had given up all physical pleasures on the altar of the revolution. For Goldman, Michel was neither a lesbian nor a heterosexual, she was an anarchist Joan of Arc.

Levetzow painted a very different portrait of Michel. He positioned sexual and gender deviance, rather than political commitment and admirable selflessness at the heart of her personality. In his essay, Levetzow argues that Michel was a classic example of a "sexual invert." "A more virile character than hers," Levetzow concluded, "cannot be found even among the most masculine of men." As a child, the doctor observes, Michel had indulged in tomboyish behavior, going so far as to play with toads, bats, and frogs. He pointed to Michel's physical appearance as proof of her lesbianism. Michel was, the doctor thought, masculine in regard, possessing, "flat lips," "bushy eyebrows," and a moustache "that would awaken the envy of a high school student." Levetzow thought her unattractive—Michel had lips that did "not invite to be kissed"—and interpreted this as a sign of Michel's inverted sexual nature.[74] In addition to the somatic and childhood signs of inversion, Michel spent her entire life in the masculine pursuits of politics. Michel's anarchist beliefs, in other words, were the result of her sexual nature. Only a sexual invert would live a life that so contradicted the imperatives of her biological sex.

Goldman's forceful repudiation of Levetzow's work must be seen as a continuation of an already established debate about Michel's sexuality. Michel had been accused (and in this context accused is the correct term) of having "tastes against nature" well before Levetzow wrote his essay. Perhaps the charge was inevitable given the facts of Michel's life. As Marie Mullaney has argued, "Pioneering women who stepped outside conventional social roles were branded as sexually variant simply because of their public activism or political commitment."[75] Rumors about Michel's relationships with other women began to surface following her imprisonment in France's prison colony of New Caledonia. In prison, Michel forged a tight relationship with a fellow inmate named Natalie Lemel. After Michel's return to France, suspicion was cast on her friendship with another colleague, Paule Minck. All three women were revolutionaries who led unconventional lives. The charge of lesbianism brought against them was directly related to their gender and their political activism. Michel was quite conscious of the fact that she was accused of being a sexual deviant. She wrote in her memoirs, "If a woman is courageous...or grasps some bit of knowledge early, men claim she is only a 'pathological' case."[76]

Goldman may also have been quick to attack Levetzow because she too faced hostile comments that focused on her sexuality and gender identity. In the late 1920s, for example, she wrote a friend, joking that since she was fond of Berkman's girlfriend "the next rumor that will go around...will be that I am a Lesbian and trying to get her away from him for myself!"[77] Like Michel, Goldman was described as masculine in appearance and behavior. Harry Kemp went so far as to compare Goldman to Theodore Roosevelt, something that neither she nor the President would have appreciated. Harry Kemp wrote that, "[Goldman] made me think of a battleship going into action."[78] Will Durant described her as "a strongly built and masculine woman." Other men echoed his description. When Durant asked a group of men attending one of Goldman's lectures, "What do you think of her?" one responded by calling her "an old hen." Another agreed, but added, "she's more like a rooster." These remarks served to belittle Goldman, and she resented them. Durant conceded that were he to have spoken directly to Goldman "she would have told me, in her sarcastic way, that a woman may have other purposes and functions in life than to please a man."[79] In her critique of Levetzow, Goldman lived up to Durant's prediction. She accused Levetzow of seeing "in women only the charmer of men, the bearer of children, and in a more vulgar sense, the general cook and bottlewasher of the household." The vigor of Goldman's response to Levetzow's article was, to some degree, a response to the many men who took Michel's and Goldman's bravery and intellect as signs of sexual and gender deviance.

It is easy to see in Goldman's response to Levetzow's essay a sign that she felt, in the words of Blanche Wiesen Cook, "a profound ambivalence about lesbianism as a lifestyle." Perhaps Goldman's zeal in attacking Levetzow indicates an ambivalence, but one can take this argument too far, and Cook does acknowledge that Goldman was not "homophobic."[80] The full extent of Goldman's thoughts on the subject have to be considered in coming to a judgment. Through the course of her life Goldman argued that in matters of love all desires, inasmuch as they are freely chosen, are deserving of social toleration. She expressed her personal views in a letter to a friend who expressed some distaste for homosexuality. "One need be no prude," Goldman wrote, "to feel diffident about phases of sex tendencies one is not familiar with." But such feelings were no basis for discrimination. Goldman herself saw "absolutely no difference in the tendency itself" and reassured her friend that "homosexuality has nothing whatever to do with depravity."[81] Goldman's sexual politics would not find much favor in the context of today's polarized sex wars; it neither satisfies those who condemn sexual difference as a sign of cultural decadence, nor those who seek to celebrate gay pride. Goldman's position on the social, ethical, and cultural place of homosexuality was very much a product of the anarchist movement in which she played so critical a role.

In formulating her sexual politics, Goldman—like other anarchist sex radicals—drew on the work of Ellis, Carpenter, Hirschfeld, and various other sexologists. They did not do so uncritically. Anarchist sex radicals favored those sexologists who they felt best reflected their own values, and they were unwilling to contest the findings of the men and women they admired. As we see with Goldman's critiques of Hirschfeld and Levetzow, anarchist sex radicals were willing to challenge sexology and sought to shape it. Through their publications, public lectures, and personal relations, the anarchists acted as conduits for new ideas about human nature and sex. They saw themselves as participants in a transatlantic debate about the moral, ethical, and social place of homosexuality—equal members in an imagined "International Institute and Society of Sexology." Through their work, anarchists contributed to the remaking of cultural and political representations of homosexuality and to ideas about what role same-sex desire had in the making of the public and the private self.

Dear Dr. Hirschfeld:

I have been familiar with your great work on sex psychology for a number of years. I have admired the brave struggle you have made for the rights of people who, by their very nature, can not find sex expression in what is commonly called "the normal way". And now that I have been fortunate enough to know you and see your efforts at close range, I am more than ever impressed with your personality and the spirit which has sustained you in your difficult task. Your readiness to give my refutation of Frhr. von Levetzow's appraisement of Louise Michel as an Uranier proves, if proofs were needed, that you have a fine sense of justice which seeks only to ascertain the truth. I thank you for that and for your able and heroic stand you have taken against ignorance and hypocrisy on behalf of light and humanism.

Before I deal with von Levetzow's article, permit me to say this: It is not prejudice against homosexuality or the aversion to homosexuals which prompts me to point out the errors in the claim of the author. If Louise Michel had ever demonstrated sexual traits to those who knew and loved her, I should be the last person to attempt to clear her from the "stigma". I may, indeed, consider it a tragedy for those who are sexually differentiated in a world so bereft of understanding for the homosexual, or so ignorant of the meaning and importance of the whole gamut of sex. But I certainly do not think such people inferior, less moral, or less capable of fine feelings and actions. Least of all should I consider it necessary to "clear" my illustrious teacher and comrade, Louise Michel, of the charge of homosexuality. Her value to humanity, her contribution to the emancipation of the slaves, is so great that nothing could and or detract from her, whatever her sexual gratifications may have been.

Letter from Emma Goldman to Magnus Hirschfeld, January 1923 (courtesy of the Kate Sharpley Library).

CHAPTER SIX:

ANARCHIST SEXUAL POLITICS IN THE POST-WORLD WAR I PERIOD

THE FIRST WORLD WAR, the Russian Revolution and the Red Scare that it sparked nearly destroyed the anarchist movement in the United States. The sexual politics that flourished within the pre-war anarchist movement was a casualty of this terrible winnowing. Movement publications such as *Mother Earth* and *The Blast* were shut down, and leading spokespersons were arrested. The end of the war gave the anarchists little relief. The rise of the Communist Party profoundly reshaped the culture of the Left, and led to the marginalization of the anarchists and their expansive political agenda. The CP was dismissive and hostile towards anarchism, and anarchists actually found themselves spending energy and resources defending themselves against communist attacks. CP activists did not believe that sexual politics were worthy of great attention, and following Stalin's rise, the sexual politics of the American CP became largely indistinguishable from the mainstream society in which it operated. Although anarchist sex radicals continued to try and break into public discourse, they were stymied by the fact that they no longer had access to publications and the same number of lecture halls. By the end of the 1920s, the anarchist sexual politics of the pre-World War I era was largely forgotten.

But anarchism did not disappear. Anarchism was a current in the artistic and social life of cities like Chicago and San Francisco. Small groups of activists persisted in advocating the ideas of libertarian socialism, including the right of individuals to choose erotic and emotional relationships free from the interference of others. Anarchists continued to present lectures, publish pamphlets, and argue for the equal treatment of same-sex love. Activists also worked to keep alive the work of their predecessors. The ideas of the pre-war anarchist sex radicals were transmitted in ways that eluded detection, and took forms that were unexpected.

The ideas of the pre-war anarchists were an important influence on sexual and cultural radicals and bohemians. The movement of the pre-war years did not reconstitute itself, but the ideas that the movement's leading ideologues crafted continued to find an audience. People like Kenneth Rexroth, Elsa Gidlow, Jan Gay, and others were influenced by the ideas of the pre-World War I anarchist sex radicals. These figures, in turn, shaped American culture. In indirect and complex ways, the sexual politics of Tucker, Goldman, Berkman, and Lloyd have had an impact on the lives of individuals that has not been sufficiently appreciated.

The anarchist movement in the United States was a casualty of the fight over whether or not the country should support the Allied Powers against the Germans and their supporters. Those who favored America's entry into World War I mobilized the police powers of the state to crush those who opposed U.S. involvement. In 1917, the year the America began to draft and send troops to war, Congress passed the Espionage Act which stated that "any person... who shall willfully cause or attempt to cause insubordination, disloyalty, mutiny, or refusal of duty in the military or naval forces of the United States, or shall willfully obstruct the recruiting or enlistment service of the United States... shall be punished by a fine of not more than $10,000 or imprisonment for not more than twenty years or both."[1] Shortly thereafter Congress passed the Alien Immigrant Act making the deportation of foreign-born radicals possible. In May of 1918, the Congress passed the Sedition Act, which made it illegal to use "unpatriotic or disloyal language."[2] Anarchists, who with a few notable exceptions (Tucker and Kropotkin among them) were against America's entry into the war, were targeted. In October 1918, for example, Congress passed the Anti-Anarchist Act, authorizing the deportation of alien anarchists.[3] According to Eric Foner, "Even more extreme repression took place at the hands of state governments...thirty-three states outlawed the possession or display of ...black flags," a symbol of the anarchist movement.[4] Federal, state, and local agents now had the power to attack those whom they deemed a threat to the nation. As Randolph Bourne observed, "With the shock of war...the State comes into its own."[5]

The fate of Berkman and Goldman is emblematic of the fate that many anarchists in the movement faced. Because of their staunch antiwar activism, they were singled out for special attention. The police did not have to look hard to find the evidence they needed to convict: On May 9, 1916 Berkman and Goldman helped to establish the No Conscription League. The League's membership issued a statement that said, "that the militarization of America is an evil that far outweighs, in its anti-social and anti-libertarian effects, any good that may come from America's participation in the war." Issuing a direct challenge to the Federal government, the League promised to "resist conscription by every means in our power, and…sustain those who, for similar reasons, refuse to be conscripted.[6]

For their statements, Berkman and Goldman were arrested and convicted of working to undermine the war effort. Harry Weinberger appealed to the Supreme Court of the United States on behalf of the two, arguing that the defendants were convicted for expressing their views on a matter of public policy, a right explicitly protected in the First Amendment to the Constitution. The Court did not accept Weinberger's petition; the government was in no mood to tolerate a broad interpretation of individual rights. The climate was hard and unyielding. On the eve of the paper's suppression, Leonard Abbott wrote in *Mother Earth* that "regimentation, uniformity [and] absolute obedience to authority…the acknowledged military standards" were the dominant values of the time.[7] Using their newly established powers, the authorities shut down anarchist publications and arrested individuals who opposed US involvement in the war. Berkman and Goldman and other less well-known anarchists were sent to prison, awaiting the end of the war for their release.

But the end of the war did not end the repression of radicals in the United States. This was due, in part, to the fact that during the war, Lenin and the Bolsheviks succeeded in establishing a communist state in Russia. There were also unsuccessful attempts to found "Red Republics" in Germany and elsewhere in Europe. The founding of the Soviet Union and the wave of revolutionary activity that swept post-war Europe terrified conservatives on both sides of the Atlantic. Many Americans thought that the revolutionary forces were gathering at the door. A wave of bombings including a spectacular explosion on Wall Street seemed to usher in a radical assault. A virulent panic swept the country.

In 1919, the American Legion, sworn to uphold Americanism and defeat Bolshevism, held its first convention. The federal government also acted. The US Attorney General, A. Mitchell Palmer, rounded up and imprisoned foreign-born radicals in a series of police actions that came to be known as the Palmer Raids. A number of anarchists, including Goldman and Berkman were among those seized. The US then decided to deport the arrestees to Russia—then the Soviet Union—the nation from which many had immigrated. Native-born radicals were spared this indignity: as anarchist Charles T. Sprading wrote Goldman in 1927, "I was saved by being born right, of both the proper stock, and in the right country."[8] But despite having eluded deportation, Sprading was not unscathed. He and other radicals were cut off from their fellow activists, and the movement within which they operated was greatly reduced.

Though they were unwilling immigrants, Goldman and Berkman approached the country of their birth with great hopes. Many Anarchists, like most on the Left, celebrated the founding of the Soviet Union. Russian anarchists played a key part in helping to overthrow both the Tsar and also the Kerenskii government that followed the abolition of Tsarist rule.[9] The Bolsheviks cultivated anarchist support by appropriating their political slogans, including, "The factories to the workers, the land to the peasants." Though the new government took actions that troubled many anarchists, they were largely dismissed as revolutionary growing pains. Before her deportation, for example, Goldman defended the Bolsheviks who, she said, "were human, like the rest of us, and likely to make mistakes."[10] Within months of her arrival in the Soviet Union, however, Goldman's illusions were shattered. She witnessed the merciless persecution of the anarchists by the Tcheka, Lenin's secret police. Berkman, whose revolutionary zeal was hotter than Goldman's, was less willing to give up his hope. Eventually, though, he too came to see that the Bolsheviks were intent on total domination. In short order, the Bolsheviks purged the anarchists, among the first of many political and social dissidents that the Soviet's ruthlessly repressed. "The Soviet government, with an iron broom," boasted Leon Trotsky, "rid Russia of anarchism."[11] Convinced, in the words of Berkman, that "the Revolution in Russia had become a mirage, a dangerous deception," he and Goldman decided to leave the country.[12]

Berkman and Goldman went into exile with their hopes crushed and a bleak political future before them. Most of those on the Left, including old allies, were enraptured by the nascent Soviet state and they had little use for the jeremiads of the anarchists. While the communists, in the words of historian Laurence Veysey, "could claim affiliation with the most hopeful large-scale revolutionary movement anywhere on the world horizon," the anarchists appeared to be a defeated lot.[13] Everywhere, the anarchists faced fierce attacks by communists who accused them of being irrelevant and anti-revolutionary. Former comrades, like the artist Robert Minor, who once designed covers for *Mother Earth*, switched allegiances. Eric Morton, an American friend of Goldman, told her that Minor, "is a real religious communist now and is developing considerable religious intolerance, referring to those who differ from his sacred doctrines as *fake* revolutionaries." [Italics in original.] Morton informed Goldman that his daughter, who was active on the Left, had heard much about her—all of it bad. "Good religious communists use you as a sort of bogey-man."[14] Goldman felt betrayed. She wrote the writer, Theodore Dreiser, that "the Russian debacle and the war have shifted all values, most of all the values of integrity and fearlessness. The very people who posed as my friends are now among my bitterest enemies."[15] The Russian Revolution utterly transformed the culture of the Left in the United States, marginalizing anarchist radicals and the ideas they had championed. American radicals were fascinated by the *élan* of the Soviet leadership and had little patience for those who warned of the dangers of Leninism.

The extent of the anarchists' marginalization is exemplified by Goldman's struggles to maintain her voice. Although she was prevented from returning to America for any extended period of time, she did manage to arrange a US speaking tour in 1934. The tour was restricted to ninety days, and she was permitted to speak only on the subjects of literature and drama. The authorities believed that, by restricting Goldman's topics, they would avoid anything controversial. This did not, however, restrict Goldman from addressing the subject of homosexuality. In a lecture on American drama, Goldman praised the play *The Children's Hour*, as well as Radcliff Hall's novel *The Well of Loneliness*, both of which portray lesbian relations. Hall's novel is, in fact, one of the best-known literary representations of lesbianism of the twentieth century. Its publication was accompanied by a sharp debate over whether or not the portrayal of homosexual relationships was, by their very nature, obscene. In addition to praising Hall's book, Goldman thought *The Children's Hour* was "beautifully written and beautifully produced."[16]

But few people heard Goldman speak during her short 1934 American tour. She no longer made headlines and the brevity of her stay precluded any sustained outreach. At this point, Goldman's politics were nearly illegible to her contemporaries. As Marian J. Morton writes, "Goldman's opposition to both capitalism and communism put her nowhere on the political spectrum."[17] *The Nation*, well aware that the center of the American Left lay in the Communist Party and its offshoots, put it quite bluntly: "Today the Anarchists are a scattered handful of survivors, and the extreme left is divided among the various communist groups…Emma Goldman is not a symbol of freedom in a world of tyrants; she is merely a wrong-headed old woman."[18]

The changing climate of radicalism in the post-war years was a critical element in the decline of anarchism. What strength anarchism enjoyed before

World War I was nurtured by the utopian, pre-Leninist socialism that some have called the "Lyrical Left." Anarchist sexual politics were well received within the Lyrical Left—and, in fact, shaped the temper of the times. People like Randolph Bourne who mixed together the personal and the political in a blaze of cultural production exemplified the Lyrical Left. Like many of his contemporaries Bourne championed "artists, philosophers, geniuses, tramps, criminals, eccentrics, aliens, freelovers and freethinkers" and all those who "violate any of the three sacred taboos of property, sex, and the State."[19] With the outbreak of the war, however, Bourne turned pessimistic, as the titles of his essays announced the "Twilight of the Idols" and the triumph of "The Disillusionment." Bourne's premature death in 1918 can be said to symbolize the end of a particular moment in the history of the US. The carnage of battle and the triumph of Leninism split apart the Lyrical Left. In his study of New York intellectual life, Thomas Bender argues that after the war, "the sort of innocent, non-doctrinaire eclectic 'revolution'" associated with people like Bourne "was no longer possible."[20] The anarchists were an important component of the Lyrical Left; its passing boded poorly for the fate of the movement. The sexual politics that had been such an important part of the anarchist movement and the Lyrical Left were traumatically foreshortened.

A number of anarchist fellow travelers abandoned their old alliances, some in quite public forums. Will Durant, for example, published a number of works in the twenties in which he made light of his former Ferrer Center associates. In *Philosophy and the Social Problem*, he acknowledged that while he "loved" the anarchist "for the fervor of his hope and the beauty of his dream," he felt that "the anarchist fails miserably in the face of interrogation." Given that thousands of Russian anarchists were, in fact, facing the brutal interrogations of the Soviet Union's secret police, Durant's words are truly ironic. Though he once admired them, Durant now believed that the anarchists had little to offer serious political thinkers. The spirit of the age was in blood and iron, not free love and libertarian conviviality. Order, not liberty, was the key to understanding political thought. "Freedom itself is a problem," Durant maintained, "not a solution." In a classic example of a backhanded compliment, he concluded, "Only children and geniuses can be truly anarchistic."[21] Hurt by Durant's criticisms, Goldman wrote an American friend to denounce her one-time comrade: "I had no faith in him from the very beginning," she wrote. "I had a feeling that he will use the movement as a stepping stone to fame and material success."[22]

Durant was not an isolated case either. After having been targeted by the government for printing allegedly seditious materials during WWI, Margaret Anderson also drifted away from her former friends, and eschewed political topics. In the twenties, she dropped discussions of anarchism and turned instead towards literary modernism. Like Durant, Anderson characterized her enthusiasm for anarchism as a youthful, immature flirtation. She said that, "In the natural course of events I had naturally turned away from anarchism."[23] This rejection of anarchism did not necessarily end her problems with the government however, as she was later arrested for publishing selections of James Joyce's *Ulysses*—a work that was considered obscene. Anderson's change of heart angered her old comrades. Leonard Abbott commented that she, "represented the tragedy of the anarchist movement in America."[24] Goldman was disappointed, admitting that her former comrade's commitment to anarchism was a passing phase and was "not actuated by any sense of social injustice."[25] By placing their hopes for social transformation in the hands of what they came to see as fair-weather friends, the anarchists believed they had made a fatal mistake.

Pre-war sex radicals who had been aligned with the anarchists also distanced themselves from their former colleagues. Birth control activist Margaret Sanger, for example, felt that her earlier association with the anarchists "was a formidable albatross from which she was determined to cut loose."[26] Before the war, Sanger worked with Goldman and the anarchists who were among her most fervent champions. Goldman sold copies of Sanger's publication while on tour and helped publicize the struggles that her comrade had with the authorities. But in the years after the war the political base of the birth control movement changed, and Sanger moved to appeal to the new base. According to historian Nancy Cott, post-war birth control advocates "were…more social and politically conservative than… [the activists of] the 1910s and more numerous."[27] The increasing conservativism of the movement and its growth were directly related. In order to grow birth control's constituency, Sanger redefined herself as a health care activist offering helpful advice on how to improve life, and not as a sex radical bent on transforming society. Sanger obscured her ties to the anarchist movement in order to make birth control palatable to a mainstream public.

The separation of Sanger's sex radicalism from the political context in which it emerged in the pre-war years was a telling development. The anarchists saw sexual liberation as only one element of "a total reconstruction of woman's role, a reconstruction which also included the abolition of the nuclear family, economic independence, and psychological self-sufficiency."[28] Included in their larger vision of social and cultural change, was the defense of homosexuality that people like Goldman, Lloyd, and Tucker articulated before World War I. Sanger and other sex activists were willing to jettison this broad agenda in order to win public acceptance for the narrowly defined right of birth control. To a great extent, their efforts were successful. Birth control, though it remained controversial, was no longer associated with free love and revolution. Many advocates for birth control built alliances with eugenicists and supported forced sterilization laws. In the 1920s, to paraphrase William O'Neill, it was possible to be a sex radical and a political conservative.[29] The anarchists were all too aware of this development. In 1927, Goldman told a Canadian newspaper "I am almost ashamed to champion [birth control] now that the staid House of Lords in Great Britain has taken it up!"[30] The defense of homosexuality that anarchist sex radicals had included in their sexual politics was not, however, shared by the House of Lords or the US Congress. Birth control may have had its advocates, but the more ambitious claims for individual sexual rights were a casualty of the limited range of cultural and radical politics in the 1920s. The scope of sexual politics in the United States was narrowed significantly once it lost the presence of its most radical advocates.

The breakdown of the anarchist movement was accelerated by the collapse of the communication networks that the anarchists had been so devoted to building. Some of this eating away at the base of the movement, particularly among the individualist anarchists, had come before the war. The first generation of native-born anarchists passed away in the late-nineteenth and early-twentieth centuries—like Ezra Heywood who died in 1893. According to Martin Blatt, Heywood's death devastated his partner, Angela who was also a leading figure in the movement. Angela "confronted the difficult challenge of supporting herself and her four children because Heywood had left virtually nothing in terms of tangible assets."[31] Much of the literature that the pre-war anarchist movement produced was no longer available. In 1908, a devastating fire destroyed Tucker's bookstore and printing press, destroying the leading producer and distributor of individualist anarchist thought. Disheartened, Tucker moved to the south of France shortly after the fire, where he lived with his free-love companion and daughter until his death in 1939. Though he intended to keep publishing *Liberty* from overseas, the publication was never successfully revived.

Although he effectively ceased working in the United States, Tucker did attempt to keep engaged. From 1913 to 1914, for example, he contributed articles to Dora Marsden's *The New Freewoman*, an English journal that espoused the ideas of the radical individualist ideas of Max Stirner. According to Bruce Clark, *The New Freewoman* "explicitly connected sexual emancipation, evolutionary progress, and libertarian politics, along lines similar to Emma Goldman's concurrent anarcho-feminist campaign."[32] The precursor to *The New Freewoman*, *The Freewoman*, was condemned as "immoral" for, among other things, carrying articles on lesbianism. Tucker, however, did not address the topic of homosexuality in his contributions to *The New Freewoman*.

Tucker's final contribution to the field of sexual politics was indirect and came via his friendship with John Henry Mackay. Born in 1864 in Scotland, Mackay was raised in Germany and lived most of his life there. He and Tucker met in 1889, likely introduced by their mutual friend, the German-American anarchist, Robert Reitzel, during one of Tucker's visits to Europe. In 1893, Mackay came to the United States, and for part of that tour, Tucker joined him in his travels, reporting to friends that they were enjoying "fine times."[33] The two were together again in 1900 during the Paris Exposition. When Tucker moved to Europe in 1908, he and Mackay were frequent guests in each other's homes. The nearly 200 letters and postcards that Mackay sent Tucker have been gathered in a collection entitled "Dear Tucker," which was compiled and annotated by the historian Hubert Kennedy. Unfortunately, Tucker's letters to Mackay are lost.

Tucker and Mackay were political and philosophical allies. Mackay was referred to in the pages of *Liberty* as Tucker's "greatest convert."[34] In 1891, Tucker translated Mackay's novel, *The Anarchists: A Picture of Civilization at the Close of the Nineteenth Century* from German and published it. The novel, which is set in London and features thinly veiled depictions of many of the well-known personalities of the Left, is a defense of individualist anarchism. In the preface to his novel, Mackay praised Tucker's work. "Oft in the lonely hours of my struggles," he wrote, he was able to turn to Tucker "to illuminate the night."[35] Tucker distributed Mackay's novel and poetry, the first English translations of which appeared in *Liberty*. On the other side of the Atlantic, Mackay helped spread Tucker's work in Germany, translating and publishing his "State Socialism and Anarchism" in 1895. He would later publish Tucker's "Are Anarchists Murderers?" Tucker wanted to translate and publish Mackay's biography of the German philosopher Max Stirner, which appeared in German in 1898, but was unable to because of the fire that destroyed his press and bookstore 1908. The plates, illustrations, and all existing copies of Mackay's work were lost—a blow that Mackay described as "a blow to our cause, which even the new work of many years will probably never succeed in overcoming."[36] The two men were ideological compatriots whose mutual support and influence was critical to the unfolding of their thought and work.

The ties between Tucker and Mackay, both social and political, are important because they enabled Mackay to develop his own sexual politics. The political tradition of individualist anarchism that the two men shared provided Mackay with the means to conceptualize his personal struggle as a political one. According to Kennedy, Mackay was sexually drawn to adolescent male youths.[37] Mackay first came to acknowledge and understand his desires in 1886 after reading Krafft-Ebing's *Psychopathia Sexualis*. After reading the work, Mackay "kept silent no longer within himself," but he did not, apparently, yet feel able to give public voice to his feelings.[38] It was not until the early-twentieth century, decades after Mackay first emerged as an anarchist activist, that he began to publish work on sexuality. Stirner's radical critique of morals, and an understanding of sexual politics that was nurtured by his relationship with Tucker, provided Mackay with the wherewithal to begin to speak publicly, however tentatively. Anarchism provided the ideological tools with which Mackay conceived of and articulated his sexual politics. According to Kennedy, Mackay came to understand that "the question of this love...[is] a social question: the fight for the individual for his freedom against whatever kind of oppression."[39]

In 1905, Mackay, using the pseudonym Sagitta, began to circulate his thoughts on what he called "the nameless love." Anarchism, especially the variants championed by Tucker, was a critical ingredient in the development of the defense of intergenerational same-sex eroticism that Mackay developed at the turn of the century. Mackay first presented his work—in the form of poetry— in *Der Eigene* (The Self-Owner), a journal whose philosophy was influenced by Stirner.[40] *Der Eigene* provided Mackay with an intellectually and culturally supportive vehicle to make his views public, but he would eventually come to regret his association with *Der Eigene*. The journal's elitist, misogynistic strain of sexual politics clashed with Mackay's more egalitarian thinking. Despite his break with *Der Eigene*, Mackay continued to champion Stirner and anarchism.

Mackay's use of a pseudonym was well considered. In 1908, the German police seized all available copies of Sagitta's writings and threatened the publisher with a prison term should he continue to circulate the work. Though Mackay came under suspicion and the police searched his house, his identity as Sagitta was not revealed. Despite these setbacks, Mackay continued to advocate for the liberalization of laws and social attitudes that governed relations between men and male youths until his death in 1933, just as the Nazis were consolidating their power. Mackay was pessimistic about his chances to change public opinion on the question of intergenerational homosexual relations. Shortly before his death he published an essay entitled "The History of a Fight for the Nameless Love," in which he wrote that "I have fought a fight, a fight in which I am beaten." Against the background of Hitler's thundering denunciations of degeneration and sexual deviance, Mackay felt that the world was entering "a long night, whose end no one sees and whose dawn none of us will experience.[41] As a final act in his political campaign, Mackay stipulated that his identity as Sagitta be made public following his death.

During what clearly were difficult years, Mackay turned to Tucker for consolation and support. Tucker seems to have been unaware of Mackay's sexual tastes before the publication of Sagitta's work. Though Mackay was well known for his love poetry—poems in which the gender of the beloved was left undefined—there is no evidence that Tucker and Mackay had discussed homosexuality. Tucker was not personally enthusiastic about this development in his friend's life, evidenced by the title page of his copies of the Sagitta writings where he wrote, "my subscription to this work shall not be taken as evidence of my sympathy with its contents."[42] Tucker clearly was put off by Mackay's sexual tastes, but did not break off relations with him. The two men continued to correspond and Tucker assisted his friend financially by purchasing copies of the "Books of Nameless Love." By supporting his friend emotionally, and by helping—albeit modestly—to underwrite the publication of his work, Tucker directly enabled Mackay's sexual politics. And Tucker did so despite his own personal ambivalence about the relations that Mackay was so keen to defend.

Tucker's friendship with Mackay was deeply felt. Rather than tactfully ignore the subject of Mackay's personal life, Tucker sought out his friend's views. In 1911, Mackay wrote Tucker that "I see out of your letter—much to my surprise—that you *want* to hear from me more and more particular details of this question, I will be only too glad to give them to you, to show you, that this love is precisely a love like your love, sexual of course, but not *only* sexual, and not a vice or an illness or a crime."[43] The "surprise" that Mackay expresses may well have reflected the fact that, even among his circle of friends, few were willing to treat with him in the full complexity of his humanity. Acknowledging the importance of their friendship, Mackay dedicated his book *The Freedomseeker*, the sequel to *The Anarchist*, to Tucker, describing his friend as "a man who in a long and incomparable life, notable for its courage, energy, and staying power, has done more for the cause of Freedom than any other living man." In a letter accompanying the book, Mackay asked Tucker to "take the book as a small tribute of gratitude for so much you have given to me."[44]

Whatever their personal differences, Tucker provided his friend with social and political support until Mackay's death. That support was critical to Mackay's formulation of his sexual politics and his ability to make his views public—albeit under a pseudonym. Tucker's views on Mackay's sexual politics were no different from those he expressed when he argued against the change in the age-of-consent laws in the United States, discussed above (in the chapter titled, "The Wilde Ones"). To excommunicate Mackay would have been to betray a double standard. Certainly heterosexual relationships that mirrored the age-disparity of the relations that Mackay advocated were not uncommon in the period when he was writing. Alexander Berkman, for example, was for a time "romantically involved" with fifteen-year-old, Becky Edolshon.[45] What, apart from gender, was the difference between the partners of Mackay and Berkman? In both cases, Tucker considered the young women and men in question to be mature enough to make decisions for themselves; they were old enough to make honest mistakes. Since Mackay was defending consensual relationships, Tucker felt it no business of his or the state to intervene. Quite the opposite, in fact: Mackay's right to pursue consensual relationships should be defended no matter what one's personal view of the nature of those relations. Tucker was clearly ambivalent—to say the very least—about Mackay's sexual choices, but he was not the least ambivalent in his feeling that Mackay had the right to defend himself against his detractors.

Tucker's few contributions to *The New Freewoman* and his support of Mackay did not register in the United States—his absence was noted. In 1926, Clarence Swartz reprinted a collection of Tucker's articles from *Liberty* for the American market, and did so because, as he said in the preface, "For a number of years practically all of the literature of Individualist Anarchism has been out of print."[46] Despite Swartz's efforts, there was little real change in the situation. Writing to his friend Joseph Ishill, William C. Owen lamented that, "our very best books…go out of circulation."[47]

Like Swartz, Ishill—a publisher working in Berkeley Heights, New Jersey—was among those who labored to keep works of interest to anarchists in print. Ishill's Oriole Press had provided a venue for anarchist sexual politics, including discussions of homosexuality. In 1929, Oriole Press produced a collection of essays celebrating the work of Havelock Ellis. Several of the essays included praise Ellis' work on the subject of homosexuality. Pierre Ramus remembered the impact that Ellis' book on "sexual inversion" had on him: "Almost twenty-six years ago, Fred Burry, a Canadian fighter for freedom following in the footsteps of Walt Whitman, loaned us in Toronto a secretly circulating [copy of *Sexual Inversion*] which in his native England was proscribed by prudery and hypocrisy and still is for the most part." Ellis' work seemed doubly special because, Ramus recalled, a friend of his "informed us that Havelock Ellis was also an admirer of Kropotkin."[48] As in the pre-war days, the contributors to Ishill's volume on Ellis cited the work of sexologists, anarchists, and poets in their work. Ramus' mention of the admiration Ellis supposedly had for Kropotkin is ironic given Kropotkin's skepticism of Ellis' work. As noted above, Kropotkin advised a number of his comrades to avoid visiting Ellis for fear that they might become swept up in the sexological project. Whatever their merits, the books put out by Oriole Press had a very small circulation. The Ellis collection was limited to 500 copies.

Though the East Coast had been the center of anarchism in the first two decades of the twentieth century, in the post-war period, Los Angeles emerged as a center of the diminished English-language anarchist movement. There, a small band of activists formed The Libertarian League, which despite its name was closer to the pre-World War I anarchists than the post-World War II Libertarians. The League, which distributed anarchist literature and published the short-lived magazine, *The Libertarian*, continued the work of their pre-war comrades. In a 1925 letter to anarchist Jo Labadie, Clarence Swartz, the League's treasurer, wrote, "I have not receded an inch from my old position, and I think I am still standing on the same foundation that Tucker and the others built for us years ago."[49] The League, whose advisory board included William Allen White and H. L. Mencken, fought for its vision despite limited resources. In his letter to Labadie, Swartz wrote, "While the magazine had to dim for lack of support, the Libertarian League is alive and functioning." In addition to trying to keep old flames alive, the League faced new battles, as Swartz told Labadie, "We are now entering the fight against Bryant and the Fundamentalists in their attack on Prof. Scopes in Tennessee."[50] The 1920s were not a friendly climate for the work of Swartz and his colleagues.

The ethical, social, and cultural place of homosexuality were among the topics the League addressed. In making their case for sexual liberalism, League members cited many of the same sources as the pre-war anarchists and used many of their same arguments. In 1932, for example, the League underwrote the publication of a short study of Edward Carpenter. Thomas Bell, the author of the study, praised Carpenter as "the greatest of modern British Anarchists." In the essay Bell discusses Carpenter's writing on "homo-sexuality" in a favorable manner adding, "though Carpenter never in so many words, so far as I know, said that he himself was of that temperament it was pretty well understood that he was."[51] Several of his friends, including Upton Sinclair, urged Bell to turn his essay into a book, but he found that publishers were uninterested. "They did not want it, as it is written for Anarchists and not for the general public," Bell told a friend.[52] Books identified as "for Anarchists" could no longer find publishers, and despite Ishill and the League's efforts, there were no anarchist publishing groups able to bring a project like Bell's to market. While Tucker's edition of Wilde's *The Ballad of Reading Gaol* and Berkman's *Prison Memoirs of an Anarchist* were reviewed by mainstream journalists, Bell found it difficult to have his work even considered by publishers.

In addition to publishing pamphlets, the League sponsored lectures on the subject of homosexuality. In the late 1920s, Bell spoke to the League's membership on the topic of Wilde's life and work. The response to the lecture was very enthusiastic, but not necessarily completely satisfactory to Bell. He found that his audience wanted to hear all about Wilde's personal life but not about his politics. Bell wrote Ishill that although the talk "was supposed to be on [Wilde] as an Anarchist...it was made too evident to me that they also were very keen to hear about him as a Man. I had to tell them over and over again the dramatic story of his later years, of the tragedy of his trial and how it came about."[53] The success of his lecture led Bell, who had been Oscar Wilde's secretary for a brief period, to write a study of Wilde. His analysis very much reflected the pre-World War I anarchist's understanding of Wilde as a political and sexual radical. In the essay he wrote about "Wilde's bold social ideals" and he treats "Wilde's homosexuality...frankly and fearlessly." Reflecting the interests of his audience, Bell went out of his way to make sure that the disgraced poet's "sexual philosophy is given fairly and fully without whitewash."[54] Bell hoped to get his study in to broader circulation, but he died in a car crash and did not live to see his manuscript in print.

The League's connection to the politics of the pre-war anarchist movement was more than ideological. John William Lloyd was on the Libertarian League's advisory board, though according to Swartz, "he had backslid some," meaning that Lloyd was less than orthodox in his anarchism.[55] Lloyd moved to California in the early 1920s and continued to write, but he was isolated, describing himself as a "literary hermit."[56] Lloyd ensconced himself in a tiny house that he had he built on a hill in the countryside outside of Los Angeles. Abba Gordin, who lived with him for nearly a year, described a typical day of his life. "Lloyd," Gordin wrote, "takes care of his trees, fig-trees, apricots, and vines, waters his flowers and plants, and sings and writes, and studies and works and hopes—and out of his window of his cabin his 'Workshop of Dreams,' and the transom of his soul, looks and sees the high mountains, covered with snow of ages and wisdom, and he is self-reliant, and as hopeful, and as serene and as sure and as tuneful as they, who have seen the beginnings of all beginnings and know the end of all ends."[57] The dreamy, spiritual tone of Lloyd's life, as described by Gordon, is reflected in Lloyd's writing (*From Terrace-Hill Overlooking: Poems of Intuition, Perception, and Prophecy*, for example), which, increasingly, turned to mysticism in the post-war years.[58] One of the last laudatory mentions of Lloyd's work appeared in 1945, in *Message of the East*, a Vedantist publication. The author of the essay, a woman known as "Sister Daya," wrote that Lloyd was a "wise man" whose "legacy of mystic philosophy is too little known."[59]

Lloyd did publish articles and essays on sexuality post-World War I, and he was encouraging to others who were writing on the subject. He was, for example, among those who encouraged Thomas Bell to expand his essay on Carpenter into a book. It appears that Lloyd wrote less on the topic of homosexuality in the years following the war. One of Lloyd's few mentions of same-sex love during this period—he uses the term "homosexuality"—occurs in a pamphlet published privately in 1931 entitled, "The Karezza Method Or Magnetation: The Art of Connubial Love." Karezza, a term first used by Alice B. Stockham, a late-nineteenth-century sex reformer, is essentially sex without male ejaculation. Karezza is similar to the ideas about male sexual behavior that John Humphrey Noyes advocated at his commune at Onieda.[60] In his pamphlet, Lloyd goes to great length discussing the putative benefits that both men and women can enjoy through the practice of karezza. One of the greatest benefits outlined was that women's sexual desires would, by virtue of the fact that coitus would be extended, have a better chance of being satisfied. It is in this context that Lloyd makes mention of same-sex love. In an aside on the nature of sexual desire and its expressions, he argues, "that some women are more masculine than the average man, and vice versa." The various combinations that occur from the mixture of feminine and masculine forces in individuals "accounts for much of the phenomena of homosexuality."[61] Homosexuals are, in this construction, men who share certain features of women or women who share certain features of men. Lloyd does not seem to be referring to visible attributes—whether a person expresses outward signs of the opposite biological sex—but to the nature of the inner sex drive.

Like many of his colleagues, Lloyd found it increasingly difficult to find publishers for his work, despite the fact that friends such as Havelock Ellis continued to champion his writing in England and in conversations with American friends. Ellis wrote Joseph Ishill that, though Lloyd "has warm admirers on this side," he was too little appreciated in the United States, and Ellis was frustrated that "publishers...are shy" of Lloyd's writings.[62] In 1929, however, Ellis succeeded in persuading George Allen and Unwin, Edward Carpenter's publisher, to bring out Lloyd's *Eneres or the Questions of Reksa*. Ellis wrote a preface to the book which says that, "Lloyd belongs to the class of 'prophets,' as in England Edward Carpenter who had a high regard for Lloyd—the class of people, that is to say, who have a 'message' to their fellow-man."[63] The metaphor of "prophecy" was apt. The themes and style of Lloyd's book are those of a work of spiritual inquiry. The title, Lloyd explains for his reader, is a reference to the structure of the text which he constructed as a dialogue between an inquisitive youth and an older man: "Eneres (pronounced E-ner-es, accent of the second syllable), the Serene—the Old Man—is myself, and Reksa—the Asker—is likewise myself."[64]

Though *Eneres* contains a brief chapter on sex, Lloyd makes no mention of homosexuality in it. Ellis does, however, mention that Lloyd had written a text entitled *The Larger Love*, which he lamented "remains for the present unpublished—it is considered unsuitable for a still too prudish generation—though until it is published the full scope of Lloyd's outlook in relation to his own time will not have been made clear."[65] According to D. A. Sachs, *The Larger Love* dealt with homosexuality in chapters entitled "The Explanation of Sexual Perversions," "Justice to the Sexual Invert," and "The God-Like are Androgyne." Ellis implies that the contents of Lloyd's work made it unacceptable to publishers, but Lloyd's work about the "larger love" was published in anarchist journals before the war. It was not the "still too prudish" nature of the public that limited Lloyd's ability to publish, rather it was the fact that Lloyd could no longer draw on the resources and audience of the pre-World War I anarchist movement.

One of Lloyd's last publications on the subject of the politics of sexuality appears in *Sex In Civilization*, a collection of articles coedited by V. F. Calverton in 1929. One of the most prominent sex radicals of the twenties, V. F. Calverton wrote and edited a number of important texts on sexuality. Though identified with the Communist Party, Calverton was not representative of the CP's sexual politics. His views, according to historian Leonard Wilcox, were "permeated with assumptions about personal growth and cultural revolution inherited from the 1910s' 'Lyrical left.'"[66] It is not surprising then that Calverton would invite Lloyd to contribute to his anthology. In his essay for *Sex and Civilization*, entitled "Sex Jealousy and Civilization," Lloyd essentially reiterates the free love ideas he developed in the anarchist movement, but he makes no mention of his former or current political affinities. Neither "anarchism" nor "libertarianism" appear in the index of *Sex and Civilization*—nor does Lloyd deal with homosexuality in his essay. In fact, Calverton's volume contains only brief and decidedly ambivalent discussions of same-sex eroticism. Lloyd did not seem eager to highlight the continuity, however diluted, his contribution to Calverton's book shared with the sexual politics of the pre-war anarchists. *Sex and Civilization* may have been a daring book for its day, but its themes and tone are no more daring than what appeared in *Lucifer the Light-Bearer* and *Liberty* in the 1890s, in *The Free Comrade* in 1902, or in *Mother Earth* in the years shortly before the war.

The leading figures of the post-World War I Left were, with few exceptions, not eager to explore the politics of personal life. Leninism, which dominated Leftist political discourse, "rejected many of the feminist and sex-radical traditions" of the pre-war left.[67] The Communist Party was—especially when compared to the pre-war anarchists—a redoubt of heteronormative attitudes. In the early twenties, there was, for a time, a popular perception that the revolution in the USSR would usher in a wave of sexual liberation and women's emancipation. Books with titles like *The Romance of New Russia,* published in 1924 by Magdeleine Marx (no relation to Karl Marx), portrayed the Soviets as pioneers of sexual freedom.[68] But despite the high hopes of Ms. Marx and others, the Soviet state was not a libidinal paradise. In the American CP, sexual politics were looked upon as a mere diversion from more serious matters. To illustrate: Malcolm Cowley, a CP intellectual, writing in the *New Republic,* chastised Calverton for indulging in supposedly petty pursuits, calling him one of "the sex boys, in their balloon of rhetoric…sailing far above the physical reality of their subject."[69] Calverton, in Cowley's eyes, was guilty of prioritizing the cultural superstructure over the economic base, a political heresy that was not permitted.

Though "a growing intolerance of the sex issue among orthodox Leftists" was already evident in the 1920s, the Stalinization of the American CP was a deathblow to the possibility that it could sponsor a radical sex politics.[70] The anarchists were sharply critical of this development, and in a short play published in 1936 in the anarchist journal *Vanguard,* David Lawrence lampooned the CP's sexual politics. Lawrence's satire, entitled "In a Soviet Village: A Morality Play," features a cast of characters including "Ivan, the Chairman of the Village Soviet," "A Sprinkling of Chekists and Red Army Men," "A Chorus of Komsomols," and "A Poet from the Dneiprostroy Union of Super-Stakhanovite Penmen." (The term Stakhanovite refers to the movement inspired by the legendary productivity of Aleksei Grigorievich Stakhanov, who was lauded by the Soviet authorities for the feat of mining 102 tons of coal in less than 6 hours.) In the play, the poet who "won the praise of Comrade Stalin, a medal, and a grant of money for producing triplets," declaims lines like: "Women's place is in the kitchen/Its time she stopped promiscuous bitchin'. The emancipated woman is a fright/Become a copulating Stakhanovite." The not so subtle attacks on the Soviet emphasis on production—sexual and otherwise—highlighted the reductive, heteronormative, and profoundly antifeminist sexual politic of Stalin and his admirers. Sexuality was seen as a productive tool of the state, not a venue for personal pleasure or expression. Women especially were to cease their "bitchin'" and set to work producing workers for Stalin.

The play features a phonograph that announces the latest party line to the assembled villagers. On this day, the radio trumpets an Orwellian sexual command:

The family is the basis of the Socialist Society. Sexual freedom is anarchy. Long live Stalinism. Lenin had only one wife...who are you to have more? Permanent marriage not permanent revolution. Who are we to interfere with the laws of Go...er, dialectical materialism.[71]

Lawrence presents the Soviets as theocrats, as eager as any prelate to judge sinners and advise chastity or marriage for their charges. He slams their regressive gender politics and implies that the productivist ideology of Stalinist Russia extends even to the bedroom, where it seems good citizens are expected to reproduce according to five-year plans. The readers of *Vanguard* no doubt also appreciated the insider jokes about the CP sprinkled throughout the play. For example, Stalin's ideological battle with Trotsky, who advocated permanent revolution and became a bitter critic of Stalin, is lampooned in the phrase "permanent marriage not permanent revolution." Lawrence also self-consciously contrasts anarchist sexual politics to those of the CP, making a tongue in cheek reference to "sexual freedom" as "anarchy."

Unlike the anarchist sex radicals, the CP took a dim view of homosexuality. When homosexuality did appear in the pages of CP publications it was most often as an occasion for satire. In 1941, Mike Quin, a leading party figure in San Francisco, wrote a story for the *People's World,* the CP's Pacific Coast daily newspaper, which portrays Rudolph Hess, Hitler, Churchill, and Roosevelt as stereotypical pansies.[72] Quin presents his story in the form of a conversation between two "common men," Mr. O'Brien and Mr. Murphy. O'Brien tells Murphy that Hess, a Nazi who parachuted into Scotland in the hopes of negotiating an end to war with the English, was "trying to land on a pansy bed" and smelled of "perfume when they picked him up." According to O'Brien, Hess was well received by the English elite. "The upper classes," he tells Murphy, "are never mad at each other in a war....The millionaires all stick together, war or no war." The evidence of the British elites' complicity with Hess is visible in the fact that both Hess and his elite English friends have "toe nails...painted red." Pictured as a gang of mad queens, class elites are portrayed as being part of a worldwide conspiracy to dominate the common man. Soon, Murphy tells his friend, Hess will journey to the US where "most of the upper-class finks wind up." Quin uses his story to suggest that working-class people everywhere need to come together against their common enemy, the upper classes. He warns his readers that there will be a battle of "red ideas against red toe-nails"—a clash, in other words, between honest working folks and decadent upper class pansies.[73] Quin's queer baiting is typical of the tactics communists used to smear fascist—and, in this case, liberal democratic—leaders and movements.[74] Of course, the temptation to use such tactics was not limited to those in the CP, but Quin's diatribe is nonetheless revealing of the sexual politics of the editors of the *People's World*.

Paradoxically, as the Left was turning towards a more conservative politics of sexuality, the American public was feeling freer to experiment and test the bounds of the crumbling Victorian sexual system. The anarchists found it hard to build an audience for radical sexual politics in a decade in which sexual liberalism and social freedom seemed to be on the rise. When Goldman came to visit Canada in the late 1920s, for example, she found herself asked about "flappers" and companionate marriages. Whereas in the pre-war years newspapers regularly denounced the anarchists as free love radicals, Goldman's ideas no longer seemed to raise the hackles of the press. The *Toronto Daily Star* reported "Miss Goldman found the women of today far advanced over those of a generation ago,"[75] and went on to claim that Goldman's ideas regarding companionate marriage had merit. "Companionate marriage," the paper declared, "would give young people a chance to find out if they were really mates." And since Goldman also advocated "easy divorce" there would be no danger of mismatched youngsters being imprisoned by the bonds of matrimony.[76] Though this is a misrepresentation of Goldman's free-love politics, it illustrates how ideas that were once radical could be assimilated into current debates and ideas. In fact, Goldman was reported as being behind almost every cultural shift of the era. In an article entitled "If you Like Jazz you're Classed as Anarchist," the *Toronto Star Weekly* recorded Goldman as characterizing jazz as "anarchistic, the very spirit of youth, essentially a revolt against outworn traditions and restrictions."[77] This analysis reduced anarchism to a playful pose and ignored Goldman's more profound critiques of economic and social relations.

But the sexual liberalism of the twenties, commented on by contemporaries and scholars alike, was an empty victory for the anarchists. People were more than happy to accept what seemed to the anarchists as dangerously watered down compromises. If all jazz fans were anarchists, then what exactly did being an anarchist mean beyond enjoying mild forms of social rebellion and cultural novelty? And if "flappers" are the penultimate expression of liberated womanhood what need was there for further critiques of the gender system? Anarchism, as presented in the Canadian press' interpretation of Goldman's ideas, is a willful, "youthful" butting against the strictures of tradition for the purposes of amusement. The political in the anarchist critiques of sexuality and gender relations had been utterly evacuated from the understanding of what Goldman, Lloyd, Tucker, and Berkman were trying to accomplish. In the twenties, radical critiques were watered down by banalities, and the politics articulated by the anarchist sex radicals were softened and sold. "Ideas that had been avant-garde in the pre-war years," writes historian Leslie Fishbein, "became the clichés of the post-war years."[78]

The anarchists were frustrated by the shallowness of what passed as sexual emancipation. Berkman wrote to Goldman about his mystification regarding the lifestyle associated with the "so called 'modern girl,' especially the American girl:"

> They have become "emancipated" from the old inhibitions, but they have not replaced them by any really earnest idea or deeper feeling. It is just a kind of superficial sexuality without rhyme or reason. More sensuality than anything else. At the bottom of it is an inner emptiness, sexual and otherwise…and… men…look upon these types of girls very lightly, even scornfully, except that they want to use them… they cannot really grow into a deeper affection for them, for there is a hidden lack of respect and understanding. They consider them light and just good enough to spend a little time with.[79]

Berkman viewed the emancipation of "the modern girl" as a sham, and the actions of modern men as reprehensible. What was missing was a political context with which to understand and guide sexual liberation. Goldman shared Berkman's disillusionment. As she told the *Toronto Daily Star*, "People refuse to see…that sex is the greatest force and the most beautiful thing in the world if its powers are rightly harnessed and directed. Where love is missing everything is missing."[80] By love, Goldman did not mean mere romantic longing. She was referring to the principles of free love and advocating relationships that were equitable, liberating, and empowering. In contrast, the freedoms enjoyed by the flapper did not challenge the power relations between men and women. The feminist basis of anarchist sexual politics was the critical missing element.

Viewed from the perspective of the politics of homosexuality, Berkman and Goldman's attack on the too easy thrills of the twenties has considerable merit. As Linda Gordon has pointed out "the sexual revolution" of the post-war period "was not a general loosening of sexual taboos but only of those on nonmarital heterosexual activity."[81] In fact, historian Gary Kinsman suggests that the sexual revolution of the twenties was a seedbed of homophobia.[82] As the rules governing heterosexual dating were liberalized, homosexuality was increasingly a focus of surveillance. Advice literature, for example, "singled out 'homosexuality' as a distinct category of sexual deviance…a pathological symptom of an individual's failure to achieve a normal state of heterosexuality."[83] This dialectic of liberalization and surveillance may help account for the popularity of the pansy performance. As George Chauncey documented, the twenties witnessed a "pansy craze"—a fascination with male homosexuality as represented by the comical, extremely fey figure of the pansy.[84] The pansy performer may have been widely celebrated, but he garnered little respect. The performance essentially involved a sophisticated audience of heterosexual couples on dates, laughing at the figure of a ridiculously over-the-top gay male figure. In staging this display of erotic and gender deviance, the pansy was illustrating the boundaries of proper conduct for his audience.[85]

Though there were more venues where gay men and lesbians could pursue their erotic and emotional needs, the expansion of that social freedom was paralleled by a contraction of the politics of homosexuality. The increase in the number of identifiable gay and lesbian venues may actually have released some of the pressure for sexual liberation that had fueled the anarchist critiques of anti-sodomy laws and other oppressive measures. Historian James Steakley, speaking of Germany, argued that the relative decline in homosexual politics in the twenties can be explained, at least in part, by the fact that "it was far easier to luxuriate in the concrete utopia of the urban subculture than to struggle for an emancipation, which was apparently only formal and legalistic."[86] There were similar developments in the United States. Prohibition forced clubs and bars into the criminal netherworld, thereby creating new opportunities for marginalized groups to gather. Speakeasies, much more so than public taverns, tolerated and even encouraged a gay and lesbian clientele.

But the increase in gay and lesbian venues had limited immediate impact on social and cultural values. Greenwich Village, for example, developed a reputation as a gay-friendly enclave, but according to Lillian Faderman the reality was less robust than the reputation. She argues that though the "Villagers prided themselves on being 'bohemian,'" their sex radicalism—dominated by heterosexual men—was tepid and uneven. "Although lesbianism was allowed to exist more openly there than it could have in most places in the United States," Faderman argues, "even in Greenwich Village sexual love between women was treated with ambivalence."[87] Though gay men and lesbians found a place in the Village, without a clearly articulated political critique of sexual norms it was difficult to challenge the "ambivalence" that permeated even the most liberal of social worlds.

There were some political activists who fought for the rights of gay men and lesbians in the inter-war decades, but they possessed neither the resources nor the political sophistication of the pre-war anarchist sex radicals. In 1925, the US's first gay rights organization, the Society for Human Rights, was established in Chicago by a small group of activists. Henry Gerber, the SHR's leader, modeled the organization on Hirschfeld's Scientific-Humanitarian Committee. Although radical in its sexual politics, the SHR was a thoroughly law-abiding organization. Seeking to minimize controversy, the SHR pledged that it stood "for law and order; it is in harmony with any and all general laws insofar as they protect the rights of others, and does in no manner recommend any acts in violation of present laws nor advocate any matter inimical to the public welfare."[88] Unfortunately, this pledge of allegiance did little to safeguard the group's members. The SHR managed to put out two issues of its journal, *Friendship and Freedom*, before reporters for the *Chicago Examiner* exposed its activities, leading to the arrest of most of the membership. Henry Gerber was also fired from his job at the Post Office. The SHR's members, isolated and without recourse, were unable to reconstitute the organization. Not until the post-World War II homophile movement would organizations similar to the SHR be established.

Despite the changing political and social climate of the twenties and the decades that followed, the ideas and influence of the pre-war anarchist sex radicals continued to be felt. Anarchists and those influenced by the pre-war anarchists had a presence in some of the gay-friendly bohemian clubs of the post-war era. In the early 1920s, for example, Kenneth Rexroth worked at The Green Mask, a Chicago club run by June Wiener, a "friend of Emma Goldman" who "came from an old Jewish Anarchist family." Wiener's girlfriend, Beryl Bolton, also worked at the club. Rexroth's own political history was shot through with anarchist influence; his grandfather considered himself an anarchist, and in his youth, Rexroth's parent's took him to cafés like Polly's Restaurant, which was frequented by members of Emma Goldman's circle. Rexroth was steeped in the history and mythology of the movement. His father, for example, made sure that the young Rexroth knew about Alexander Berkman's fourteen-year prison ordeal.[89]

The atmosphere of The Green Mask combined literary and political modernism with sexual and gender liberalism. The club hosted poetry readings and lectures by Sherwood Anderson and the lawyer Clarence Darrow and housed, in Rexroth's words, "a small permanent family of oddities," including "a hermaphrodite violinist"; "[the] great female impersonators Bert Savoy, Julian Eltinge…[and] Carole Normand, 'The Creole Fashion Plate,' known to her friends as 'The Queer Old Chafing Dish'"; "[a] little Mexican fairy known as Theda Bara, and her knife-toting pal, who weighed about four hundred pounds, the Slim Princess"; as well as "a very light, freckled-faced Negro… who claimed to be the illegitimate son of a British admiral and a Haitian princess." This faux aristocrat "had dyed red hair, ultraconservative clothes in the height of fashion, and wore an egg-shaped eyeglass without ribbon or rim."[90] The mix of high and low culture and the truly wild social scene fostered by the club was, at least in part, a product of the political background of the club's owner.

Rexroth also visited a more sober club—in all senses of the word—called the Gray Cottage, located next door to a bookshop run by a Dutch man who had been one of the leaders of the Rotterdam Commune, the Gray Cottage was owned by Ruth Norlander and Eve Adams, who "wore men's clothes and for years traveled about the country selling *Mother Earth, The Masses*, and other radical literary magazines." *Mother Earth* had been suppressed during World War I, but the magazine's message continued to resonate. According to Rexroth, both women "were convinced libertarians and part of the movement." Their club "was a great deal more intellectual and radical than the Green Mask." Though the Gray Cottage was "the most bohemian of the bohemian tearooms of the Chicago North Side," it attracted a less spectacular crowd than the Green Mask. Norlander and Adam's cafe "attracted few customers from show business…and none of the tough homosexuals who came into the Green Mask." The Gray Cottage's customers "were cast more upon the pattern of Edward Carpenter…than lady prizefighters and drag queens and cheap burlesque girls."[91] At the Gray Cottage, the ideology of libertarian socialism was foregrounded, while at the Green Mask anarchism expressed itself in the creation of a social space free from society's norms and rules.

It is not surprising that the Green Mask and the Gray Cottage were located in Chicago, considering Rexroth's claims that among the writers, artists, and activists he associated with in Chicago at the time, "Most people called themselves anarchists."[92] The city was home to the Free Society group, which according to anarchist historian Sam Dolgoff was "the most active anarchist propaganda group in the country."[93] Rexroth frequented the Dill Pickle, a club located near "Bughouse Square, where every variety of radical sect…was preached from a row of soapboxes every night in the week when it wasn't storming." The "political radicals among [the Bughouse Square speakers] hung out at the Dill Pickle and constituted the inner core of club membership."[94] There is no direct evidence that the founders of the Society for Human Rights were connected to anarchist circles but the general mood of Chicago's gay scene was shot through with anarchist ideas and personalities.

The sexual politics of the pre-war anarchists was a persistent influence in the social worlds Rexroth moved in. The Dill Pickle and Bughouse Square were places where sex was openly discussed, though more often than not in a ribald tone. One of the Dill Pickle's leading characters, for example, "had an amazing talent for getting really important scholars to talk for him—under a lewd title, such as "Should the Brownian Movement Best Be Approached from the Rear?"[95] Browning was a slang term for anal sex. Rexroth also knew "a little man with tousled yellow curls" who "had been a famous war resister but by the time I knew him he had only one subject on the soapbox...the pleasures of oral sex, and its answers to the Problems of Malthus and Marx."[96] Despite their creative engagement with Marx, the denizens of the Dill Pickle and the Bug Club were not representative of the local CP-dominated socialist scene. According to Rexroth, the "Anarchist and IWW freelance soapboxers" he enjoyed listening to were "completely disillusioned with the organized radical movement."[97]

Chicago was also the home of Goldman's old lover and tour manager, Ben Reitman. Like Rexroth, Reitman was a member of the Dill Pickle and a figure in Chicago's demimonde. Though no longer an anarchist, Reitman remained interested in the subject of sexuality and radical politics and was a frequent visitor to anarchist meetings. In 1931, he reprised his old role, helping to sell anarchist literature at a gathering held in honor of Kropotkin. Reitman devoted a considerable amount of time to working with those on the margins of society and, according to Dolgoff, had a well-deserved reputation as "a distinguished physician, specializing in venereal and allied diseases." In addition to his medical practice, Reitman was the director of the Chicago School for Social Pathology. Dolgoff was impressed with the fact that Reitman "was deeply concerned with the plight of the 'misfits,' the prostitutes, the homeless, the hobos, the tramps, the derelicts, the 'dregs of society,' who, when I knew him, crowded the flop houses and dingy saloons of the skidrow on West Madison Street."[98]

Reitman showed a continuing fascination with the life of gay men and lesbians. In 1937, he helped "Box Car Bertha" write *Sister of the Road*, a book that told the story of Bertha's "fifteen years of wandering, a hobo, traveling from one end of the country to the other."[99] At the end of Bertha's narrative Reitman added an appendix intended to answer the question "what makes sisters of the road?" Among the reasons Reitman gave are "sex irregularities." He believed, he told Goldman in a letter, that "homosexual women...make up a large proportion of the hitch-hiking, intellectual women of the day."[100] These same women, according to Reitman, had an affinity for radical politics. The sisters of the road included "anarchist communists of the Emma Goldman, Alexander Berkman, Peter Kropotkin types," as well as "Individualist anarchists of the Max Stierner [sic], Tucker, and Frederick Nietzsche types."[101] His findings should be taken with a grain of salt, as Reitman's work tells us far more about Chicago's bohemian world of sexual and radical politics than about the life of female hoboes in the 1920s and 1930s. Reitman extrapolated from the world he knew, one where homosexuality and anarchism existed in overlapping social circles, and placed that experience on the larger world.

Reitman's daughter, Jan Gay, was also interested in the ethical, social and cultural place of homosexuality. She believed that science was the golden road to sexual freedom, and she had a "commitment to science as a significant avenue to social reform."[102] Just as Goldman and Lloyd had in their day, Gay sought out and worked with the European sexologists she admired—in particular the German sexologist Magnus Hirschfeld. Beginning in the 1920s, Gay interviewed hundreds of lesbians in Europe and America using techniques and strategies she learned from Hirschfeld. Her mentor clearly thought highly of her, for Reitman wrote Goldman that his daughter was "writing a book with Prof. Magnus Hirschfeld, [entitled] "Women without Men."[103] Unfortunately, it appears the book was never completed.

When she returned to the United States, Gay continued her studies in sexology. In the mid-1930s, Gay played a key role in founding the Committee for the Study of Sex Variants, an American organization led by Robert Latou Dickinson. Eventually Gay's findings were incorporated into George W. Henry's *Sex Variants: A Study of Homosexual Patterns*, published in 1941. But the publication of *Sex Variants* was not the triumph for Gay that it should have been. Apart from a few minor acknowledgements, Henry made no mention of Gay's work. Dejected and feeling betrayed, Gay stopped her research on homosexuality.[104]

Gay's work on homosexuality was greatly influenced by the pre-war anarchists. She and her father were in contact well into her adulthood, and through him, Gay was connected to the legacy of anarchist sex radicalism of which he was a part. Gay was likely brought into contact with Hirschfeld, the greatest influence in her intellectual development, through the efforts of the pre-war anarchist sex radicals. In the same year that Reitman wrote Goldman about his daughter, Goldman received a letter from Gay to which she responded warmly. "I was interested and delighted," Goldman writes Gay, "to hear that you had met my good friend, Dr. Magnus Hirschfeld, and glad to see that you are about to do a book with him. I daresay it will prove to be of value."[105] The fact that Gay kept both her father and Goldman abreast of her work with Hirschfeld reflects the fact that she understood that her relationship with Hirschfeld owed something to the relationship he had with her father and her father's colleagues.

Gay was not the only lesbian intellectual of her era whose life and work was shaped by the political legacy of libertarian socialism. Anarchism also played a critical role in the life of poet, Elsa Gidlow. Born in 1898, Gidlow spent a considerable part of her life in a struggle to "get a room of my own" and "find my kind of people."[106] In 1923, she published *On a Gray Thread*, the first volume of explicitly lesbian poetry in North America. In 1926, Gidlow moved to the San Francisco Bay Area where she lived until her death in 1986. During her time in the Bay Area, Gidlow was an active member of the lesbian community and of the region's diverse artistic and political worlds. Anarchism was a subtle current within the overlapping social milieus that Gidlow moved. She counted among her friends, Kenneth Rexroth—who himself had moved to the Bay Area—with whom she formed a "friendship based on respect for one another's poetry, political orientation, and sexual orientation."[107] The libertarian values of the worlds of radical art, anarchism, and the sexual culture of the Bay Area were interwoven. Sometimes this could be expressed in silly, but telling ways. For example, the Bay Area poet Jack Spicer and his lover John Ryan once referred to themselves as the "Interplanetary Services of the Martian Anarchy."[108] The name of this fabulous society of two, plays on the freedom or "anarchy" that the Bay Area's social and artistic world afforded Spicer, Ryan, Gidlow, and Rexroth.

Gidlow's engagement with anarchism came, ironically, in the immediate aftermath of WWI and the Russian Revolution. As thousands were streaming out of the movement—either because they were drawn to communism or their dreams of social revolution were shattered—Gidlow embraced the ideals of the pre-war anarchists. The war seemed to be particularly troubling for Gidlow and her friends: "Our fledgling adult consciousness," she wrote, "was lit for the start by war's murderous phosphorescence. Every value we had absorbed became suspect." The revolution in Russia did not seduce Gidlow; while many saw Lenin as a harbinger of heaven on earth, Gidlow looked askance at those who argued that "a new Russian dictatorship must be countenanced and the 'liquidation' (a disinfected new term) of individuals justified." Troubled, Gidlow looked for answers—and found them—in the intellectual tradition of libertarian socialism. "Emma Goldman," she would later recall, "had dawned on my horizon." In the very year that the Buford set sail, Gidlow told her friends, "I believe I am an anarchist."[109]

While her embrace of Goldman's legacy was heartfelt, Gidlow's anarchism was significantly different from that of the pre-war movement. Though she believed that "society must be radically transformed, not for any one group or class, but for all of us," in practice, Gidlow's anarchism reflected her desire for personal liberation.[110] Her commitment to anarchism was rooted in her personal experience, not in an engagement with the kinds of issues—gradual reform versus revolution, the merits of various methods of propaganda, and individual versus collective ownership of the means of production—that exercised her predecessors. In her memoirs she admitted, "neither I nor my companions were ready to take to the streets, soap boxes, or brave jail." Gidlow and her friends "could not see salvation in any brand of politics." A forlorn crew adrift in a sea, their "abiding faith was in art, in the fruits of the spirit, in personal integrity and responsibility to one another."[111] This was an inward-looking anarchism, one that served as a guide for interpersonal relationships, not revolutionary social change. To be sure, Goldman and the pre-war anarchists put great stress on the politics of personal life, but they did so in the context of a mass movement with broad economic and social goals. But by the time Gidlow encountered anarchism, the movement—with the exception of a few small, active groups—was greatly reduced. Gidlow's libertarianism was a powerful, yet attenuated variant, of its pre-war mother.

Gidlow's profession of anarchism was intimately related to her sense of personal rebellion. In 1928, she mused in the pages of her journal on the relationship between her politics, her place in society, and her personality:

> Another ghost of memory: I wonder what has become of that good little hunchback, Frank Genest, who once called me—poor little shy, silent me at eighteen!—an "enemy of society!" I hardly knew what "society" was: hardly knew it existed. Perhaps that was enough to make me its enemy in his eyes. My natural "anarchism" was perhaps evident. I don't think I ever had any particular feeling of enmity towards society, even when I found out what it was. Simply, I always knew I was alone; knew I always should be; took it for granted in fact; knew that I must act out of my own need and vision, ignoring authority. Does that make me an anarchist?[112]

It would be hard to imagine Berkman or Tucker writing about anarchism in the way that Gidlow does here. Eschewing anarchist critiques of society, Gidlow adopts the pose of the outsider, someone who "always knew I was alone; knew I always should be." She makes no reference to economic injustice, strategies for propaganda either by word or deed, or the need to challenge state power. In fact, Gidlow exhibits some discomfort with identifying herself as an anarchist. Her use of quotation marks around the word anarchism signals a certain distance, indicating to the reader that she does not mean anarchism, an ideology of fundamental social and political change, but "anarchism," the natural expression of a youthful, rebellious spirit. Gidlow's anarchism was quite different than the one that flourished in the context a broad, international and active movement in the decades prior to the First World War.

Gidlow's anarchism, her gender and sexual politics, and her identity as a poet reinforced each other. As a lesbian and an artist, she felt doubly alienated from the society in which she lived. Gidlow turned to the legacy of Goldman to create new forms of expression with which to understand and appreciate herself as a woman whose emotional and sexual life was built around her relationships with other women. Her willingness to defy convention was, in part, a product of her understanding the need for individuals to be free to construct their own rules of personal and social conduct. This was magnified by her self-image as an artist, an individual who was able to see that "drabness, tedium, injustices were not the whole of life."[113] For Gidlow, both artists and lesbians were in conflict with the world in which they lived. They were anarchists by default. She felt that "perhaps the artist, the lesbian artist in particular, always will have to survive within the interstices of the chicaneries and despotism of any power structure."[114] The norms and rules of that society were, she believed, explicitly hostile to her desires and work. Anarchism challenged power structures and empowered individuals. It was, in short, particularly suited to Gidlow's intertwined identity as a radical, a poet, a lesbian, and a feminist.

Gidlow understood anarchism as a doctrine of individual empowerment, not as the ideological product of a mass movement. This is the critical difference between hers and Emma Goldman's anarchism. The activists of the pre-war movement addressed questions of sexuality in the course of pursuing broad social change. Gidlow was interested in anarchism because it allowed her to explore and expand the boundaries of her life. This take on anarchism was shared by many who gravitated to it in the post-World War I decades. These men and women, writes Sam Dolgoff, "did not conceive anarchism as an organized social revolutionary movement with a mass base and a definite ideology, but as a bohemian 'lifestyle.'" Dolgoff was disturbed by this development that he believed, "meant regression to a form of organization not much above local groups and an intimate circle of friends."[115] But what Dolgoff lamented was precisely what Gidlow and others sought—a refuge from what they perceived to be a hostile, unpalatable world. The work of Goldman, Berkman, Tucker, and other anarchist sex radicals served as a valuable resource for people who—in the spirit, if not in the form of their anarchist predecessors—continued to insist on the right of all women and men to live their life according to their own lights.

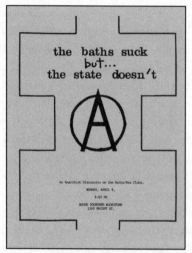

the baths suck
but...
the state doesn't

An Anarchist Discussion on the Baths/Sex Clubs.
MONDAY, APRIL 9,
8:00 PM
BOUND TOGETHER BOOKSTORE
1369 HAIGHT ST.

CONCLUSION:

ANARCHISM, STONEWALL, AND THE TRANSFORMATION OF THE POLITICS OF HOMOSEXUALITY

IN THE LAST THIRD of the twentieth century anarchism, was rediscovered by a new generation of activists, bohemians, and alienated youth, and was most visible on college campuses. Near the end of 1960s, a friend of George Woodcock, a leading figure of the anarchist revival, told him that his students had seemingly all become anarchists. When the professor asked the 160 students in his Contemporary Ideologies class to identify themselves "ninety of them chose anarchism in preference to democratic socialism (which came in next with twenty-three votes), liberalism, Communism, and conservatism." Of course, this was a biased group, they were in a class taught by Woodcock's friend, someone who we can assume was fairly open to discussions of anarchism. Woodcock notes that the student's enthusiasm was shared by many of their teachers. "Since 1960 more serious and dispassionate studies of anarchism have appeared than during the previous sixty years of the century." [1] Goldman, especially, has been the subject of this wave of scholarly interest. There have been a number of Goldman biographies published since 1960, and The Emma Goldman Papers Project has undertaken the systematic collection of texts documenting her life and work.

There are, however, important differences between anarchism at the turn of the century and the anarchism of the late-twentieth century. "The anarchists of the 1960s," Woodcock argues, "were not the historic anarchist movement resurrected; they were something quite different, a new manifestation of the idea."[2] At the turn of the century, anarchists could identify themselves with a worldwide, mass movement. Tucker, Lloyd, Goldman, Berkman, Abbott, and their comrades believed in, and struggled for, a social revolution that would transform every aspect of life. Today's anarchists, like Rexroth, Gidlow, and the denizens of the Green Mask, were more likely to be relatively isolated individuals or members of small groups. For the most part, today's anarchists have given up on the idea that a revolution—in the traditional sense of the word—is possible, much less that it is imminent. Contemporary anarchists have not reconstituted the level of organization, scale, and mission that the pre-World War I anarchists had. Instead, many focus on building a counter-culture within the body of the present social order.

The political culture of the two periods—the context in which the respective anarchist movements operate—is also quite different. At the turn of the twentieth century, the Left was a vital and visible force within American society. Socialists governed cities, ran candidates, and shaped public discourse to a far greater degree than in today's America. The anarchists were not, of course, thrilled with the idea of elected socialist representatives, but they benefited from the fact that radical alternatives were taken seriously. During the years when Tucker, Lloyd, Goldman, and Berkman were active, the Left constituted a significant force in American political culture. Hundreds of thousands of Americans subscribed to socialist publications, voted for socialist candidates, claimed membership in socialist organizations—including anarchist groups—and socialism was a powerful force in organized labor. Although the Left enjoyed a burst of life in the late 1960s and early 1970s, it has not regained the place it had in American society at the turn of the century. The anti-Vietnam War and Civil Rights movements of the last third of the century were influenced by Left activists, but unlike the earlier period of political activism, they did not take the form of a mass movement rooted in the American working class.

Contemporary anarchism, like its predecessor, is not monolithic; it is fraught with ideological and stylistic differences. Many of today's anarchists tend to stress the spontaneous, the eclectic, the temporary, and the irrational. Hakim Bey, for example, has called for anarchists to fashion "a practical kind of 'mystical anarchism,' …a democratization of shamanism, intoxicated and serene."[3] Bey is best known for advocating the concept of the Temporary Autonomous Zone (TAZ), a space within which spontaneous expressions of desire and play can take place. The TAZ is not meant to be a beachhead from which revolutionary plans can be formulated and enacted. Bey compares TAZs to the libratory power of an insurrectionary moment, and argues that the revolution is almost always a call to bring back hierarchy, order, and authority. To be sure, there are anarchists, Murray Bookchin being the most notable example, who vigorously oppose Bey's vision of anarchism.

Murray Bookchin identified himself with "an idealistic, often theoretically coherent Left that militantly emphasized its internationalism, its rationality in its treatment of reality, its democratic spirit, and its vigorous revolutionary aspirations."[4] Note, however, that Bookchin spoke of this Left in the past tense; the title of the essay in which he discussed his ideological beliefs is entitled "The Left That Was: A Personal Reflection." Bookchin is refers to the culture of the Left that flourished at the turn of the century before the Russian Revolution—a Left that no longer really exists, and in his view, is in danger of degenerating into mere petulant egotism.

Bookchin's critique generated an intense debate between, what Bob Black dubbed the "traditionalistic anarchists—leftist, workerist, organizationalist, and moralist—and an even more diverse (and an ever more numerous) contingent of anarchists who have in one way or another departed from orthodoxy, at least in Bookchin's eyes." Black attacked Bookchin as a self-appointed scold who was unable to fully divest himself of the influences of Marxism.[5] In some ways, the battle between Black and Bookchin—taken as representative of poles within anarchist thought—repeated the endemic battles between communist- and individualist anarchists. But the rupture between the camps bespeaks a deep cultural and ideological division that is unique to the present and not merely a rehashing of old arguments. I do not mean to take sides in this debate, rather I wish to point out that the culture, ideas, social basis, rhetoric, and style of anarchism that exists today is quite different than that which flourished in the United States in the decades prior to WWI. Bookchin may have been wrong in his critique of contemporary anarchism, but he was right to note that the rhetoric and goals of today's anarchists differs markedly from that of the turn-of-the-century anarchists who were largely united in their belief in the value of reason, progress, and universal applicability of social goals and concepts.

The sexual and gender politics of the turn-of-the-century anarchists is one of the reasons that they have found admirers since the late 1960s. Alix Kates Shulman, for example, found a ready audience for the discussions of Goldman's sexual politics that she began producing in the early 1970s. Shulman, who admired Goldman's defiance of "the sexual hypocrisy of Puritanism," found her political commitments to women's liberation mirrored in the libertarian ideals of the anarchists. "Anarchism by definition," she wrote, "and radical feminism as it has evolved, are both fundamentally and deeply anti-hierarchical and anti-authoritarian."[6] Shulman would go on to publish a biography of Goldman and edit a collection of Goldman's own writings which had fallen out of print.[7] Of course, Goldman's notoriety extended well beyond radical circles. Like Che Guevera, whose likeness adorns t-shirts sold in malls, Goldman's radicalism has been significantly blunted by the omnivorous appetite of the market place; she is in danger of becoming yet another radical-chic commodity.[8]

Goldman is by far the most republished turn-of-the-century anarchist, but she is not the only person whose work found new readers. Lloyd's pamphlet on Karezza, or male continence, was republished in California in 1973 and again, in French, in Montréal in 2000. This is not to say that this new audience was always aware of the ideological roots of the works they were reading. Lloyd's work proved particularly appealing to those readers who identified his work as an example of Eastern religious and philosophic traditions. The Canadian pamphlet identifies Lloyd's work as an example of "Occidental tantric" thought, and was published by Ganesha Press, the name of which refers to a Hindu god.[9]

Gay liberationists, radical feminists, and lesbian feminists (not exclusive categories by any means) were all drawn to the work of the turn-of-the-centuries' anarchist sex-radicals. The texts of the pre-WWI anarchist sex radicals found new readers among contemporary sex radicals. For example, Jonathan Ned Katz's groundbreaking collection of primary documents entitled *Gay American History*, published in 1976, included excerpts from Goldman's autobiography, Sperry's letters to Goldman, and selections from Berkman's *Prison Memoirs*. Anarchists occasionally find themselves featured in the gay press, like the 1990 inaugural issue of *The Slant*, a periodical serving Marin County in the San Francisco Bay Area, which featured a quote by Edward Carpenter, who is identified as a "gay English anarchist." [10] The gay press provides a venue for some of the early work on the sexual politics of the anarchists. For example, in 1981, Hubert Kennedy published an article on John Henry Mackay in *The Alternate*, a monthly publication which described itself as "the news magazine for today's Gay America" and which, in addition to publishing feature articles, boasted extensive personal ads.[11] And *Gayme*, a publication that, like Mackay did, defends intergenerational relations between men and youths, reprinted an excerpt from Hakim Bey's *TAZ: The Temporary Autonomous Zone, Ontological Anarchy* in 1994. The brief description of the excerpt that appears in *Gayme's* table of contents states that Bey argues that "revolution may be in disrepute...but people on the erotic and political fringe can still insurrect." [12] Bey might contest whether or not revolution is in disrepute, but for the editors of *Gayme*, the larger scope of Bey's politics are a bit beside the point. What is important is that Bey's ideas are useful to "people on the erotic and political fringe."

The rediscovery of some of the anarchists' politics by LGBT activists did not signal a renaissance of the turn-of-the-century anarchist movement. Katz's book is not an anarchist anthology; it is a gay liberation anthology. The ideas of the anarchists were attractive to gay liberationists and lesbian feminists to the extent that they reflected the libertarian sexual politics of those particular movements, but the larger political goals of the anarchists are not particularly attractive to contemporary gay and lesbian political activists. Though there were and are anarchists active in both gay liberation and lesbian feminist groups the majority of men and women active in LGBT activism do not reject American traditions of representative democracy or capitalism. For example, when, in 1989, the Stonewall Gay Democratic Club chose "Absolute Sovereignty of the Human Body" as its theme for the annual LGBT Pride Parade one could easily hear a strong echo of the language of individualist anarchism.[13] Afterall, Josiah Warren, a key figure in the development of the movement, was famed for extolling "the sovereignty of the individual," and surely Warren would approve of the Stonewall Gay Democrats championing "the right of consenting adults" and their stated desire to brandish the "banner of individual freedom."[14] But, of course, the Stonewall Gay Democrats were affiliated with the Democratic Party; they were most assuredly not anarchists no matter how much they might sound like them. The pull of the contemporary gay and lesbian movement's liberal political culture acts to tame whatever revolutionary impulse remains in the anarchist texts and ideas that still circulate in the movement.

This is not to discount the important, and as yet under-appreciated ways, that turn-of-the-century anarchists' work has shaped contemporary gay and lesbian politics and culture. Elsa Gidlow, for example, was an important figure in the post-WWII Bay Area's lesbian community, and her work was, at least in part, inspired by the ideas of the anarchists she read in her youth. Her willingness to rebel against dominant social values and her insistence on the rights of individuals to fulfill their desires and needs reflects the spirit of Goldman that so influenced her in her youth. In the pre-Stonewall era, Gidlow was a supporter of the Daughters of Bilitis, the first American lesbian rights organization. In the 1970s, she published a number of important lesbian feminist works including *Sapphic Songs* and *Ask No Man Pardon: The Philosophical Significance of Being Lesbian*. Gidlow made her home, Druid Heights, into a center of the women's community and a retreat for artists and writers. "Women," Gidlow wrote, "often came to me at Druid Heights to share their dilemmas, especially those they have as lesbians in a culture that excludes them and [that has] family patterns they cannot fit into."[15]

But here again the connections between Gidlow's politics and those of Goldman and her comrades are complicated. Though the inspiration for establishing Druid Heights had roots in Gidlow's larger political ideas, the retreat was not an anarchist center. Though Gidlow discusses the influence anarchism had on her life in her autobiography, her memoir is not an anarchist text compared to Goldman's autobiography, *Living My Life*, or Berkman's *Prison Memoirs of an Anarchist*. Anarchism was part of Gidlow's political inheritance, but as the lesbian feminist community grew, the ideas generated by its leading ideologists—Gidlow being one of them—began to displace the bohemian anarchism of her youth. Like Gidlow, though, many lesbian feminists and gay liberationists embraced a broad politics that addressed questions of economic justice, as well as social equality for homosexuals, but the modern homosexual rights movement is largely a single-issue interest group operating within the context of American liberal democracy. Today's sex radicals may know Goldman for her claim—an apocryphal one—that "It's not my revolution if I can't dance," but they are less likely to be familiar with her impassioned critiques of capitalism. The anarchists were radicals who dealt with issues of sexuality as part of their larger revolutionary goals. With few exceptions, today's gay and lesbian activists seek inclusion within the boundaries of American culture, rather than the fundamental restructuring of that culture. They may find inspiration in the spirit of freedom expressed by the anarchists but they are not revolutionaries.

The difference between the contemporary LGBT rights movement and the sexual politics of turn-of-the-century anarchist movement is most glaringly illustrated in the place of marriage in the respective movements. The anarchist homosexual politics discussed in this book were grounded in a critique of marriage. The claim that neither representatives of the state nor other regulatory agents should have any authority over the relationship or sexual choices of "sovereign individuals" was the fundamental core of anarchist sexual politics. And that claim was forged within the context of a critique of marriage. When Oscar Wilde was arrested, the anarchists rose to his defense because they had already come to understand that state regulation of relationships—whether between members of the opposite or same sex—was a problem. Anarchist politics of homosexuality grew out of a rejection of marriage.

Given this history, it is ironic that the right to marry—to enter into state and church sanctioned, legally binding unions—has recently become a leading cause for the LGBT movement. In his book, *Why Marriage?: The History Shaping Today's Debate Over Gay Equality*, historian George Chauncey writes that the debate over same-sex marriage is "fully engaged" and constitutes "a decisive moment for our generation."[16] Championed by LGBT activists and denounced by cultural conservatives, the battle over whether or not gay men and lesbians can marry is being fought in newspaper headlines, court dockets, and state initiatives. It is true that not all LGBT activists see the battle for same-sex marriage as a positive development: historian John D'Emilio, in a recently published article entitled, "The Marriage Fight is Setting Us Back," laments that, with their impulse towards "de-center[ing] and de-institutionaliz[ing] marriage," the sexual politics of gay liberation, lesbian feminist, and queer activists has been forgotten in the rush to the altar. He notes that the fight for gay marriage, which has been marked by the passage of constitutional bans of same-sex marriage, has actually "created a vast body of *new* antigay law."[17] D'Emilio's voice is, for the moment, a decisively marginalized one. The push for marriage looks to remain "fully engaged" for the foreseeable future.

It is easy to imagine that Tucker, Berkman, and Lloyd might look poorly on the quest for gay marriage. After all, those who wish to see same-sex marriage put on equal footing with opposite-sex marriage do not hesitate to make use of the tools of the state to pursue and enforce their position. It is less clear how the turn-of-the-century anarchists would view the contemporary LGBT movement. Most likely they would see it as limited; they wanted to create a whole new world, not reform and amend law and social attitudes. Goldman, for example, was critical of single-issue style homosexual politics. She despaired of what she saw as "one predominant tendency among homosexuals:…their attempt to claim every outstanding personality for their creed." This was, Goldman believed, a classic case of overcompensation in the face of oppression. "It may be psychologically conditioned in all persecuted people to cling for support to the exceptional types of every period," she wrote, but "while seemingly a benign impulse, this tendency to celebrate one's own" could lead to parochialism. "Persecution breeds sectarianism; this in return makes people limited in their scope, and very often unfair in their appraisement of others."[18] Goldman expressed the same idea somewhat less diplomatically in 1924 when she wrote Havelock Ellis that she could not tolerate the "narrowness" of many of the lesbians she met; they were a "crazy lot" whose fixation on the conditions of their own oppression to the exclusion of all other matters grated on her.[19] It is safe to say that Goldman's reaction to the Louise Michel case, and her frustration with the "narrowness" of the lesbians she met while in exile was shaped by the fact that she herself was frustrated in her political goals. Goldman's life in exile was a nearly continuous experience of frustration, which she may well have been venting on the very "victims of oppression" that she championed. But nonetheless, Goldman's critique reflects the different political goals and

ideas of the anarchist sex radicals and those activists who pursue single-issue
sexual politics.

Ultimately, it does not matter if the anarchists were the direct forbearers
of the contemporary LGBT rights movement, or whether they would align
themselves with those who support gay marriage. To truly understand and appreciate the lives and work of Tucker, Goldman, Lloyd, Abbott, Berkman, and
their comrades they need to be seen within the context of their own time. In
post-Stonewall America, it is hard to appreciate the originality and bravery of
the anarchist sex radicals. In their day, they were nearly alone in their defence of
people's right to express their erotic feelings free from the threat of arrest and
social ostracism. When Oscar Wilde was thrown in prison for "crimes against
nature," the anarchists rose to his defense, while others cheered his fall. They refused to let his voice be silenced, and they worked to ensure that others did not
share his cruel fate. In the decades that followed, anarchist sex radicals lectured,
wrote, and argued about the fundamental political and moral questions raised
by the Wilde trial. Almost alone among their contemporaries, the anarchist sex
radicals addressed the issue of homosexuality within the context of their larger
political goals: no mainstream politician did so; no major independent intellectual did so; no leading American scientific figure did so; and no social critic saw
the question of the social, ethical, and cultural place of same-sex love as worthy
of their time and energy. The work of the anarchist sex radicals was unique and
valuable. It is time we acknowledge and honor their accomplishments.

NOTES

Introduction (pages 1–12)

1   On Bentham and Fourier, see *We Are Everywhere: A Historical Sourcebook of Gay and Lesbian Politics*, eds. Mark Blasius and Shane Phelan (New York: Routledge, 1997), 15–33 and Saskia Poldervaart, "Theories About Sex and Sexuality in Utopian Socialism," in *Gay Men and Sexual History of the Political Left*, eds. Gert Hekma, Harry Oosterhuis, and James Steakley (New York: Harrington Park Press, 1995), 41–67.

2   See Barry D. Adam, *The Rise of a Gay and Lesbian Movement* (Boston: Twayne, 1987); Phyllis Grosskurth, *The Woeful Victorian: A Biography of John Addington Symonds* (New York: Holt, Rinehart & Winston, 1964); John Lauritsen and David Thorstad, *The Early Homosexual Rights Movement, 1864–1935* (New York: Times Change Press, 1974); James Steakley, *The Homosexual Emancipation Movement in Germany* (New York: Arno Press, 1975); Jeffrey Weeks and Sheila Rowbotham, *Socialism and the New Life: The Personal and Sexual Politics of Edward Carpenter and Havelock Ellis* (London: Pluto Press, 1977); Jeffrey Weeks, *Coming Out: Homosexual Politics in Britain from the Nineteenth Century to the Present* (London: Quartet Books, 1990) and *Sex, Politics, and Society: The Regulation of Society Since 1800*, second edition (London: Longman, 1989); *Lesbians in Germany, 1890s–1920s*, eds. Lillian Faderman and Brigitte Eriksson (Tallahassee, FL: Naiad Press, 1990); and Charlotte Wolff, *Magnus Hirschfeld: A Portrait of a Pioneer in Sexology* (London: Quartet Books, 1986)

3   See Peter Boag, *Same-Sex Affairs: Constructing and Controlling Homosexuality in the Pacific Northwest* (Berkeley: University of California Press, 2003); John C. Burnham, "Early References to Homosexual Communities in American Medical Writings," *Medical Aspects of Human Sexuality* 7, no. 8 (August 1973), 34, 40–41, 46–49; George Chauncey, *Gay New York: Gender, Urban Culture, and the Making of the Gay Male World, 1890–1940*

(New York: Basic Books, 1994); John D'Emilio, "Capitalism and Gay Identity," in *The Lesbian and Gay Studies Reader*, eds. Henry Abelove, Michele Aina Barale, and David M. Halperin (New York: Routledge, 1993), 467–476; John D'Emilio and Estelle B. Freedman, *Intimate Matters: A History of Sexuality in America* (New York: Harper and Row, 1988); Martin Duberman, *About Time: Exploring the Gay Past* (New York: Meridian, 1991); Lisa Duggan, *Sapphic Slashers: Sex, Violence, and American Modernity* (Durham, NC: Duke University Press, 2000); Jonathan Ned Katz, *Gay American History: Lesbians and Gay Men in the U.S.A* (New York: Thomas Crowell, 1976); Jonathan Ned Katz, *Gay/Lesbian Almanac: A New Documentary* (New York: Harper and Row, 1983); Jonathan Ned Katz, *Love Stories: Sex Between Men Before Homosexuality* (Chicago: University of Chicago Press, 2001); Steven Maynard, "Through a Hole in the Lavatory Wall: Homosexual Subcultures, Police Surveillance, and the Dialectics of Discovery in Toronto, 1890–1930," *Journal of the History of Sexuality* 5, no. 2 (October 1994), 207–242; Lawrence Murphy, "Defining the Crime Against Nature: Sodomy in the United States Appeals Courts, 1810–1940," *Journal of Homosexuality* 19, no. 1 (1990), 49–66; Michael D. Quinn, *Same-Sex Dynamics among Nineteenth Century Americans: A Mormon Example* (Urbana: University of Illinois Press, 1996); Siobhan Somerville, *Queering the Color Line: Race and the Invention of Homosexuality in American Culture* (Durham, NC: Duke University Press, 2000); and Jennifer Terry, *An American Obsession: Science, Medicine, and Homosexuality in Modern Society* (Chicago: University of Chicago Press, 1999).

4   John Lauritsen, "Edward Irenaeus Prime-Stevenson (Xavier Mayne) (1868–1942) in *Before Stonewall: Activists for Gay and Lesbian Rights in Historical Context*, ed. Vern L. Bullough (New York: Harrington Park Press, 2002), 35–40.

5   Earl Lind, *The Female Impersonators* (New York: The Medico-Legal Journal, 1922), 151.

6   Ibid., 164, 146.

7   Chauncey, *Gay New York*, 43.

8   Katz, *Gay American History*, 366. More recently, Katz seems to take Lind's claims more seriously. See Katz, *Love Stories*, 297–307. I think that Katz's more skeptical initial appraisal is correct.

9   Elizabeth Lapovsky Kennedy and Madeline Davis, *Boots of Leather, Slippers of Gold: The History of a Lesbian Community* (New York: Routledge, 1993), 186.

10   Quoted in *Yearbook for Sexual Intermediate Types* (Berlin: Scientific Humanitarian Committee, 1923).

11   Emma Goldman, "Anarchism: What it Really Stands For," in *Anarchism and Other Essays* (New York: Dover, 1969 [1917]), 62.

12   Quoted in William O. Reichert, *Partisans of Freedom: A Study in American Anarchism* (Bowling Green: Bowling Green University Press, 1976), 417.

13   Margaret Marsh, *Anarchist Women: 1870–1920* (Philadelphia: Temple University Press, 1981), 3.

14   James Joll, *The Anarchists* (Boston: Little, Brown & Company, 1964), 162.

15   Emma Goldman, letter to Hirschfeld, January 1923.

16   Richard Cleminson has published a number of essays on the politics of homosexuality in the Spanish anarchist movement in the 1930s and edited a collection of articles on homosexuality from *Revista Blanca*. See Richard Cleminson, *Anarchism, Ideology, and Same-Sex Desire* (London: Kate Sharpley Library, 1995); Richard Cleminson, "Male Inverts and Homosexuals: Sex Discourse in the Anarchist Revista Blanca" in *Gay Men*

and the Sexual History of the Political Left, 259–272; and Anarquismo y Homosexualidad: Antologia de Articulos de la Revista Blanca, Generacion Consciente, Estudios e Iniciales, ed. Richard Cleminson (Madrid: Ediciones Libertarias, 1995). Hubert Kennedy has done a great deal of work on German anarchist, John Henry Mackay, who, writing under the pseudonym Sagitta, produced a number of defenses of intergenerational same-sex love in the early-twentieth century. See Hubert Kennedy, *Anarchist of Love: The Secret Life of John Henry Mackay* (New York: Mackay Society, 1983) and *Dear Tucker: The Letters of John Henry Mackay to Benjamin R. Tucker*, ed. Hubert Kennedy (San Francisco: Peremptory Publications, 1991). See also Walter Fahnders, "Anarchism and Homosexuality in Wilhelmine Germany: Senna Hoy, Erich Mühsam, John Henry Mackay," in *Gay Men and the Sexual History of the Political Left*, 117–153. There is no monographic study of anarchism and the politics of homosexuality for Europe or any single European nation.

17 Candace Falk, *Love, Anarchy and Emma Goldman* (New York: Holt, Rinehart and Winston, 1984); Alice Wexler, *Emma Goldman: An Intimate Life* (New York: Pantheon Books, 1984); and Bonnie Haaland, *Emma Goldman: Sexuality and the Impurity of the State* (Montréal: Black Rose Books, 1993). See also Blanche Wiesen Cook, "Female Support Networks and Political Activism: Lillian Wald, Crystal Eastman, Emma Goldman." *Chrysalis* 3 (1977), 43–61. Cook and Haaland do grapple with these questions, though to different ends. Cook's study is short, while Haaland's work is longer, largely historiographical, and interpretive and it does not rely on significant archival research. Though I disagree with Haaland on a number of points, I have nonetheless found her book to be very useful. Marsh's study of anarchist women also has material on anarchism and the politics of homosexuality.

18 Quoted in Everett Marshall, *Complete Life of William McKinley and the Story of His Assassination* (Chicago: Historical Press, 1901), 76. Marshall's book contains an interview with Goldman.

Chapter 1 (pages 13–41)

1 Ann Uhry Abrams, "The Ferrer Center: New York's Unique Meeting of Anarchism and the Arts," *New York History*, July 1978, 311. Abrams does not discuss Durant's lectures at any length.

2 Will Durant and Ariel Durant, *A Dual Autobiography* (New York: Simon and Schuster, 1977), 38.

3 Will Durant, *Transition: A Sentimental Story of One Mind and One Era*, (Garden City: Garden City Publishing, 1927), 168.

4 Will and Ariel Durant, *A Dual Autobiography*, 39.

5 The only clearly erotic relationship that Durant speaks of in his biography is his love for and marriage to a young Ferrer Center student named Ida Kaufman. Kaufman, who Durant affectionately called "Puck," a name given her by schoolmates, followed Durant to Columbia after he left the Ferrer Center for the halls of academia. Kaufman changed her name to Ariel Durant and co-authored many of Will Durant's historical texts.

6 Katz, *Gay and Lesbian Almanac*, 16.

7 Durant, *Transition*, 167.

8 Ibid.

9 Emma Goldman quoted in S. D., "Farewell," *Free Society*, 13 August, 1899, 2. This article provides excerpts of Goldman's speeches.

10   Dr. Georg Merzbach, "We Have Won a Great Battle," in Katz, *Gay American History*, 381–382.

11   Emma Goldman quoted in S. D., "Farewell," *Free Society*, 13 August 1899, 2.

12   Marsh, *Anarchist Women*, 69–70.

13   Richard Sonn, *Anarchism* (New York: Twayne, 1992), 46.

14   Peter Kropotkin, "Anarchism," in *Kropotkin's Revolutionary Pamphlets*, ed. Roger Baldwin (New York: Benjamin Blom, 1968), 284–285.

15   Seymour Martin Lipset and Gary Marks, *Why Socialism Failed in the United States: It Didn't Happen Here* (New York: W. W. Norton, 2000), 22.

16   Ibid., 23.

17   J. F. Finn, "AF of L Leaders and the Question of Politics in the Early 1890s," *American Studies*, 7:3, 243. See also Frank H. Brooks, "Ideology, Strategy and Organization," 59.

18   Margaret Marsh, *Anarchist Women*, 90.

19   Ibid., 77.

20   Hal D. Sears, *The Sex Radicals: Free Love in High Victorian America* (Lawrence, Kansas: The Regents Press of Kansas, 1977), 22.

21   "Rapports du Congrès Antiparlémentaire International de 1900" in *Les Temps Nouveaux* Supplément Littéraire (November 1900), n.p. Translations are my own.

22   Sonn, *Anarchism*, 11.

23   Marsh, *Anarchist Women*, 10.

24   Harvey Klehr and John Earl Haynes, *The American Communist Movement: Storming Heaven Itself* (New York: Twayne Publishers, 1992), 7.

25   Daniel Pick, *Faces of Degeneration: A European Disorder, c. 1848–1918* (New York: Cambridge University Press, 1989), 131. Pick's work focuses on Europe, but similar ideas were common on both sides of the Atlantic.

26   Paul Avrich, *The Haymarket Tragedy* (Princeton: Princeton University Press, 1984), 401. It should also be mentioned that the Haymarket Tragedy inspired many prominent individuals to join the anarchist ranks, Emma Goldman, Voltairine de Cleyre, and Ricardo Flores Magón, among them.

27   Theodore Roosevelt, "First Annual Address," in *The State of the Union Messages of the Presidents, 1790–1966*, volume 2, 1861–1904, ed. Fred L. Israel (New York: Chelsea House, 1966), 2016, 2017, 2024.

28   Marsh, 8.

29   Quoted in Richard Drinnon, *Rebel in Paradise: A Biography of Emma Goldman* (Boston: Beacon Press, 1961), 323.

30   Emma Goldman, "En Route," *Mother Earth*, December 1908, 353.

31   Hutchins Hapgood, *A Victorian in the Modern World* (New York: Harcourt, Brace, and Company, 1939), 202.

32   Floyd Dell, *Woman as World Builders: Studies in Modern Feminism* (Chicago: Forbes and Company, 1913), 58.

33   Floyd Dell, *Intellectual Vagabondage; An Apology for the Intelligentsia* (New York: George H. Doran, 1926), 158–159.

34   David Kennedy, *Birth Control in America: The Career of Margaret Sanger* (New Haven: Yale University Press, 1970), 12–13. Kennedy's comment is true in terms of the English-language anarchists examined in this study. His remarks are less apt when describing the non-English language movement and foreign movements.

35   Isabel Meredith, *A Girl Among the Anarchists*, Introduction by Jennifer Shaddock (Lincoln, Neb.: University of Nebraska Press, 1992), 18.

36   Ibid., 56.

37   Emma Goldman to Ben L. Reitman, 28 August 1912, *Emma Goldman Papers: A Microfilm Edition*. 20,0000 documents in 69 Reels. Candace Falk, Ronald J. Zboray, et al., eds. (Alexandria: Chadwyck-Healey, Inc., 1991), reel 6.

38   Mabel Dodge Luhan, *Movers and Shakers* (Albuquerque: University of New Mexico Press, 1985 [1936]), 59.

39   Hapgood, *A Victorian in the Modern World*, 201.

40   Quoted in Barbara Strachey, *Remarkable Relations: The Story of the Pearsall Smith Family* (London: Victor Gollancz, 1981), 207.

41   See Angus McLaren, "Sex and Socialism: The Opposition of the French Left to Birth Control in the Nineteenth Century," *Journal of the History of Ideas*, July–September 1976, 485; and David Bergman, *Gaiety Transfigured: Gay Self-Representation in American Literature* (Madison: University of Wisconsin Press, 1991), 143.

42   Frederic Trautmann, *The Voice of Terror: A Biography of Johann Most* (Westport, Conn.: Greenwood Press, 1980), 92. Despite being an important and colorful figure in American anarchism, Most has not received the level of historical attention that one would expect.

43   Will Durant, "An Afternoon With Kropotkin." Unpublished manuscript, Joseph Ishill Papers.

44   Hubert Kennedy, "Johann Baptist von Schweitzer: The Queer Marx Loved to Hate," in *Gay Men and the Sexual History of the Political Left*, 90.

45   Harry Kelly, "Anarchism: A Plea for the Impersonal," *Mother Earth*, February 1908, 559.

46   See *Anarchy!: An Anthology of Emma Goldman's Mother Earth*, for a sample of the kinds of essays that appeared regularly in Goldman's journal.

47   Emma Goldman to F. Heiner, 1–8 June 1934, *Emma Goldman Papers*, reel 31.

48   Emma Goldman, *Living My Life*, 555.

49   On Parker, see the introductory notes to the article in *Anarchy: An Anthology of Emma Goldman's Mother Earth*, ed. Peter Glassgold, (Washington, D.C.: Counterpoint, 2001), 124.

50   R.A.P., "Feminism in America," *Mother Earth*, February 1915, 392–394.

51   Mari Jo Buhle, *Women and American Socialism, 1870–1920* (Urbana: University of Illinois Press, 1981), 249.

52   L. Glen Seretan, "Daniel DeLeon and the Woman Question," in *Flawed Liberation: Socialism and Feminism*, ed. Sally M. Miller (Westport: Greenwood Press, 1981), 6.

53   Nick Salvatore, *Eugene V. Debs: Citizen and Socialist* (Urbana: University of Chicago Press, 1982), 229.

54   Emma Goldman, "En Route," *Mother Earth*, December 1908, 353.

55   Benjamin R. Tucker, *State Socialism and Anarchism*, ed. James J. Martin (Colorado Springs: R. Myles, 1972), 21–22.

56   loc. cit.

57   loc. cit.

58   Laurence Veysey, *The Communal Experience: Anarchist and Mystical Countercultures in America* (New York: Harper and Row, 1973), 430.

59   C. L. James, "Sex Radicalism," *The Demonstrator*, 5 April 1905, 3.

60   William Thurston Brown, *The Evolution of Sexual Morality* (Portland: The Modern School, n.d.), 11.

61   James S. Denson, "Sexual and Economic Reform—A Question of Precedence," *Free Society*, 24 April 1898. n.p.

62   Ego, "Relation of the Sexes," *The Alarm*, 24 November 1888. n.p.

63   Quoted in Jesse F. Battan, "'The Word Made Flesh': Language, Authority and Sexual Desire in Late-Nineteenth Century America," in *American Sexual Politics: Sex Gender, and Race Since the Civil War*, eds. John Fout and Maura Shaw Tantillo (Chicago: Chicago University Press, 1993), 113.

64   John William Lloyd, *Psalms of the Race Root* (n.p., n.d.), 1–4.

65   loc. cit.

66   Michael Monahan, *The Papyrus: A Magazine of Individuality*, March 1905, 15.

67   Chauncey, *Gay New York*, 33.

68   Quoted in Howard P. Chudacoff, *The Age of the Bachelor: Creating an American Subculture* (Princeton, N.J.: Princeton University Press, 1999), 183.

69   Marilyn Yalom, *A History of the Wife* (New York: Harper Collins, 2001), 286.

70   Glenda Riley, *Divorce: An American Tradition* (New York: Oxford, 1991), 115.

71   Emma Goldman, "Marriage and Love," in *Anarchism and Other Essays*, 228.

72   Quoted in Paul Avrich, *An American Anarchist: The Life of Voltairine de Cleyre* (Princeton, N.J.: Princeton University Press, 1978), 160.

73   Voltairine de Cleyre, "Sex Slavery," in *Women Without Superstition: "No Gods—No Masters," The Collected Writings of Women Freethinkers of the Nineteenth and Twentieth Centuries*, ed. Annie Laurie Gaylor (Madison: Freedom From Religion Foundation, 1997), 363.

74   John William Lloyd, *The Free Comrade*, April 1911, 117.

75   Quoted in S. D., "Farewell," *Free Society*, 13 August 1899, 2.

76   Marsh, *Anarchist Women*, 91.

77   Will Durant and Ariel Durant, *A Dual Autobiography*, 46.

78   Victoria Woodhull, "The Principles of Social Freedom," in *The Victoria Woodhull Reader*, ed. by Madeline B. Stern (Weston, Mass.: M& S Press, 1974), 23–24.

79   In fact, with few exceptions, the non-libertarian left did not deal with the subject of homosexuality until the 1970s, when they were forced to confront the new sexual politics of the post-Stonewall period. The Communist Party and many of the various Trotskyite and Maoist sects failed to articulate a defense of same-sex relations. Well into the 1970s, the CP, Revolutionary Communist Party, and other Marxist-Leninist groups were openly hostile to gay men and women. See David Thorstad, "Homosexuality and the American Left: The Impact of Stonewall," in *Gay Men and the Sexual History of the Political Left*, 319–349.

80   James Steakley, "Iconography of a Scandal: Political Cartoons and the Eulenburg Affair in Wilhelmin Germany," in *Hidden from History: Reclaiming the Gay and Lesbian Past*, eds. Martin Duberman, Martha Vicinus, and George Chauncey (New York: New American Library, 1989), 223.

81   Ibid., 239.

82   "A German Muckraker," Wilshire's, January 1908, 11.

83   "Observations and Comments," *Mother Earth*, November 1907, 366.

84   loc. cit.

85   Hal Sears, *The Sex Radicals: Free Love in Victorian America* (Lawrence: The Regents Press of Kansas), 226.

86   Lois Waisbrooker, *My Century Plant* (Topeka, Kansas: Independent Publishing Company, 1896), 11. Waisbrooker was born in 1820; the shift in the anarchist position on

homosexuality that occured at the turn of the century was, to some extent, a generational one.

87 Moses Harman, *Digging for Bedrock* (Valley Falls, Kansas: Lucifer Publishing Company, 1890), 168.

88 C. L. James, "Anarchism: The Discussion of Its Principles Continued," *The Alarm*, 8 August 1885, 3.

89 "Only Books that Teach Anarchy are Sold in this Sixth Avenue Shop," *New York Herald*, April 12, 1908, 6.

90 Irving C. Rosse, "Homosexuality in Washington, D.C." in Katz, *Gay American History*, 42.

Chapter Two (pages 43–68)

1 Goldman, *Living My Life*, 269. Barry Pateman suggests that Goldman may have exaggerated her efforts on Wilde's behalf in this passage. It may well be that she amplified her record, but the essential truth of her claim remains: she defended Wilde when it was not popular to do so.

2 Quoted in John Ehrenberg, *Proudhon and His Age* (New Jersey: Humanities Press, 1996), 109.

3 Benjamin R. Tucker, "The Criminal Jailers of Oscar Wilde," *Liberty*, 15 June 1895, 4.

4 See Sears, *The Sex Radicals: Free Love in Victorian America*, 81–96.

5 Ibid., 110–111.

6 See Martin Henry Blatt, *Free Love and Anarchism: The Biography of Ezra Heywood* (Urbana: University of Illinois Press, 1989).

7 Emma Goldman, "Anarchism: What It Really Stands For," *Anarchism and Other Essays* (New York: Dover, 1969 [1917]), 55.

8 "Roosevelt is not Friend of Labor," *The Oregonian*, June 3, 1907

9 "Mild Comedy at the Tabor; Virile Talk at Woman's Club: Emma Goldman," *Denver Post*, 22 April 1912.

10 Emma Goldman to Ben Capes, 23 June 1925, *Emma Goldman Papers*, reel 15.

11 Alexander Berkman, *What is Communist Anarchism* (New York: Dover Publication, 1972 [1929]) 59–60.

12 See Avrich, *The Haymarket Tragedy*, 353.

13 Max Nettlau, *A Short History of Anarchism* (London: Freedom Press, 1996 [1935]), 213

14 Quoted in Karl Beckson, *London in the 1890s: A Cultural History* (New York: Norton, 1992), 20.

15 See Beckson, 3–31. And Mark Bevir, "The Rise of Ethical Anarchism in Britain, 1885–1900," *Historical Research* (June 1996): 143–165.

16 While a number of very good studies have examined the relationship between artists and anarchism in Europe—particularly Paris—very few studies of the American cultural landscape have done so. An exception to this, is the excellent book, Henry F. May, *The End of American Innocence: A Study of the First Years of Our Own Time, 1912–1917* (New York: Columbia University Press, 1992 [1959]).

17 Who authored *Catechism* is a matter of some historical debate. Paul Avrich argues that it was largely the work of Nechaev, although certainly Bakunin had a great influence on the work. On the relationship between the two men see Paul Avrich, *Anarchist Portraits* (Princeton: Princeton University Press, 1988), 32–52.

18 Sergei Nechaev, *Catechism of the Revolutionist* (London: Aldgate Press, 1989), 4.

19   E. H. Carr, *Michael Bakunin* (New York: Vintage, 1961), 392.

20   George Woodcock, *Anarchism: A History of Libertarian Ideas and Movements* (New York: Penguin, 1986), 143.

21   Hubert Kennedy, "Johann Baptist von Schweitzer: The Queer Marx Loved to Hate," in *Gay Men and the Sexual History of the Political Left*, 86–89. My discussion of Bakunin and Nechaev's relationship is heavily indebted to Kennedy.

22   Eileen Boris, *Art and Labor: Ruskin, Morris, and the Craftsman Ideal in America* (Philadelphia: Temple University Press, 1986), xi.

23   *Bangor Maine Commercial*, October 4, 1882, quoted in Rose Snider "Oscar Wilde's Progress Down East," *New England Quarterly*, XIII (1940): 11.

24   Oscar Wilde quoted in Jeffrey Escoffier, "Oscar Wilde's Politics: The Homosexual as Artist as Socialist," *The Gay Alternative*, 10 (1975), 6.

25   George Woodcock, "Introduction" Oscar Wilde, *The Soul of Man under Socialism* (London: Porcupine Press, n.d.), vii–viii.

26   Christopher Hitchens, "Oscar Wilde's Socialism" *Dissent* (Fall, 1995): 516.

27   Oscar Wilde, *The Soul of Man under Socialism*, reprinted in George Woodcock, *Oscar Wilde: The Double Image* (Montréal: Black Rose Books, 1989), 257–258.

28   Emma Goldman to Ben Capes, June 23, 1925, *Emma Goldman Papers*, reel 15.

29   Benjamin R. Tucker, "On Picket Duty," *Liberty*, April 4, 1891, 1.

30   Terence V. Powderly, "Editorial," *Journal of the Knights of Labor* quoted in Benjamin R. Tucker, *Instead of a Book: By a Man Too Busy to Write One* (New York: Benjamin R. Tucker, 1893), 37.

31   See Terence V. Powderly, *Thirty Years of Labor, 1859 to 1889* (Philadelphia, 1890), 271–288.

32   "A Criticism and Reply," *Liberty*, December 26, 1885, 1.

33   On the *Desert News* see Quinn, *Same-Sex Dynamics Among Nineteenth-Century Americans*, 314-315.

34   Benjamin Tucker, "On Picket Duty," *Liberty*, April 20, 1895, 1.

35   See Thomas Beer, *The Mauve Decade: American Life at the end of the Nineteenth Century* (New York: Alfred Knopf, 1926), 126–129. Beer thanks "Mr. Charles Cleary Nolan for the use of his…Wildiana and his monstrous collections of American religious eloquence." (Beer, 267).

36   Richard Ellman, *Oscar Wilde* (New York: Alfred Knopf, 1988), 458.

37   Quoted in "The Oscar Wilde Revival," *Current Literature*, November 1906, 521.

38   Elsa Barker, "Oscar Wilde," *Current Literature*, July 1907, 106.

39   On the Alice Ward / Freda Mitchell case, see Duggan, *Sapphic Slashers*.

40   Havelock Ellis, *Studies in the Psychology of Sex: Volume II: Sexual Inversion* (Philadelphia: F. A. Davis Company, 1928), 352. See also Ed Cohen, *Talk on the Wilde Side: Towards a Genealogy of a Discourse on Male Sexuality* (New York: Routledge, 1993), 98–99.

41   On personal correspondence, see Helen Lefkowitz Horowitz, *The Power and Passion of M. Carey Thomas* (New York: Alfred Knopf, 1994), 286–287; and Cohen, *Talk on the Wilde Side*, 98. On "The Sins of Oscar Wilde" see Ellman, *Oscar Wilde*, 575.

42   Cohen, *Talk on the Wilde Side*, 1.

43   Goldman, *Living My Life*, 269.

44   Tucker, "On Picket Duty," *Liberty*, 20 April 1895, 1.

45   Octave Mirabeau, "Oscar Wilde's Imprisonment," *Liberty*, 13 July 1895, 6–7.

46 Richard Sonn, *Anarchism and Cultural Politics in Fin de Siecle France* (Lincoln: University of Nebraska Press, 1989), 176. See also Alexander Varias, *Paris and the Anarchists: Aesthetes and Subversives During the Fin de Siecle* (New York: St. Martin's Press, 1996).

47 Sears, *The Sex Radicals*, 226–227.

48 Tucker, "The Criminal Jailers of Oscar Wilde," 4–5.

49 loc. cit.

50 Chauncey, *Gay New York*, 43, 84–85, 88–96, 140–141.

51 Tucker, "The Criminal Jailers of Oscar Wilde," 4–5.

52 On the Footes, see Blatt, *Free Love and Anarchism*, and Sears, *The Sex Radicals*.

53 E. B. Foote Jr., "Liberty Run Wilde," *Liberty*, 13 July 1895, 6.

54 Cohen, *Talk on the Wilde Side*, 198.

55 Quoted in *Hidden Heritage: History and the Gay Imagination: An Anthology*, ed. Bryne Fone (New York: Avocation Press, 1980), 197.

56 Tucker, "A 'Liberal' Comstock," *Liberty*, 13 July 1895, 2–3.

57 James F. Morton Jr., "The Many Roads to Liberty," *The Agitator*, 15 February 1911.

58 Robert E. Riegel, "Changing American Attitudes Toward Prostitution," *Journal of the History of Ideas* (July–September 1968), 451.

59 Tucker, *Instead of a Book*, 161.

60 Linda R. Hirshman and Jane E. Lanson, *Hard Bargains: The Politics of Sex* (New York: Oxford University Press, 1998), 131.

61 Tucker, "A 'Liberal' Comstock," 2–3.

62 *The Firebrand*, 21 August 1895.

63 Ellman, *Oscar Wilde*, 532.

64 Oscar Wilde, "The Ballad of Reading Gaol," in Oscar Wilde, *The Soul of Man and Prison Writings*, ed. Isobel Murray (New York: Oxford University Press, 1990), 170.

65 Tucker, "The Ballad of Reading Gaol," *Liberty*, March 1899, 5.

66 loc. cit.

67 Quoted in Beckson, *London in the 1890s*, 229.

68 Tucker, "The Ballad of Reading Gaol," 5.

69 Benjamin Tucker to Henry Bool, May 21, 1899, Ishill Collection.

70 Oscar Wilde, "The Ballad of Reading Gaol," *The Literary World*, 19 August 1899, 268.

71 See "The Critics on Oscar Wilde's Poem," *Liberty*, May 1899, 4, 5, 8.

72 Chauncey, *Gay New York*, 10.

73 "The Ennobling Influence of Sorrow (From Oscar Wilde's 'De Profundis')," *Mother Earth*, July 1906, 13.

74 Goldman, "The Unjust Treatment of Homosexuals," in Katz, *Gay American History*, 379.

75 Goldman, "The Tragedy at Buffalo," *Mother Earth*, October 1906, 11.

76 John William Lloyd, *The Dwellers in the Vale Sunrise* (Westwood, Mass: Ariel Press, 1904), 4.

77 Ibid., 20.

78 Ibid., 165–175. See also Veysey, *Communal Experience*, 27.

79 Veysey, *Communal Experience*, 20.

80 See Robert K. Martin, "Knights-Errant and Gothic Seducers: The Representation of Male Friendship in Mid-Nineteenth-Century America," in *Hidden From History: Reclaiming the Gay and Lesbian Past*, eds. Martin Duberman, Martha Vicinus, and George Chauncey Jr. (New York: Meridian, 1989). Native Americans, whom Lloyd saw as the apotheosis of the "natural man," fascinated him. "The American aborigine," he wrote,

"was the noblest savage of his time, if not all time." Lloyd believed that Indian society was a prime example of anarchist ideas put into practice. "Here," he wrote, "we find a remarkable condition of individual liberty and responsibility, equality, fraternity, and solidarity." (*Liberty*, 23 November 1889, 6.) In the early 1900s, Lloyd traveled to the Southwest—"at the invitation of my gentle and warm-hearted Pima friend, Edward Herbert Weston"—and wrote a study, entitled *Aw-aw Tam Indian Nights*, in which he chronicled the "mystic and legendary tales" of the "simple, kindly, hospitable people" he lived with. See John William Lloyd, *Aw-aw-tam Indian Nights; Being the Myths and Legends of the Pimas of Arizona* (Westfield, NJ: The Lloyd Group, 1911).

81   James Gifford, *Daynesford's Library: American Homosexual Writing, 1900–1913* (Amherst: University of Massachusetts Press, 1995), 12–13.

82   Rose Florence Freeman, "Oscar Wilde," *The Free Spirit*, Vol. I, Issue I, 1919, 18–20.

83   Ben Reitman, "Vengeance," *Mother Earth*, July 1916, 529.

84   "The Prisoners," *Free Society*, August 25, 1901, 1.

Chapter Three (pages 69–95)

1   Richard Drinnon, *Rebel in Paradise: A Biography of Emma Goldman* (Boston: Beacon Press, 1961), 160.

2   Leonard Abbott in *The Centenary of Walt Whitman's "Leaves of Grass," Selected Excerpts From the Writings of Various Authors*, ed. Joseph Ishill (Berkeley Heights, N.J.: Oriole Press, 1955), 55.

3   Emma Goldman, "On the Road," *Mother Earth*, April, 1907, 65. On the history of *Mother Earth*, see Peter Glassgold, "Introduction: The Life and Death of *Mother Earth*," in *Anarchy: An Anthology of Emma Goldman's Mother Earth*, ed. Peter Glassgold (Washington, D.C.: Counterpoint, 2001), xv–xxxvi.

4   Leonard Abbott in *The Centenary of Walt Whitman's "Leaves of Grass,"* 55.

5   W.F.B., "Literature: Review of Milla Tupper Maynard's Walt Whitman," *Free Society*, March 8, 1903, 3.

6   William Thurston Brown, *Walt Whitman: Poet of the Human Whole* (Portland: The Modern School, n.d.), 27.

7   Katz, *Love Stories*, 249.

8   Leonard Abbott, "The Anarchist Side of Walt Whitman," *The Road To Freedom*, March, 1926, 2.

9   John Addington Symonds, *Sexual Inversion: A Classic Study of Homosexuality* (New York: Bell Publishing Company, 1984 [1896]), 183. See also John Addington Symonds, *Walt Whitman: A Study* (London: John C. Nimmo, 1893).

10   Edward Carpenter in *The Centenary of Walt Whitman's "Leaves of Grass,"* 30.

11   Katz, *Love Stories*, 257–271.

12   Walt Whitman, "A Woman Waits For Me," *The Complete Poetry and Prose of Walt Whitman: Two Volumes in One* with an introduction by Malcolm Cowley (Garden City: Garden City Books, 1948), 124.

13   Quoted in Byrne R. S. Fone, *A Road to Stonewall, 1750–1969: Male Homosexuality and Homophobia in English and American Literature* (New York: Twayne Publishers, 1995), 43.

14   Benjamin Tucker in *The Centenary of Walt Whitman's "Leaves of Grass,"* 66–74.

15   Jonathan Ned Katz, *Love Stories*, 6.

16   Ibid., 335.

17 For a discussion of the periodization of this change, see Steven Seidman, *Romantic Longings: Love in America, 1830–1980* (New York: Routledge, 1991), 109–117. See also "Introduction," In *Hidden From History: Reclaiming the Gay and Lesbian Past*, eds. Martin Bauml Duberman, Martha Vicinus, and George Chauncey Jr. (New York: New American Library, 1989), 5.

18 Eve Kosofsky Sedgwick, *Between Men: English Literature and Male Homosocial Desire* (New York: Columbia University Press, 1985), 202. Sedgwick focuses on English readers of Whitman, among them John Addington Symonds and Edward Carpenter.

19 Benjamin Tucker, "Obscenity and the State," *Liberty*, 27 May 1882, 2.

20 Benjamin Tucker, "On Picket Duty," *Liberty*, October 28, 1882, 1.

21 *Walt Whitman: The Correspondence: Volume IV: 1886–1889*, ed. Edwin Havilland Miller (New York: New York University Press, 1969), 372.

22 Quoted in Tucker in *The Centenary of Walt Whitman's "Leaves of Grass,"* 73.

23 John William Lloyd, "Mount Walt Whitman," *Egoism*, May 1892, 1.

24 John William Lloyd, "A Poet of Nature," *Liberty*, May 7, 1892, 3

25 C. H. Cheyse, "Dawn Thought," *Discontent*, April 10, 1901, 1.

26 Lloyd, *The Free Comrade*, October 1902, 6.

27 Ibid., 5.

28 Ibid., 3.

29 Edward Carpenter, *Ioläus: An Anthology of Friendship* (New York: Pagan Press, 1982 [1902]), 188.

30 Edward Carpenter, *Towards Democracy* (London: Gay Men's Press, 1985 [1885]), 415.

31 Havelock Ellis, *My Life* (London: Neville Spearman, 1967), 163.

32 John William Lloyd, *The Free Comrade*, October 1910, 46.

33 Katz, *Gay American History*, 364.

34 John William Lloyd, *The Free Comrade*, October 1902, 6–7.

35 Carpenter, *Ioläus*, 188–189.

36 John William Lloyd, *The Free Comrade*, October 1902, 7.

37 Ibid., 6–7.

38 Earl Lind, *Autobiography of an Androgyne* (New York: Medico-Legal Journal, 1918), 212–213. On the figure of the fairy, see George Chauncey, *Gay New York*. In his laudable attempt to emphasize the resistance and inventiveness of the men he studied, Chauncey acknowledges, but downplays, the violence fairies dealt with on a near-daily basis. How, for example, did tradespeople, landlords, and employers outside the sex and entertainment businesses treat fairies? Also absent from Chauncey's study is any exploration of the religion's role in shaping the view of same-sex sexuality. There is admittedly little information on such matters, but absence of negative reports hardly supports the contention there was relatively little prejudice. The very sources that seem to indicate a relative tolerance of fairies among the working class are also filled with examples of incredible violence and hatred.

39 Lind, *Autobiography of an Androgyne*, 117.

40 Alan Sinfield, *The Wilde Century: Effeminacy, Oscar Wilde, and the Queer Moment* (New York: Columbia University Press, 1994), 110.

41 Lloyd, *The Free Comrade*, October 1902, 7.

42 Chushichi Tsuzuki, *Edward Carpenter, 1844–1929: Prophet of Human Fellowship* (Cambridge, UK: Cambridge University Press, 1980), 115.

43 John William Lloyd, *The Free Comrade*, September 1901, 7.

44 Lloyd, *The Free Comrade*, August 1902, 6.

45 Lloyd, *The Free Comrade*, May 1902, 6.

46 Bryne R. S. Fone, *A Road to Stonewall: Male Homosexuality and Homophobia in English and American Literature, 1750–1969* (New York: Twayne Publishers, 1995), 95.

47 Lloyd, *The Free Comrade*, October 1902, 3.

48 Stanley Pierson, "Edward Carpenter: Prophet of a Socialist Millennium," *Victorian Studies* (March 1970), 306.

49 Lloyd, *The Free Comrade*, October 1902, 5.

50 Charles B. Willard, *Whitman's American Fame: The Growth of His Reputation in America After 1892* (Providence, R.I.: Brown University, 1950), 32. See also Harold Blodgett, *Walt Whitman in England* (New York City: Russell and Russell, 1973).

51 John William Lloyd, "The Overlook," *Ariel*, March 1907, 7.

52 On the U.S. and England, see Willard and Blodgett. On Canada, see Gary Kinsman, *The Regulation of Desire: Homo and Hetero Sexualities*, revised edition (Montréal: Black Rose Books, 1996), 123–124.

53 William James, *The Varieties of Religious Experience* (New York: Longmans, Green and Co., 1902), 85.

54 Oscar Lovell Trigg, *The Changing Order: A Study of Democracy* (Chicago: Charles H. Kerr & Company, 1905), 267.

55 John William Lloyd, *The Free Comrade*, July 1911, 157–158.

56 Quoted in Clara Barrus, *Whitman and Burroughs: Comrades* (Port Washington, NY: Kennikat Press, 1968 [1931]), 313.

57 Nick Salvatore, *Eugene V. Debs: Citizen and Socialist* (Urbana, Ill.: University of Illinois Press, 1982), 88.

58 Malcolm Cowley, "Introduction," *The Complete Poetry and Prose of Walt Whitman*, 10.

59 William O Reichert, "Edward C. Carpenter's Socialism in Retrospective," *Our Generation* (Fall/Winter, 1987–88), 187.

60 Quoted in Chushichi Tsuzuki, *Edward Carpenter, 1844–1929: Prophet of Human Fellowship* (Cambridge: Cambridge University Press, 1980), 97–98.

61 Will S. Monroe, "Walt Whitman and Other American Friends of Edward Carpenter," in *Edward Carpenter: In Appreciation*, ed. Gilbert Beith (London: George Allen & Unwin, 1931), 152.

62 Leonard Abbott, "J. William Lloyd: Brother of Carpenter and Thoreau," *The Comrade*, July 1902, 225.

63 Leonard Abbott, "Edward Carpenter, A Radical Genius," *The Road to Freedom*, September 1931, 7.

64 Leonard Abbott, "Edward Carpenter: A Recollection and a Tribute," *The Free Spirit*, May 1919, 39.

65 Paul Avrich, *The Modern School* (Princeton: Princeton University Press, 1980), 172.

66 Leonard Abbott, *The Free Comrade*, July 1910, 11.

67 John William Lloyd, "The Overlook," *Ariel*, January 1909, 23.

68 Ibid., 25.

69 Ibid., 27.

70 Marsh, *Anarchist Women*, 172.

71 John William Lloyd, "The Overlook," *Ariel*, January 1909, 27–28.

72 John William Lloyd, *The Free Comrade*, September–October 1911, 175–177.

73 See "Literary Notes," *The Agitator*, 15 July 1911.

74 George Sylvester Viereck, "The Ethical Dominant in American Poetry," *Current Literature*, September 1911, 323–324.

75   loc. cit. It is possible that, in the original Berlin lecture, of which Lloyd may have had some knowledge, Viereck used the term "homosexuality" when discussing Whitman.

76   Elmer Gertz, *Odyssey of a Barbarian: The Biography of George Sylvester Viereck* (Prometheus Books, 1978), 34.

77   George S. Viereck, *My Flesh and Blood: A Lyrical Autobiography with Indiscreet Annotations* (New York: Liveright, 1931), 58.

78   Gertz, 34–35.

79   See James Steakley, *The Homosexual Emancipation Movement in Germany* (New York: Arno Press, 1975).

80   Veysey, *Communal Experience*, 89, n. 22. Veysey had access to papers held by Abbott's son, William Morris Abbott.

81   Gertz, *Odyssey of a Barbarian* 55–59, 83.

82   George S. Viereck, "The Ballad of the Golden Boy" in *The Candle and the Flame* (New York: Moffat, Yard and Company, 1912), 25-28. See also "Marginalia," in *The Candle and the Flame*, 108.

83   M. D. O'Brien, "Socialism and Infamy: the Homogenic or Comrade Love Exposed: An Open Letter in Plain Words for a Socialist Prophet," in *Nineteenth-Century Writings on Homosexuality: A Sourcebook*, ed. Chris White (London: Routledge, 1999), 23.

84   David Goldstein and Martha Moore Avery, *Socialism: The Nation of Fatherless Children* (Boston: Thomas J. Flynn and Company, 1911), 164–165. Like many critics of the Left, the authors blend together members of the Socialist Party, utopians, and anarchists in one huge free-love conspiracy.

85   David Reynolds, *Walt Whitman's America: A Cultural Biography* (New York: Knopf, 1995), 198.

86   José Martí, "Walt Whitman," in *Marti on the U.S.A.*, selected and translated by Luis A. Baralt (Carbondale, Ill.: Southern Illinois University Press, 1966), 10.

87   "Whitman and War," *The Chap Book*, 15 February 1898, 290. See also Fone, *A Road To Stonewall*, 182–189.

88   Walter Grunzweig, "Whitman in the German-Speaking Countries," in *Walt Whitman and the World*, eds. Gay Wilson Allen and Ed Folsom (Iowa City, Iowa: University of Iowa Press, 1995), 165.

89   "The Feminine Soul in Whitman," *Current Literature*, July 1906, 53–56. The author of this article is not identified, but it must have been Viereck, who read German and was quite interested in sexology. The author of the *Current Literature* article clearly had an understanding of German and was also familiar with the work of Ellis, John Addington Symonds, Ulrich, Hirschfeld, and other sexologists.

90   Jeffrey Weeks, *Coming Out: Homosexual Politics in Britain from the Nineteenth Century to the Present* (London: Quartet Books, 1990), 81.

91   loc. cit.

92   Emma Goldman to Ben Capes, 12 November 1927, *Emma Goldman Papers*, reel 19.

93   Earl Lind, *The Female-Impersonators*, 36.

94   Henry O'Higgins, *Alias Walt Whitman* (Newark: The Carteret Book Club, 1930), 39, 35. This short work is a reprint of the *Harper's* article.

95   Emma Goldman to Evelyn Scott, 21 December 1927, in *Nowhere at Home: Letters from Exile of Emma Goldman and Alexander Berkman*, eds. Richard and Anna Maria Drinnon (New York: Schocken Books, 1975), 141.

96   loc. cit.

97   loc. cit.

Chapter Four (pages 97–125)

1   Ben Reitman, "Speech Delivered at Lenox Hall after His Release from Prison," *Mother Earth*, August 1916, 583.

2   Ibid., 581

3   loc. cit.

4   Ibid., 583.

5   loc. cit.

6   Louis Dwight, "The Sin of Sodom is the Vice of Prisoners," in Katz, *Gay American History*, 27–28.

7   Kate Richards O'Hare, "Prison Lesbianism," in Katz, *Gay American History*, 69.

8   Katz, *Gay American History*, 578, n. 69.   .

9   Emma Goldman, "The Unjust Treatment of Homosexuals," in Katz, *Gay American History*, 379.

10   Goldman, *Living My Life*, 667. See also Haaland, *Emma Goldman*, 174–176.

11   Leonard Abbott, "An Intellectual Giant," *Mother Earth*, December, 1912, 328.

12   Peter Kropotkin, *In Russian and French Prisons* (Montréal: Black Rose Books, 1991 [1906]), 335–336.

13   Quoted in "What the Critics Say," *Mother Earth*, March 1913, n.p.

14   Bayard Boyesen, "Prison Memoirs," *Mother Earth*, February 1913, 424.

15   Alex Kershaw, *Jack London: A Life* (New York: St. Martin's Press, 1997). Kershaw suggests that London had a sexual relationship with another prisoner during his jail stay (36–38.)

16   Hutchins Hapgood, "As Introductory," in Alexander Berkman's *Prison Memoirs of an Anarchist* (New York: Mother Earth Publishing Association 1912), ix–xi.

17   Berkman, *Prison Memoirs*, 263.

18   John William Ward, "Violence, Anarchy, and Alexander Berkman," *New York Review of Books* (November, 5 1970), 27.

19   Hutchins Hapgood, "As Introductory," x.

20   "Two Indictments of Our Prison System," *Current Literature*, December 1912, 673.

21   Quoted in "What the Critics Say," *Mother Earth*, March 1913. n.p.

22   Alexander Berkman, "October 19th, 1912," Alexander Berkman Archive, International Institute of Social History.

23   Emma Goldman, *Living My Life*, 979–980.

24   Edward Carpenter, "Introduction," Alexander Berkman, *Prison Memoirs of an Anarchist* (London: The C. W. Daniel Company, 1926), n.p.

25   Emma Goldman to Alexander Berkman, 28 May 1925, *Emma Goldman Papers*, reel 15.

26   See, for example, Berkman's relationship with Wingie. Wingie's interest in Berkman has a physical component, but Berkman remains ignorant of this. At one point, Wingie gives Berkman's "cheek a tender pat," and Berkman steps back, "with the instinctive dislike of a man's caress." Berkman's phrase seems to indicate that he believes that physical touch between men is "instinctively" uncomfortable. Unlike Red, however, Wingie does not push the matter; he is embarrassed by his clumsy attempt at seduction. He tells Berkman, with "a faint flush stealing over his prison pallor," that he was only "trying" him. Berkman, clearly clueless, wonders what all this could mean. "What could he have meant," he writes, "by 'trying' me?" See Berkman, *Prison Memoirs*, 144–145.

27   Ibid., 160–165.

28   Ibid.,. 169–171.
29   Ibid., 173.
30   Ibid., 325.
31   Ibid., 243.
32   Ibid., 173.
33   Ibid., 257.
34   See Boag, *Same-Sex Affairs*.
35   Chauncey, *Gay New York*, 95.
36   loc. cit.
37   loc. cit.
38   Berkman, *Prison Memoirs of an Anarchist*, 316, 319.
39   Ibid., 321–4.
40   Ibid., 343.
41   Ibid., 350.
42   See Blanche Weisen Cook, "The Historical Denial of Lesbianism." *Radical History Review* 20 (Spring–Summer 1979): 60–65.
43   Berkman, *Prison Memoirs*, 403.
44   Boyesen, "Prison Memoirs," 423.
45   Berkman, *Prison Memoirs*, 401–402.
46   Ibid., 403–408.
47   Ibid., 440.
48   On David and Jonathan see Quinn, *Same-Sex Dynamics and Nineteenth-Century Americans*, 112–113.
49   Berkman, *Prison Memoirs*, 430–434.
50   Ibid., 437–439.
51   Ibid., 438.
52   Ibid., 429.
53   Ibid., 433.
54   Edward Carpenter, *Homogenic Love and its Place in a Free Society*, (London: Redundancy Press, 1980 [1895]), 14–15.
55   Berkman, *Prison Memoirs*, 440.
56   Ibid., 478.
57   Goldman, *Living My Life*, 484.
58   Emma Goldman to unknown, 25 September 1911, *Emma Goldman Papers*, reel 17.
59   See advertisement in *Mother Earth*, January 1911, n. p.
60   Oscar Wilde, "The Ennobling Influence of Sorrow," *Mother Earth*, July 1906, 14.
61   Goldman, "The Unjust Treatment of Homosexuals," in Katz, *Gay American History*, 379.
62   Goldman, "Prisons," in *Anarchism and Other Essays*, 111.
63   Marie Ganz, *Rebels: Into Anarchy and Out Again* (New York: Dodd, Mead, and Company, 1919), 224. Ganz would quickly renounce her former colleagues, an ideological journey chronicled in her memoir.
64   Berkman, *Prison Memoirs*, 434.
65   Reb Raney, "Alexander Berkman in San Francisco," *Mother Earth*, June 1915, 152.
66   loc. cit.
67   Billie McCullough, "Alexander Berkman in Los Angeles," *Mother Earth*, May 1915, 113.

68   Emma Goldman and Alexander Berkman, *A Fragment of the Prison Experience of Emma Goldman and Alexander Berkman* (New York: Stella Comyn, 1919), 20.

69   Goldman, "Prison," 116.

70   See David Nicoll, *Life in English Prisons: Mysteries of Scotland Yard* (London: Kate Sharpley Library, 1992), 22.

71   Quoted in Tsuzuki, *Edward Carpenter*, 114.

72   Berkman, *Prison Memoirs*, 225

73   Jeffrey Weeks, *Coming Out: Homosexual Politics in Britain from the Nineteenth Century to the Present* (London: Quartet Books, 1990), 71.

74   Ibid., 131–132.

75   Emma Goldman to Edward Carpenter, 29 October 1925, *Emma Goldman Papers*, reel 15.

76   Emma Goldman to Alexander Berkman, May 15–16, 1927, *Emma Goldman Papers*, reel 18.

77   Edward Carpenter, "Introduction," in Berkman, *Prison Memoirs*, n.p.

Chapter Five (pages 127–152)

1   John William Lloyd, *The Free Comrade*, August 1902, 5–6.

2   Marsh writes that "Lloyd thought of himself as a social scientist seeking the means by which society could be made both virtuous and free." Marsh, *Anarchist Women*, 82.

3   Emma Goldman, "En Route," *Mother Earth*, December 1908, 353.

4   Emma Goldman, "What I Believe," in *Red Emma Speaks*, 57.

5   Hulda Potter-Loomis, *Social Freedom: The Important Factor in Human Evolution* (Chicago: M. Harman, n.d.), 6–7. See Veysey, *Communal Experience*, 29.

6   On the relative underdevelopment of American sexological work as compared to European sexology, see Bert Hansen, "American Physicians' 'Discovery' of Homosexuals: 1880–1900: A New Diagnosis in a Changing Society," in *Framing Disease: Studies in Cultural History*, eds. Charles E. Rosenberg and Janet Goldin (Rutgers, New Jersey: Rutgers University Press, 1992).

7   "Observations and Comments," *Mother Earth*, August 1911, 166.

8   Emma Goldman to Magnus Hirschfeld, January 1923, *Emma Goldman Papers*, reel 13.

9   John William Lloyd to Joseph Ishill, March 30, 1922, Ishill Collection.

10 . John William Lloyd, "Havelock Ellis: The Listener," unpublished manuscript, Ishill Collection.

11   Emma Goldman, *Living My Life*, 173.

12   Emma Goldman to Magnus Hirschfeld, January 1923, *Emma Goldman Papers*, reel 13.

13   John William Lloyd, "Havelock Ellis: The Most Satisfactory Great Man I Ever Met," in *Havelock Ellis: An Appreciation*, ed. Joseph Ishill (Berkeley Heights, N.J.: Oriole Press, 1929), 167.

14   Bolton Hall, "Havelock Ellis: A Most Radical and a Most Courageous Pioneer," in *Havelock Ellis: An Appreciation*, 202–203.

15   Haaland, *Emma Goldman*, 165.

16   Lillian Faderman and Brigitte Erikson, "Introduction," *Lesbians in Germany: 1890s–1920s* (Tallahassee, FL.: Naiad Press, 1990), x–xi. See also Sheila Jeffries, *The Spinster and Her Enemies: Feminism and Sexuality, 1880–1930* (London: Pandora, 1985).

17   Katz, *Gay American History*, 129.

18   Vernon A. Rosario, "Homosexual Bio-Histories: Genetic Nostalgias and the Quest for Paternity," in *Science and Homosexualities*, ed. Vernon A. Rosario (New York: Rout-

ledge, 1997), 3. See also Henry L. Minton, *Departing from Deviance: A History of Homosexual Rights and Emancipatory Science in America* (Chicago: University of Chicago Press, 2002).

19 Vernon A. Rosario, "The Science of Sexual Liberation," *The Gay and Lesbian Review: Worldwide* (November–December, 2002), 37–38.

20 Harry Oosterhuis, *Step Children of Nature: Krafft-Ebing, Psychiatry and the Making of Sexual Identity* (University of Chicago Press, 2000), 186.

21 Edward Carpenter, "Custom," *Liberty*, 2 February 1889, 7.

22 loc. cit.

23 Emma Goldman to Ben Reitman, 13 July 1912, *Emma Goldman Papers*, reel 6.

24 Goldman, *Living My Life*, 575.

25 Vern Bullough, *Science in the Bedroom: A History of Sex Research* (New York: Basic Books, 1994), 81.

26 Emma Goldman to Havelock Ellis, 27 December 1924, *Emma Goldman Papers*, reel 14.

27 Havelock Ellis, *My Life*, 300

28 On the Legitimation League and Ellis see Jeffrey Weeks, *Sex, Politics and Society: The Regulation of Sexuality Since 1800*, second edition (London: Longman, 1989), 180–181.

29 Emma Goldman to Joseph Ishill, 23 July 1928, *Emma Goldman Papers*, reel 20.

30 Goldman, *Living My Life*, 173.

31 Hapgood, *A Victorian in the Modern World*, 466.

32 Bonnie Haaland agrees that sexology was influential in shaping Goldman's sexual politics, but sees this influence as pernicious. This damage takes the form, Haaland argues, of false consciousness. "While Goldman obviously felt she had been liberated by the sexologists, as witnessed by her willingness to talk openly about sexual matters, she was at the same time, contributing to the sexologists' pathologization of sexuality by classifying sexual behaviors as perversions, inversions, etc." In other words, Goldman was merely repeating the misrepresentations of the sexologists. (Haaland, *Emma Goldman*, 165.)

33 Emma Goldman to Joseph Ishill, 31 December 1912, *Emma Goldman Papers*, reel 6.

34 See advertisement, "The Sexual Question by August Forel," *Mother Earth*, November 1915.

35 Helene Stöcker, "The Newer Ethics," *Mother Earth*, March 1907, 17–23.

36 Falk, *Love, Anarchy, and Emma Goldman*, 423–424.

37 See Boag, *Same-Sex Affairs* and Chauncey, *Gay New York*.

38 Ben Reitman, *Sister of the Road: The Autobiography of Box-Car Bertha as Told to Ben Reitman* (New York: Sheridan House, 1937), 283.

39 Roger A. Bruns, *The Damndest Radical: The Life and World of Ben Reitman, Chicago's Celebrated Social Reformer, Hobo King, and Whorehouse Physician* (Urbana: University of Illinois Press, 1987), 16.

40 Christine Stansell, *American Moderns: Bohemian New York and the Creation of a New Century* (New York: Henry Holt and Company, 2001), 132.

41 Harry Kemp, *Tramping on Life: On Autobiographical Narrative* (Garden City, NJ: Garden City Publishing Company, 1922), 286–287.

42 See Martin Duberman, *Stonewall* (New York: Dutton, 1993); and Terence Kissack, "Freaking Fag Revolutionaries: New York's Gay Liberation Front, 1969–1971," *Radical History Review* 62 (1995), 104–134.

43   Abe Isaak Jr., "Report from Chicago: Emma Goldman," *Free Society*, 9 June 1901, 3.

44   Emma Goldman to Ellen A. Kennan, 6 May 1915, *Emma Goldman Papers*, reel 9.

45   Margaret Anderson, *My Thirty Years' War: The Autobiography, Beginnings and Battles to 1930* (New York: Covici Friede), 55.

46   Goldman, *Living My Life*, 531.

47   Emma Goldman, *Mother Earth*, October 1914, 253.

48   Goldman, *Living My Life*, 531.

49   Will and Ariel Durant, *A Dual Autobiography*, 37.

50   Dr. J. Allen Gilbert, "Homosexuality and Its Treatment," in *Gay/Lesbian Almanac: A New Documentary*, ed. Jonathan Ned Katz (New York: Harper and Row, 1983), 272.

51   Almeda Sperry to Emma Goldman, 1 November 1912, *Emma Goldman Papers*, reel 6.

52   Almeda Sperry to Emma Goldman, 18 October 1912, *Emma Goldman Papers*, reel 6.

53   Cook, "Female Support Networks and Political Activism," 57. See also Haaland, *Emma Goldman*, 172–174.

54   Katz, *Gay American History*, 523.

55   Wexler, *Emma Goldman*, 309, n. 35. See also Stansell, *American Moderns*, 296–297.

56   Emma Goldman to Nunia Seldes, 4 October 1912, *Emma Goldman Papers*, reel 6.

57   Almeda Sperry to Emma Goldman, 21–22 October 1912, *Emma Goldman Papers*, reel 6.

58   Emma Goldman to Ellen A. Kennan, 6 May 1915, *Emma Goldman Papers*, reel 9.

59   Peter Glassgold, "Introduction: The Life and Death of *Mother Earth*," in *Anarchy!: an Anthology of Emma Goldman's Mother Earth*, ed. Peter Glassgold (Washington D.C.: Counterpoint, 2001), xxvi.

60   Emma Goldman, "Agitation En Voyage," *Mother Earth*, June 1915, 155.

61   Anna W., "Emma Goldman in Washington," *Mother Earth*, May 1916, 517.

62   Margaret Anderson quoted in Katz, *Gay/Lesbian Almanac*, 363–366.

63   Anna W., "Emma Goldman in Washington," *Mother Earth*, May 1916, 517.

64   Goldman, *Living My Life*, 556.

65   loc. cit.

66   Ibid., 555.

67   Josephine DeVore Johnson to William H. Warren, 5 August 1915, *Emma Goldman Papers*, reel 56.

68   John Donald Gustav-Wrathall, *Take the Young Stranger by the Hand: Same-Sex Relations and the YMCA* (Chicago: Chicago University Press, 1998), 161.

69   Boag, *Same-Sex Affairs*, 3. Boag's is the most extensive study of the scandal and of homosexuality in the turn-of-the-century Northwest.

70   Wrathall, *Take the Young Stranger by the Hand*, 165.

71   George Edwards, "A Portrait of Portland," *Mother Earth*, November 1915, 312–313.

72   Goldman, The Unjust Treatment of Homosexuals," in Katz, *Gay American History*, 376.

73   Emma Goldman to Havelock Ellis, 27 December 1924, *Emma Goldman Papers*, reel 14.

74   Quoted in Marie Mullaney, "Sexual Politics in the Career and Legend of Louise Michel," *Signs* (Winter 1990), 310–311.

75   Ibid., 300.

76   Ibid., 322. Haaland argues that Goldman and Michel were sexually attracted to each other, that they were "lovers." (Goldman, *Living My Life*, 166–168). See Haaland, *Emma Goldman*, 168.

77   Emma Goldman to Emily Holmes Coleman, December 16, 1928, *Emma Goldman Papers*, reel 28.

78   Kemp, *Tramping Through Life*, 285.

79   Will Durant, *Transitions*, 151–152.

80   Cook, "Female Support Networks and Political Activism," 56. See also Mullaney, "Sexual Politics in the Career and Legend of Louise Michel," 312–313; and Haaland, *Emma Goldman*, 164–177.

81   Emma Goldman to Thomas Lavers, 27 January 1928, *Emma Goldman Papers*, reel 19.

Chapter Six (pages 153–180)

1   Quoted in Kathleen Kennedy, *Disloyal Mothers and Scurrilous Citizens: Women and Subversion During World War I* (Bloomington: Indiana University Press, 1999), xiii.

2   David Rabban, *Free Speech in its Forgotten Years* (Cambridge: Cambridge University Press, 2001), 267.

3   Falk, 288.

4   Eric Foner, *The Story of American Freedom* (New York: W. W. Norton, 1999), 178.

5   Randolph Bourne, "The State," in *The Radical Will: Randolph Bourne, Selected Writings: 1911–1918*, ed. By Olaf Hansen (New York: Urizen Books, 1977), 356.

6   "No Conscription! Statement of the No Conscription League," in *Life of an Anarchist: The Alexander Berkman Reader*, ed. Gene Fellner (New York: Four Walls Eight Windows, 1992) 155–156.

7   Leonard D. Abbott, "The War Hysteria and Our Protest," *Mother Earth*, August 1917, 204.

8   Charles T. Sprading to Emma Goldman, August 6, 1927, *Emma Goldman Papers*, reel 18.

9   On the complex relationship between the Bolsheviks and the anarchists, see Paul Avrich, *The Russian Anarchists* (Princeton: Princeton University Press, 1967).

10   Goldman, *Living My Life*, 698.

11   Quoted in Joll, *The Anarchists*, 191.

12   Berkman, "The Russian Tragedy," in *Life of an Anarchist: The Alexander Berkman Reader*, 244.

13   Veysey, *Communal Experience*, 166.

14   Eric Morton to Emma Goldman, February 3, 1925 in *Nowhere at Home*, 42.

15   Emma Goldman to Theodore Dreiser, September 29, 1926, *Emma Goldman Papers*, reel 16.

16   "Drama Developing New Social Trend," *The Montréal Gazette*, March 6, 1935.

17   Marian J. Morton, *Emma Goldman and the American Left: Nowhere at Home* (New York: Twayne Publishers, 1992), 138.

18   Ibid., 138.

19   Randolph Bourne, "Old Tyrannies," in *The Radical Will*, 172.

20   Thomas Bender, *New York Intellect: A History of Intellectual Life in New York City, from 1750 to the Beginnings of Our Own Time* (New York: Knopf, 1987), 245–246.

21   Will Durant, *Philosophy and the Social Problem* (New York: The World Publishing, 1927), 208–209. Durant's book is dedicated to Alden Freedman.

22   Emma Goldman to Joseph Ishill, December 29, 1927, *Emma Goldman Papers*, reel 19.

23   Quoted in Marsh, *Anarchist Women*, 42. Marsh's discussion of Anderson shaped my own interpretation of the post-war fate of anarchist sexual politics.

24   Anderson, *My Thirty Years War*, 190.

25　Goldman, *Living My Life*, 531.

26　Burns, *The Damndest Radical*, 173.

27　Nancy Cott, *The Growth of Modern Feminism*, (New Haven: Yale University Press, 1987), 91.

28　Marsh, *Anarchist Women*, 94.

29　O'Neill writes that in the 1920s, it became "possible to take a radical stand on sex and a conservative one on women's social role." See William O'Neill, *Everyone was Brave: The Rise and Fall of Feminism in America* (New York: Quadrangle, 1969), 312.

30　"Emma Goldman Pays Visit to Hamilton," *The Spectator*, May 10, 1927.

31　Martin Henry Blatt, *Free Love and Anarchism: The Biography of Ezra Heywood* (Urbana: University of Illinois Press, 1989), 173.

32　Bruce Clark, *Dora Marsden and Early Feminism: Gender, Individualism, Science* (Ann Arbor: University of Michigan Press, 1996), 69. See also S. E. Parker, "The New Freewoman: Dora Marsden and Benjamin R. Tucker," in *Benjamin R. Tucker and the Champions of Liberty: A Centenary Anthology*, eds. Michael E. Coughlin, Charles H. Hamilton, and Mark A. Sullian (St. Paul: Michael E. Coughlin and Mark Sullivan Publishers, 1986) 149–157.

33　B.R.T. to Joseph Labadie, August 12, 1893. Joseph Ishill papers, Harvard.

34　John William Lloyd, "The Story of Auban," *Liberty*, August 6, 1892, 4.

35　John Henry Mackay, *The Anarchists: A Picture of Civilization at the Close of the Nineteenth Century* (Boston, Mass: Benjamin R. Tucker, 1891), ix.

36　John Henry Mackay, *Max Stirner: His Life and Work*, translated by Hubert Kennedy (Concord, CA: Peremptory Publications, 2005) xii.

37　Mackay, according to historian Hubert Kennedy, was attracted to adolescents aged fourteen to seventeen. See Hubert Kennedy, *Anarchist of Love: The Secret Life of John Henry Mackay* (New York: Mackay Society, 1983), 25.

38　Quoted in Hubert Kennedy, *Anarchist of Love*, 5.

39　Ibid., 22. Kennedy states that it was Mackay's "acceptance of the philosophy of individualism that allowed him to fully accept himself as a boy-lover."

40　See *Homosexuality and Male Bonding in Pre-Nazi Germany*, eds. Harry Oosterhuis and Hubert Kennedy (Harrington Park Press, 1991). It is unclear what kind of circulation—if any—*Der Eigene* had in the United States. Interestingly, a photo of a youth from San Francisco appeared in a 1906 edition of the journal. See "photo by Dr. A Wilhemi" in *Männer von hinten, Band 1: Photographie, 1900–1920* (Berlin: Janssen Verlag, 1994), 9.

41　John Henry Mackay, *Fenny Skaller and other Prose Writings from the Books of the Nameless Love*, translated Hubert Kennedy (Amsterdam: Southernwood Press, 1988), 134.

42　Thomas A. Riley, *Germany's Poet-Anarchist: John Henry Mackay* (NY: Revisionist Press, 1972), 111.

43　Mackay to Tucker, February 4, 1911, in *Dear Tucker: The Letters of John Henry Mackay to Benjamin R. Tucker*, ed. Hubert Kennedy (San Francisco: Peremptory Publications, 1991), 44.

44　Ibid., Mackay to Tucker, 5 November 1920, 73.

45　Alice Wexler, *Emma Goldman in America* (Beacon, 1984), 135.

46　Clarence Swartz, "Preface," in Benjamin Tucker, *Individual Liberty*, ed. Clarence L. Swartz (New York: Vanguard Press, 1926), v.

47　William C. Owen to Joseph Ishill, December 30, 1923, Ishill Collection.

48 Pierre Ramus, "Havelock Ellis: The Greatest Investigator of the Mysteries of Sex," in *Havelock Ellis: An Appreciation*, 261–262.

49 Clarence Swartz to Joseph Labadie, June 8, 1925, Labadie Collection.

50 loc. cit. John T. Scopes, a biology teacher, was being prosecuted by the state of Tennessee for teaching Darwinism, which was contrary to accepted biblical accounts of human creation.

51 Thomas H. Bell, *Edward Carpenter: The English Tolstoi* (Los Angeles: The Libertarian Group, 1932) 3, 15. The pamphlet was published following a Testimonial Dinner held in Bell's honor by "all the local Libertarian organizations," and was intended to honor "Thomas H. Bell's fifty years of social activity, all but the first three or four devoted to the Libertarian Movement."

52 Thomas Henry Bell to Joseph Ishill, July 29, 1930, Ishill Collection.

53 Thomas Henry Bell to Joseph Ishill, August 14, 1930, Ishill Collection.

54 Cassius V. Cook, "Synopsis: Thomas H. Bell, Author, Oscar Wilde without Whitewash" (Los Angeles: Rocker Publication Committee, n.d.), 7. This pamphlet was intended to solicit funds to help pay for the publication of Bell's book on Wilde. A copy can be found in the Ishill Collection.

55 Clarence Swartz to Joseph Labadie, June 8, 1925, Labadie Collection.

56 Biographical Notes, "John William Lloyd," in *Sex in Civilization*, Eds. V. F. Calverton and S. D. Schmalhausen (New York: AMS Press, 1976 [1929]), 687.

57 Abba Gordin, "J. William Lloyd," *The Road to Freedom*, April 1932, 33. This is the second of a two-part article, the first of which appears in the March 1932 issue of *The Road to Freedom*.

58 John William Lloyd, *From Hill-Terrace Outlooking: Poems of Intuition, Perception, and Prophecy* (Los Angeles: Samuel Stebb, 1939).

59 Quoted in Veysey, *Communal Experience*, 33.

60 See Lawrence Foster, "Free Love and Feminism: John Humphrey Noyes and the Oneida Community." *Journal of the Early Republic* 1 (Summer 1981): 165–183.

61 John William Lloyd, "The Karezza Method or Magnetation: The Art of Connubial Love" (privately published, 1931).

62 *The Unpublished Letters of Havelock Ellis to Joseph Ishill*, ed. Joseph Ishill (Berkeley Heights, N. J.: Oriole Press, 1954), 68, 82.

63 Havelock Ellis, "Introduction," in John William Lloyd, *Eneres or the Questions of Reksa* (London: George Allen and Unwin, 1929), 11.

64 John William Lloyd, "A Foreword," *Eneres*, n.p.

65 Ellis, "Introduction," *Eneres*, 17.

66 Leonard Wilcox, "Sex Boys in a Balloon: V. F. Calverton and the Abortive Sexual Revolution," *Journal of American Studies* 23 (1989), 9.

67 Linda Gordon, *Woman's Body, Woman's Right* (NY, 1977), 209–210. See also, Mari Jo Buhle, "Free Love," in *The Encyclopedia of the Left: Second Edition*, eds. Mari Jo Buhle, Paul Buhle, and Dan Georgakas (New York: Oxford University Press, 1998), 24; Buhle, *Women and American Socialism*, 323; and Constance Coiner, *Better Red: The Writings and Resistance of Tillie Olsen and Meridel Le Sueur* (Oxford: Oxford University Press, 1995).

68 Magdeleine Marx, *The Romance of New Russia* (New York: Thomas Seltzer, 1924).

69 Quoted in Wilcox, "Sex Boys in a Balloon: V. F. Calverton and the Abortive Sexual Revolution," 21.

70 Ibid., 20. See also Laura Engelstein, "Soviet Policy Towards Male Homosexuality: Its Origins and Historical Roots," in *Gay Men and the Sexual History of the Political Left*,

155–178 and Patrick Pollard, "Gide in the U.S.S.R.: Some Observations on Comradeship," in *Gay Men and the Sexual History of the Political Left*, 179–195.

71   David Lawrence, "In a Soviet Village: A Morality Play," *Vanguard*, Aug/Sept. 1936, 7–8.

72   Quin wrote his satirical essay in the months between the Nazi-Soviet pact and the German invasion of the USSR, a period when the CP turned against its Popular Front allies. During the Popular Front, which lasted from 1935 to 1939, the Communist party allied itself with a broad array of progressive forces, going so far as to support President Roosevelt in his reelection bid. In 1939, Stalin signed a peace treaty with Hitler and joined with Germany in attacking Poland. He called upon Western European and American communists to return to a policy of revolutionary ultraism. This shocking development led many liberals and non-communist socialists to resign from Popular Front organizations and vow to never again work with communists. The abrupt disavowal of the Popular Front illustrates how the "Communist party's position in American life...was always hostage to Soviet foreign policy." (Klehr and Haynes, *The American Communist Movement*, 92.) Quin's text is a quintessential product of the short-lived Nazi-Soviet pact, but its mobilization of homophobia as a political tool was reflective of the culture and sexual politics of the CP.

73   Mike Quin, "A Pansy Parachuter," in *On The Drumhead: A Selection from the Writing of Mike Quin: A Memorial Volume*, ed. Harry Carlisle (San Francisco: Pacific Publishing Foundation, n.d.), 118–119. Alan Berube's work on the San Francisco-based Marine Cooks and Stewards Union, a union that had a significant CP presence, is a striking exception to this pattern. In their fight to gain control of the union, CP organizers openly appealed to the gay men working onboard ships. However, it is unclear that the CP's overall view of the subject—the party line advocated across the country—on homosexuality was affected by this particular battle. Quin, after all, was a leading figure in San Francisco's CP. While the activities of the rank and file are important to document, the CP "was not merely a collection of people who shared membership in a social organization. It was a Leninist party with certain goals, visions, and plans, however perfectly or imperfectly these were realized or carried out by the membership." (Klehr and Haynes, *The American Communist Movement*, 5.) In other words, it matters what the party line was because the CP was an organization that enforced a uniformity of belief and action. Any evaluation of the merits or demerits of the CP on a given issue must take this into consideration. If the CP came to power, what would have been their policy on homosexuality? I would argue that the sentiments expressed in Quin's story would have been the governing principles for policy. Having said that, the relationship between the CP and the politics of homosexuality are complex. For example, Harry Hay, one of the founders of the gay rights group, the Mattachine Society, was radicalized by his experience in the CP. However, Hay had to leave the CP in order to pursue his sexual politics. It would have been impossible for Hay to do otherwise, as the CP had a policy of actively discouraging the membership of gay men and women who would not remain silent about their private lives.

74   See Lauritsen and Thorstadt, *The Early Homosexual Rights Movement*, 61–62; Andrew Hewitt, *Political Inversion: Homosexuality, Fascism, and the Modernist Imaginary* (Stanford: Stanford University Press, 1996); and Harry Oosterhuis, "The 'Jews' of the Antifascist Left: Homosexuality and Socialist Resistance to Nazism," in *Gay Men and the Sexual History of the Political Left*, 227–257.

75 "Emma Goldman, in Canada, Puts O.K on Flapper," *The Toronto Daily Star*, November 6, 1926.

76 "Emma Goldman Advocates Companionate Marriage, *The Toronto Daily Star*, February 9, 1927.

77 "If you Like Jazz You're Classed as Anarchist," *The Toronto Star Weekly*, December 19, 1926.

78 Leslie Fishbein, *Rebels in Bohemia* (Chapel Hill: University of North Carolina, 1982), 206.

79 Alexander Berkman to Emma Goldman, August 1929, in *Nowhere at Home*, 161.

80 "Emma Goldman Advocates Companionate Marriage, *The Toronto Daily Star*, February 9, 1927

81 Gordon, *Woman's Bodies, Woman's Right*, 392.

82 Kinsman, *The Regulation of Desire*, 69–71.

83 Steven Seidman, *Romantic Longings: Love in America, 1830–1980* (New York: Routledge, 1991), 88–89.

84 Chauncey, *Gay New York*, 301–329.

85 This dynamic is very much like that described by the historians of "whiteness." See Noel Ignatiev, *How the Irish Became White* (New York: Routledge, 1995); and David Rodiger, *The Wages of Whiteness and the Making of the American Working Class*, revised edition (London: Verso, 1999).

86 Steakley, *The Homosexual Emancipation Movement in Germany*, 81–82.

87 Lillian Faderman, *Odd Girls and Twilight Lovers: A History of Lesbian Life in Twentieth-Century America* (New York: Penguin, 1991) 82.

88 "Charter: Society for Human Rights, Inc.," in Katz, *Gay American History*, 387.

89 See Linda Hamalian, *A Life of Kenneth Rexroth* (New York: Norton, 1991), 3–5.

90 Kenneth Rexroth, *An Autobiographical Novel* (New York: Doubleday, 1966) 162–167

91 Ibid., 260.

92 Ibid., 169.

93 Sam Dolgoff, *Fragments: A Memoir* (Cambridge: Refract Publications, 1986), 39.

94 Rexroth, *An Autobiographical Novel*, 137.

95 Ibid., 136.

96 Ibid., 140.

97 Ibid., 138.

98 Dolgoff, *Fragments*, 51–52.

99 Reitman, "Preface," *Sister of the Road*, n.p.

100 Ben Reitman to Emma Goldman, March 11, 1934, *Emma Goldman Papers*, reel 30.

101 Reitman, *Sister of the Road*, 310.

102 Minton, *Departing From Deviance*, 46.

103 Ben Reitman to Emma Goldman, February 9, 1931, *Emma Goldman Papers*, reel 23.

104 Gay did, however, continue work on sexuality. In 1932, she published *On Going Naked*, a study of nudism that was banned in a number of states. The book was the basis for a film, *This Naked World*, which was released in 1935.

105 Emma Goldman to Jan Gay, February 13, 1931, *Emma Goldman Papers*, reel 23. Goldman refers to Gay by her birth name, "Helen."

106 Elsa Gidlow, *Elsa: I Come With My Songs* (San Francisco: Booklegger Press, 1986), 66. See Kinsman, 65, 124.

107 Hamalian, *A Life of Kenneth Rexroth*, 47.

108   Lewis Ellinghman and Kevin Killian, *Poet Be Like God: Jack Spicer and the San Francisco Renaissance* (Hanover: Wesleyan University Press, 1998), 57.

109   Gidlow, *Elsa*, 81–82.

110   Ibid., 300.

111   Ibid., 82.

112   Elsa Gidlow, December 26, 1928, unpublished journal, 66–67. Archives of the Gay, Lesbian, Bisexual, Transgender Historical Society of Northern California, Elsa Gidlow Collection.

113   Gidlow, *Elsa*, 67.

114   Ibid., 301.

115   Dolgoff, *Fragments*, 93.

Conclusion (pages 181–188)

1   George Woodcock, "Anarchism Revisited," in *Anarchism and Anarchists* (Kingston, Ontario: Quarry Press, 1992), 44.

2   Ibid., 45. See also Martin Duberman, "Anarchism Left and Right," *Partisan Review*, (Fall, 1966), 615; David E. Apter, "The Old Anarchism and the New—Some Comments," *Government and Opposition*, (Autumn, 1970), 403; and Paul Goodman, "The Black Flag of Anarchism," *New York Times Magazine*, (July 14, 1968), 10–22. Veysey, on the other hand, argues that there exists "a more continuous underground tradition" that ties the Old and the New anarchism together (Veysey, 40–41).

3   Hakim Bey, *T.A.Z.: The Temporary Autonomous Zone, Ontological Anarchism, Poetic Terrorism* (New York: Autonomedia, 1991), 63.

4   Murray Bookchin, *Social Anarchism or Lifestyle Anarchism: An Unbridgeable Chasm* (San Francisco: AK Press, 1995), 66.

5   Bob Black, *Anarchy After Leftism* (Columbia, MO: C.A.L. Press, 1997), 12.

6   Alix Kates Shulman, "Emma Goldman's Feminism: A Reappraisal," in *Red Emma Speaks*, 17. See Alix Kates Shulman, *To the Barricades: The Anarchist Life of Emma Goldman* (New York: Ty Crowell Co., 1971).

7   Ibid., 16.

8   See Oz Frankle, "Whatever Happened to 'Red Emma'? Emma Goldman from Alien Rebel to American Icon," *The Journal of American History* (December 1996): 903–942.

9   See John William Lloyd, *The Karezza Method; or Magnetation* (Hollywood: Phoenix Press, 1973) and John William Lloyd, *Karezza, L'Art de L'Amour: La Voie de L'Extase Sexuelle: Un Tantrisme Occidental* (Montréal: Editions Ganesha, 2000). Veysey noted that in the twenties and thirties Lloyd found readers among adherents of Eastern religious traditions.

10   *The Slant*, February 1990, 5.

11   Hubert Kennedy, "John Henry Mackay: Anarchist of Love," *The Alternate* (March 1981): 27–31.

12   Hakim Bey, "Temporary Autonomous Zones," *Gayme* (September 1994): 26–28.

13   Richmond Young, "Stonewall Demo Club," Letters to the Editor, *Sentinel*, June 22, 1989.

14   loc. cit.

15   Gidlow, *Elsa*, 301.

16   George Chauncey, *Why Marriage?: The History Shaping Today's Debate Over Gay Equality* (New York: Basic Books, 2004), 3.

17   John D'Emilio, "The Marriage Fight is Setting Us Back," *The Gay and Lesbian Review*, November–December, 2006, 10–11.

18   Emma Goldman "The Unjust Treatment of Homosexuals," in Katz, *Gay American History*, 377.

19   Emma Goldman to Havelock Ellis, 27 December 1924, *Emma Goldman Papers*, reel 14.

SELECTED BIBLIOGRAPHY

MANUSCRIPT SOURCES:

Helena Born Papers, Tamiment Library, New York University.
Elsa Gidlow Papers, Archives of the Gay, Lesbian, Bisexual, Transgender Historical Society, San Francisco.
Joseph Ishill Collection, Houghton Library, Harvard University
Labadie Collection, Hatcher Library, University of Michigan, Ann Arbor
Benjamin R. Tucker Papers, Manuscripts and Archives Division, New York Public Library, Astor, Lenox and Tilden Foundations.

PERIODICALS:

The Adult, London, England (1897–1899).
The Alarm. Chicago and New York (1884–1889).
Ariel, New York (n.d.).
The Blast, San Francisco and New York (1916–1917).
The Clarion, New York (1932–1934).
The Coming Era, Dallas (1898).
The Comrade, New York (1901–1905).
Current Literature, New York (1888–1912).
The Demonstrator, Home, Washington (1903–1908).
The Eagle and the Serpent, London and Chicago (1898–1902, 1927).
Ego, Clinton, Iowa (1921–1923).
Egoism, San Francisco and Oakland (1891–1897).
The Egoist, Clinton, Iowa (1923–1924).
Fair Play, Valley Falls, Kansas and Sioux City, Iowa (1888–1908).

Free Society, San Francisco; Chicago; and New York (1897–1904).
The Firebrand, Portland, Oregon (1895–1897).
The Free Comrade, Wellesley, Massachusetts (1900–1902, 1910–1912).
The Free Spirit, New York (1919–1921).
I, Wellesley, Massachusetts (1898–1900).
L'En Dehors, Orleans, France (1922–1939).
Liberty, Boston and New York (1881–1908).
The Literary World, London (1868–1919).
Lucifer the Light-Bearer, Valley Falls, Kansas; Topeka, Kansas; and Chicago (1883–1907).
Man!, San Francisco (1933–1940).
The Modern School, New York and Stelton, New Jersey (1912–1922).
Mother Earth, New York (1906–1917).
The Papyrus, New York (n.d.)
The Radical Review, New Bedford, Massachusetts (1877–1878).
The Road to Freedom, Stelton, New Jersey, and New York (1924–1932).
The Spectator, Hamilton, Canada (n.d.).
The Storm!, New York (1976–1988).
The Torch, London, England (1891–1895).
Vanguard, New York (1932–1939).
Wilshire's, Los Angeles (1900–1915).
Why?, Tacoma, Washington (1913–1914).
Why?, New York (1942–1947).
The Word, Princeton and Cambridge, Massachusetts (1872–1893).

PUBLISHED PRIMARY SOURCES:

Anderson, Margaret, ed. *The Little Review Anthology*. New York: Hermitage House, 1953.
———. *My Thirty Years: The Autobiography, Beginnings and Battles to 1930*. New York: Covici, Friede, 1930.
Avrich, Paul, ed. *Anarchist Voices: An Oral History of Anarchism in America*. Princeton: Princeton University Press, 1995.
Bakunin, Michael, *God and State*. Translated by Benjamin R. Tucker, with a new introduction by Paul Avrich. New York: Dover Publications, 1970.
Beith, Gilbert, ed. *Edward Carpenter: In Appreciation*. London: George Allen and Unwin, 1931.
Bell, Thomas, *Edward Carpenter: The English Tolstoi*. Los Angeles: The Libertarian Group, 1932.
Berkman, Alexander, *The Bolshevik Myth*. New York: Boni and Liveright, 1925.
———. *Life of An Anarchist: The Alexander Berkman Reader*. ed. Gene Fowler. New York: Four Walls Eight Windows, 1992.
———. *Now and After: The ABC of Communist Anarchism*. New York: Vanguard Press, 1929.
———. *Prison Memoirs of An Anarchist*. Introduction by Hutchins Hapgood. New York: Mother Earth Publishing Association, 1912.
———. *Prison Memoirs of An Anarchist*. Introduction by Edward Carpenter. London: C. W. Daniel Co., 1926.
———. *What is Communist Anarchism?* New York: Dover, 1972,
Berman, Paul, ed. *Quotations from the Anarchists*. New York: Praeger Publications, 1975.

Bey, Hekim, *T.A.Z.: The Temporary Autonomous Zone, Ontological Anarchism, Poetic Terrorism*. New York: Autonomedia, 1991.

Bookchin, Murray, *Social Anarchism or Lifestyle Anarchism: An Unbridgeable Chasm*. San Francisco and Edinburgh: AK Press, 1995.

Brown, William Thurston, *The Evolution of Sexual Morality*. Portland: The Modern School, 1912.

————. *Walt Whitman: Poet of the Human Whole*. Portland: The Modern School, 1912.

Born, Helena. *Whitman's Ideal Democracy*. Boston: Everett Press, 1902.

Bourne, Randolph, *The Radical Will: Randolph Bourne, Selected Writings: 1911–1918*. ed. Olaf Hansen. New York: Urizen Books, 1977.

Brooks, Frank H., ed. *The Individualist Anarchists: An Anthology of Liberty (1881–1908)*. New Brunswick: Transaction Publishers, 1994.

Calverton, V. F. and S. D. Schmalhausen, eds. *Sex in Civilization*. New York: AMS Press, 1976.

Carpenter, Edward, *Angel's Wings; A Series of Essays on Art and its Relation to Life*. New York: Macmillian, 1898.

————. *Homogenic Love and Its Place in a Free Society*. London: Redundancy Press, 1980.

————. *The Intermediate Sex: A Study of Some Transitional Types of Men and Women*. New York: Mitchell Kennerley, 1912.

————. *Ioläus: An Anthology of Friendship*. New York: Pagan Press, 1982.

————. *Towards Democracy*. London: Gay Men's Press, 1985.

Cook, Cassius V., "Synopsis: Thomas H. Bell, Author, Oscar Wilde Without Whitewash," Los Angeles: Rocker Publishing Committee, n.d.

de Cleyre, Voltairine, "Sex Slavery," in *Women Without Superstition: "No Gods—No Masters:" The Collected Writings of Women Freethinkers of the Nineteenth and Twentieth Centuries*, ed., Annie Laurie Gaylor. Madison: Freedom From Religion Foundation, 1997.

Dell, Floyd, *Women as World Builders: Studies in Modern Feminism*. Chicago: Forbes, 1913.

————. *Intellectual Vagabondage; An Apology for the Intelligentsia*. New York: George H. Doran, 1926.

Durant, Will, *Philosophy and the Social Problem*. New York: The World Publishing, 1927.

————. *Socialism and Anarchism*. New York: Albert and Charles Boni, 1914.

————. *Transitions: A Sentimental Story of One Mind and One Era*. New York: Boni and Liveright, 1927.

Durant, Will and Ariel Durant, *A Dual Autobiography*. New York: Simon and Schuster, 1977.

Ellis, Havelock, *My Life*. London: Neville Spearman, 1967.

————. *Studies in the Psychology of Sex: Volume II: Sexual Inversion*. Philadelphia: F. A. Davis Company, 1928.

————. *The Unpublished Letters of Havelock Ellis to Joseph Ishill*, ed. Joseph Ishill. Berkeley Heights, N.J.: Oriole Press, 1954.

Faderman, Lillian and Brigitte Erikson, eds. *Lesbians in Germany: 1890s–1920s*. Tallahassee, Fl.: Naiad Press, 1990.

Flynn, Elizabeth G., *The Rebel Girl*. New York: International Publishers, 1973.

Fone, Bryne R. S., ed. *Hidden Heritage: History and Gay Imagination, An Anthology.*
New York: Avocation, 1980.

Ganz, Marie, *Rebels: Into Anarchy and Out Again.* New York: Dodd, Mead, and
Company, 1919.

Gertz, Elmer, *The Biography of George Sylvester Viereck.* New York: Prometheus
Books, 1978.

Gidlow, Elsa, *Elsa: I Come With My Songs.* San Francisco: Booklegger Press, 1986.

Goldman, Emma. *Anarchism and Other Essays.* New York: Mother Earth Publishing
Association, 1910.

————. *Emma Goldman: A Documentary History of the American Years: Volume One:
Made For America, 1890–1901,* Forward by Leon Litwack, Falk, Candace,
Barry Pateman, et al. eds., Berkeley: University of California Press, 2003.

————. Emma *Goldman Papers: A Microfilm Edition: 20,000 Documents in 69 Reels,*
Falk, Candace, Ronald J. Zboray, et all., eds. Alexandria, Virginia: Chadwyck-
Healey, 1990–1993.

————. *Living My Life,* Garden City: Garden City Publishing Company, 1934.

————. *My Disillusionment in Russia.* London: C. W. Daniel Co., 1925.

————. *Nowhere at Home: Letters from Exile of Emma Goldman and Alexander
Berkman,* eds. Richard and Anna Maria Drinnon. New York: Schocken Books,
1975.

————. *Red Emma Speaks: Selected Writings and Speeches by Emma Goldman.* Alix
Kates Shulman, ed., New York: Schocken Books, 1983.

Goldman, Emma and Alexander Berkman. *A Fragment of the Prison Experience of
Emma Goldman and Alexander Berkman.* New York: Stella Comyn. 1919.

Goldstein, David and Martha Moore Avery, *Socialism: The Nation of Fatherless
Children.* Boston: Thomas J. Flynn and Company, 1911.

Hapgood, Hutchins, *An Anarchist Woman.* New York: Duffield and Co., 1909.

————. *A Victorian in a Modern World.* New York: Harcourt, Brace, 1939.

————. *Spirit of Labor.* New York: Duffield, 1907.

Harman, Lillian, "Some Problems of Social Freedom," in *Freedom, Feminism, and the
State,* ed. Wendy McElroy. New York: Holmes and Meier, 1991.

Harmon, Moses, *Digging for Bedrock.* Valley Falls, Kansas: Lucifer Publishing
Company, 1890.

Hartland, Claude, *The Story of a Life: For the Consideration of the Medical Community*
San Francisco: Grey Fox Press, 1985.

Hoffman, Robert L, ed. and trans., *Anarchism.* New York: Atherton, 1970.

Horowitz, Irving L. ed. *The Anarchists.* New York: Dell, 1964.

Ishill, Joseph, ed. *The Centenary of Walt Whitman's "Leaves of Grass (1855–1955)," Selected
Excerpts From the Writings of Various Authors.* Berkeley Heights, N.J.: The Oriole
Press, 1955)

————. ed. *Free Vistas: A Libertarian Outlook on Life and Letters, 2 Volumes.*
Berkeley Heights, N.J.: Oriole Press, 1933–1937.

————. ed. *Havelock Ellis: An Appreciation,* Berkeley Heights, N.J.: Oriole Press, 1929.

James, William, *The Varieties of Religious Experience.* New York: Longmans, Green
and Company, 1902.

Katz, Jonathan, ed. *Gay American History: Lesbians and Gay Men in the U.S.A.* New
York: Thomas Crowell, 1976.

————. ed. Gay/Lesbian Almanac: A New Documentary. New York: Harper and Row, 1983.

Kemp, Harry, Tramping On Life: An Autobiographical Narrative. Garden City, N.J.: Garden City Publishing Company, 1922.

Krimmerman, Leonard and Lewis Perry, eds., Patterns of Anarchy: A Collection on the Anarchist Tradition. New York: Anchor Books, 1966.

Kropotkin, Peter, In French and Russian Prisons. Montréal: Black Rose Books, 1991.

————. Kropotkin's Revolutionary Pamphlets. Edited with a new introduction by Roger N. Baldwin. New York: Vanguard Press, 1927.

————. Memoirs of a Revolutionist. Boston: Houghton, Mifflin Co., 1899.

————. Mutual Aid: a Factor in Evolution. London: Heinemann, 1902.

Lind, Earl, Autobiography of an Androgyne. New York: Medico-Legal Journal, 1918.

————. The Female Impersonators. New York: Medico-Legal Journal, 1922.

Lloyd, John William, Aw-aw-tam Indian Nights; Being the Myths and Legends of the Pimas of Arizona. Westfield, NJ: The Lloyd Group, 1911.

————. Dawn Thoughts on Reconciliation. Westfield, N.J.: The Lloyd Group, 1904

————. The Dwellers in the Vale Sunrise. Westwood, Mass.: Ariel Press, 1904.

————. Eneres: Or the Questions of Reksa. Introduction by Havelock Ellis. London: George Allen and Unwin, 1929.

————. From Hill-Terrace Outlooking: Poems of Intuition, Perception, and Prophecy. Los Angeles: Samuel Stebb, 1939.

————. The Karezza Method or Magenetation: The Art of Connubial Love. Los Angeles: Privately Published, 1931.

————. Maxims and Meditations of John William Lloyd. Roscoe, CA: J. W. Lloyd, 1940.

————. Psalms of the Race Root. Privately Published, n.d. [1902?]

————. The Natural Man: A Romance of the Golden Age. Newark: Benedict Prieth, 1902

Luhan, Mabel, Movers and Shakers: Volume Three of Intimate Memoirs. New York: Harcourt, Brace, 1936.

Marshall, Everett, Complete Life of William McKinley and the Story of His Assassination. Chicago: Historical Press, 1901.

Martí, José, "Walt Whitman," in Marti on the U.S.A., selected and translated by Luis A. Baralt. Carbondale, Ill.: Southern Illinois University Press, 1966.

Marx, Madeleine, The Romance of New Russia. New York: Thomas Selzer, 1924.

Mayne, Xavier [Edward Irenaeus Prime Stevenson]. The Intersexes: A History of Similisexualism as a Problem in Social Life. New York: Arno Press, 1975.

Meredith, Isabel, A Girl Amongst the Anarchists, Introduction Jennifer Shaddock. Lincoln, Neb: Nebraska University Press, 1992.

Monroe, Will S., "Walt Whitman and Other American Friends of Edward Carpenter," in Edward Carpenter: In Appreciation, ed. Gilbert Beith. London: George Allen and Unwin, 1931.

Nechaev, Sergei, Catechism of a Revolutionist. London: Aldgate, 1989.

Nicoll, David, Life in English Prisons: Mysteries of Scotland Yard. London: Kate Sharpley Library, 1992.

Perlin, Terry M, ed. Contemporary Anarchism. New Brunswick, N.J.: Transaction Books, 1979.

Perry, Bliss. *Walt Whitman: His Life and Work*. Boston: Houghton, Mifflin, 1906.
Potter-Loomis, Hulda, *Social Freedom: The Most Important Factor in Human Evolution*. Chicago: M. Harman, n.d.
Powderly, Terence V., *Thirty Years of Labor*. Columbus: Excelsior Publishing House, 1890.
O'Brien, M. D., "Socialism and Infamy: The Homogenic or Comrade Love Exposed: An Open Letter in Plain Words for a Socialist Prophet," in *Nineteenth-Century Writings on Homosexuality: A Sourcebook*, ed. Chris White. London: Routledge, 1999.
O'Higgins, Henry, *Alias Walt Whitman*. Newark: Carteret Book Club, 1930.
Quin, Mick, *On the Drumhead: A Selection of Writing of Mike Quin: A Memorial Volume*, ed. Harry Carlisle. San Francisco: Pacific Publishing Foundation, 1948.
Reitman, Ben, *Sister of the Road: The Autobiography of Box-Car Bertha as Told to Ben Reitman*. New York: Sheridan House, 1937.
Rexroth, Kenneth, *An Autobiographical Novel*. New York: Doubleday, 1966.
Roosevelt, Theodore, "First Annual Address," in *The State of the Union Messages of the Presidents, 1790–1966, Volume 2, 1866–1904*, ed. Fred L. Israel. New York: Chelsea House, 1966.
Sachs, Emanie, *The Terrible Siren: Victoria Woodhull, 1838–1927*. New York: Harper and Row, 1928.
Sanger, Margaret, *An Autobiography*. New York: W. W. Norton, 1938.
Shatz, Michael, ed. *The Essential Works of Anarchism*. New York: Quadrangle, 1972.
Silverman, Henry, ed. *American Radical Thought: The Libertarian Tradition*. Lexington, Mass.: D. C. Heath, 1970.
Sprading, Charles T, ed. *Liberty and the Great Libertarians*. Los Angeles, 1913.
Stoehr, Taylor, ed. *Free Love in America: A Documentary History*. New York: AMS Press, 1979.
Symonds, John Addington. *The Memoirs of John Addington Symonds*. ed. Phyllis Grosskurth. London: Hutchinson, 1984.
———. *Sexual Inversion: A Classical Study of Homosexuality*. New York: Bell Publishing Company, 1984.
———. *Walt Whitman: A Study*. London: John C. Nimmo, 1893.
Trigg, Oscar Lovell, *The Changing Order: A Study of Democracy*. Chicago: Charles Kerr and Company, 1913.
Tucker, R. Benjamin, *Individual Liberty*, ed. Clarence Lee Swartz; New York: Vanguard Press, 1926.
———. *Instead of a Book: By a Man Too Busy to Write One*. New York: Haskell House Publishers, 1969 reprint of 1897.
———. *State Socialism and Anarchism, How Far They Agree, and Wherein They Differ*. Introduction by James Martin. Colorado Springs: R. Myles, 1972.
———. *The Attitude of Anarchism Toward Industrial Combinations*. New York: Tucker Publishing Company, 1903.
Viereck, George Sylvester, *The Candle and the Flame*. New York: Moffat, Yard, and Company, 1912.
———. *My Flesh and Blood; a Lyrical Autobiography with Indiscreet Annotations*. New York: H. Liveright, 1931.
———. *Nineveh and Other Poems*. New York: Moffat, Yard, and Company, 1912.

Waisbrooker, Lois, *My Century Plant*. Topeka, Kansas: Independent Publishing
    Company, 1896.
Whitman, Walt, *The Complete Poetry and Prose of Walt Whitman: Two Volumes in One*.
    Garden City: Garden City Books, 1954.
————. *The Correspondence: Volume IV: 1886–1889.*, ed. Edwin Havilland Miller.
    New York: New York University Press, 1969.
Wilde, Oscar. *The Soul of Man and Prison Writings*. Edited Isobel Murray. New York:
    Oxford University Press, 1990.
————. *The Soul of Man under Socialism*. London: Porcupine Press, n.d.
Woodhull, Victoria, "The Principles of Social Freedom," in *The Victoria Woodhull
    Reader*, ed. Madeline B. Stern. Weston, Mass.: M and S Press, 1974.

SECONDARY SOURCES:

Anderson, Carlotta R. *All-American Anarchist: Joseph A. Labadie and the Labor
    Movement*. Detroit: Wayne State University Press, 1998.
Austen, Roger. *Genteel Pagan: The Double Life of Charles Warren Stoddard*, ed. John
    W. Crowley. Amherst: University of Massachusetts Press, 1991.
————. *Playing the Game: The Homosexual Novel in America*. Indianapolis: Bobbs–
    Merrill, 1977.
Avrich, Paul. *An American Anarchist: The Life of Voltairine de Clyre*. Princeton:
    Princeton University Press, 1978.
————. *Anarchist Portraits*. Princeton: Princeton University Press, 1988.
————. *The Haymarket Tragedy*. Princeton: Princeton University Press, 1984.
————. *The Modern School Movement*. Princeton: Princeton University Press, 1980.
————. *The Russian Anarchists*. Princeton: Princeton University Press, 1967.
Abelove, Henry, Michele Aina Barale, and David M. Halperin, eds. *The Lesbian and Gay
    Studies Reader*. New York: Routledge, 1993.
Abrams, Ann Uhry. "The Ferrer Center: New York's Unique Meeting of Anarchism and
    Art." *New York History* 15 (July 1978): 298–325.
Barrus, Clara. *Whitman and Burroughs: Comrades*. Port Washington, N.Y.: Kennikat
    Press, 1968.
Battan, Jesse F. "'The Word Made Flesh': Language, Authority and Sexual Desire in
    Late-Nineteenth Century America." In *American Sexual Politics: Sex, Gender and
    Race Since the Civil War*. Edited John Fout and Maura Shaw Tantillo. Chicago:
    University of Chicago Press, 1993): 110–134.
Beckson, Karl. *London in the 1890s: A Cultural History*. New York: Norton, 1992.
Bederman, Gail, *Manliness and Civilization: A Cultural History of Gender and Race in
    the United States, 1880–1917*. Chicago: University of Chicago Press, 1995.
Beemyn, Brett, ed. *Creating a Place for Ourselves: Lesbians, Gays, and Bisexual
    Community Histories*. New York: Routledge, 1997.
Beer, Thomas. *The Mauve Decade: American Life at the End of the Nineteenth Century*.
    New York: Knopf, 1926.
Bender, Thomas. *New York Intellect: A History of Intellectual Life in New York City,
    from 1750 to the Beginnings of Our Own Time*. New York: Knopf, 1987.
Bergman, David. *Gaiety Transformed: Gay Self-Representation in American Literature*.
    Madison: University of Wisconsin Press, 1991.
Bevir, Mark. "The Rise of Ethical Anarchism in Britain, 1885–1900." *Historical
    Research* 21 (June 1996): 143–165.

Blatt, Martin Henry. Free *Love and Anarchism: The Biography of Ezra Heywood*. Urbana: University of Illinois Press, 1989.

Boag, Peter, *Same-Sex Affairs: Constructing and Controlling Homosexuality in the Pacific Northwest*. Berkeley: University of California Press, 2003.

Boris, Eileen. *Art and Labor: Ruskin, Morris, and the Craftsmen Ideal in America*. Philadelphia: Temple University Press, 1986.

Buhle, Paul, "Anarchism and American Labor." *International Labor and Working Class History* 20 (Spring 1983): 21–34.

Buhle, Mari Jo. "Free Love." In *The Encyclopedia of the Left: Second Edition*, eds. Mari Jo Buhle, Paul Buhle, and Dan Georgakas. New York: Oxford University Press, 1998.

———. *Women and American Socialism, 1870–1920*. Urbana, Ill.: University of Illinois Press, 1979.

———. *Women and the American Left: A Guide to Sources*. Boston: Hall, 1983.

Bullough, Vern L. "Challenges to Societal Attitudes toward Homosexuality in the Late-Nineteenth and Early-Twentieth Centuries." *Social Science Quarterly* 58 (June 1977): 29–44.

———. *Science in the Bedroom: A History of Sex Research*. New York: Basic Books, 1994.

Burnham, John C. "Early References to Homosexual Communities in American Medical Writings." *Medical Aspects of Human Sexuality* 7, no. 8 (August 1973): 34, 40–41, 46–49.

———. "The Progressive Revolution in American Attitudes Toward Sex." *Journal of American History* 59, no. 4 (March 1973): 885–908.

Burns, Roger A. *The Damndest Radical: The Life and World of Ben Reitman, Chicago's Celebrated Social Reformer, Hobo King, and Whorehouse Physician*. Urbana: University of Illinois Press, 1987.

Brooks, Frank. "American Individual Anarchism: What It Was and Why It Failed." *Journal of Political Ideologies* 1 (1966): 75–95.

———. "Ideology, Strategy and Organization: Dyer Lum and the American Anarchist Movement." *Labor History* 34 (winter 1993): 79–80.

Carr, E. H. *Michael Bakunin*. New York: Octagon, 1975.

Chalberg, John. *Emma Goldman: American Individualist*. New York: Harper and Collins, 1991.

Chauncey, George Jr., "Christian Brotherhood or Sexual Perversion? Homosexual Identities and the Construction of Sexual Boudaries in the World War I Era." In *Hidden From History: Reclaiming the Gay and Lesbian Past*, eds. Martin Duberman, Martha Vicinus, and George Chauncey, Jr., 294–317. New York: Meridian, 1989.

———. "From Sexual Inversion to Homosexuality: Medicine and the Changing Conceptualization of Female Deviance." In *Passion and Power: Sexuality in History*, eds. Kathy Peiss and Christina Simmons with Robert A. Padgug, 87–117. Philadelphia: Temple University Press, 1989.

———. *Gay New York: Gender, Urban Culture, and the Making of the Gay Male World, 1890–1940*. New York: BasicBooks, 1994.

Chudacoff, Howard P. *The Age of the Bachelor: Creating an American Subculture*. Princeton: Princeton University Press, 1999.

Clark, Bruce. *Dora Marsden and Early Feminism: Gender, Individualism, Science.* Ann
    Arbor: University of Michigan Press, 1996.
Cleminson, Richard. *Anarchism, Ideology, and Same-Sex Desire.* London: Kate Sharpley
    Library, 1995.
————. *Anarchism, Science and Sex: Eugenics in Eastern Spain, 1900–*
    1937. Bern: Peter Lang, 2000.
————. "Male Inverts and Homosexuals: Sex Discourse in the Anarchist Revista
Blanca," In *Gay Men and the Sexual History of the Political Left,* eds. Gert
    Hekma, Harry Oosterhuis, and James Steakley. New York: Harrington Park Press,
    1995.
Cohen, Ed. *Talk on the Wilde Side: Towards a Genealogy of Discourse on Male
    Sexualities.* New York: Routledge, 1993.
Coiner, Constance. *Better Red: The Writings and Resistance of Tillie Olson and Meridel
    Le Sueur.* New York: Oxford University Press, 1995.
Cook, Blanche Wiesen. "Female Support Networks and Political Activism: Lillian Wald,
    Crystal Eastman, Emma Goldman." *Chrysalis* 3 (1977): 43–61.
————. "The Historical Denial of Lesbianism." *Radical History Review*
    20 (Spring–Summer 1979): 60–65.
Cott, Nancy. *The Grounding of Modern Feminism.* New Haven: Yale University Press,
    1987.
Coughlin, Michael, Charles Hamilton, and Mark Sullivan, eds. *Benjamin R. Tucker and
    the Champions of "Liberty": A Centenary Anthology.* St. Paul: Michael Coughlin,
    Publisher, 1987.
DeLeon, David. *The American as Anarchist: Reflections on Indigenous Radicalism.*
    Baltimore: Johns Hopkins Press, 1976.
D'Emilio, John, "Capitalism and Gay Identity." In *The Lesbian and Gay Studies Reader.*
    Edited by Henry Abelove, Michele Aina Barale, and David M. Halperin, 467–
    476. New York: Routledge, 1993.
————. *Sexual Politics, Sexual Communities: The Making of a Homosexual Minority in
    the United States, 1940–1970.* Chicago: University of Chicago Press, 1983.
D'Emilio, John and Estelle B. Freedman. *Intimate Matters: A History of Sexuality in
    America.* New York: Harper and Row, 1988.
Destler, Chester M. *American Radicalism, 1865–1901.* New York: Octagon Books,
    1963.
Donaldson, Randall Paul. "Robert Reitzel (1849–1898) and his German-American
    Periodical *De arme Teufel.*" Ph.D. diss., John Hopkins University, 1976.
Duberman, Martin. , *About Time: Exploring the Gay Past, Rev. Ed.* New York:
    Meridian, 1991.
————. "Anarchism Left and Right." Partisan Review (Fall 1966):
————. *Left Out: The Politics of Exclusion, Essays, 1964–2002.* Boston: South End
    Press, 2002.
————. ed. *A Queer World: The Center for Lesbian and Gay Studies Reader.* New York:
    New York University Press, 1997.
Duberman, Martin, Martha Vicinus, and George Chauncey Jr., eds. *Hidden from History:
    Reclaiming the Gay and Lesbian Past.* New York: Meridian, 1990.
Dubofsky, Melvyn. *We Shall Be All: A History of the Industrial Workers of the World.*
    New York: Quadrangle, 1969.

Duggan, Lisa. "Making It Perfectly Queer." *Socialist Review* 22, no. 1 (January–March 1992): 11–31.

———. *Sapphic Slashers: Sex, Violence, and American Modernity*. Durham, N.C.: Duke University Press, 2000.

Drinnon, Richard. *Rebel in Paradise: A Biography of Emma Goldman*. Boston: Beacon Press, 1961.

Ellman, Richard, *Oscar Wilde*. New York: Knopf, 1988.

Ehrenberg, John. *Proudhon and His Age*. New York: Humanities Press, 1996.

Ellingham, Lewis and Kevin Killian. *Poet Be Like God: Jack Spicer and the San Francisco Renaissance*. Hanover: Wesleyan University Press, 1998.

Escoffier, Jeffrey. "Oscar Wilde's Politics: The Homosexual as Artist as Socialist." *The Gay Alternative* 10 (1975): 4–15.

Faderman, Lillian. *Odd Girls and Twilight Lovers: A History of Lesbian Life in Twentieth-Century America*. New York: Columbia, 1991.

———. *Surpassing the Love of Men: Romantic Friendship and Love Between Women from the Renaissance to the Present*. New York: William Morrow, 1981.

Falk, Candance. *Love, Anarchy, and Emma Goldman*. New York: Holt, Reinhart, and Winston, 1984.

Fine, Sidney, "Anarchism and the Assassination of McKinley." *American Historical Review* 60 (1955): 777–799.

Fishbein, Leslie. *Rebels in Bohemia: The Radicals of the Masses, 1911–1917*. Chapel Hill: University of North Carolina Press, 1982.

Fone, Byrne R. S. *A Road to Stonewall, 1750–1969: Male Homosexuality and Homophobia in English and American Literature*. New York: Twayne, 1995.

Foner, Eric. *The Story of American Freedom*. New York: Norton: 1999.

Foucault, Michel. *The History of Sexuality. Vol 1, An Introduction*. New York: Pantheon, 1978.

Frankle, Oz. "Whatever Happened to 'Red Emma'? Emma Goldman from Alien Rebel to American Icon." *The Journal of American History* 83 (December 1996): 903–942.

Gifford, James. *Dayneford's Library: Homosexual Writing, 1900–1913*. Amherst: University of Massachusetts Press, 1995.

Gordon, Linda, *Woman's Bodies, Woman's Right: Birth Control in America*. New York: Penguin, 1977.

Greenberg, David F., *The Construction of Homosexuality*. Chicago: University of Chicago Press, 1988.

Grittner, Frederick K. *White Slavery: Myth, Ideology, and American Law*. New York: Garland, 1990.

Goodway, David, ed. *For Anarchism: History, Theory and Practice*. London: Routledge, and Kegan Paul, 1988.

Grosskurth, Phyllis. *The Woeful Victorian: A Biography of John Addington Symonds*. New York: Holt, Rinehart, and Winston, 1964.

Grunzweig, Walter. "Whitman in the German-Speaking Countries." In *Walt Whitman and the World*, eds. Gay Wilson Allen and Ed Folsom. Iowa City: University of Iowa Press.

Guérin, Daniel. *Anarchism: From Theory to Practice*. New York: Monthly Review Press, 1970.

Gustav-Wrathall, John Donald. *Take the Young Stranger by the Hand: Same-Sex Relations and the YMCA*. Chicago: University of Chicago Press, 1998.

Gutman, Herbert G. Introduction to *Liberty*. Westport, Conn.: Greenwood Press, 1970.

Haaland, Bonnie. *Emma Goldman: Sexuality and the Impurity of the State*. Montréal: Black Rose Books, 1993.

Hale, Nathan G. *Freud and the Americans: The Beginnings of Psychoanalysis in the United States, 1876–1917*. New York: Oxford University Press, 1971.

Hamalian, Linda. *A Life of Kenneth Rexroth*. New York: Norton, 1991.

Hansen, Bert. "American Physicians' 'Discovery' of Homosexuals: 1880–1900: A New Diagnosis in a Changing Society." In *Framing Disease: Studies in Cultural History*, eds. Charles E. Rosenberg and Janet Goldin. Rutgers: Rutgers University Press, 1992.

Hekma, Gert, Harry Oosterhuis, and James Steakley, eds. *Gay Men and the Sexual History of the Political Left*. New York: Harrington Park Press, 1995.

Hewitt, Andrew. *Political Inversion: Homosexuality, Fascism, and the Modernist Imaginary*. Stanford: Stanford University Press, 1996.

Higham, John. "The Reorientation of American Culture in the 1890s." In *The Origins of Modern Consciousness*, edited by John Weiss, 25–48. Detroit: Wayne State University Press, 1965.

Hillquit, Morris. *History of Socialism in the United States*. New York: Dover Publications, 1971.

Hirschman, Linda R., and Jane E. Lanson. *Hard Bargains: The Politics of Sex*. New York: Oxford University Press, 1998.

Hitchens, Christopher. "Oscar Wilde's Socialism." *Dissent* (Fall 1995): 516.

Horowitz, Helen Lefkowitz. *The Power and the Passion of M. Carey Thomas*. New York: Knopf, 1994.

Howe, Irving. *Socialism and America*. New York: Harcourt, Brace Jovanovich, 1977.

———. *World of Our Fathers*. New York: Simon and Schuster, 1976.

Ignatiev, Noel. *How the Irish Became White*. New York: Routledge, 1995.

Jacker, Corinne. *The Black Flag of Anarchy*. New York: Charles Scribner's Sons, 1968.

Jackson, Charles O., ed. *The Other Americans: Sexual Variance in the National Past*. Westport, Conn.: Prager, 1996.

Jeffries, Sheila. *The Spinster and Her Enemies: Feminism and Sexuality, 1880–1930*. London: Pandora, 1985.

Joll, James. *The Anarchists*. Boston: Little, Brown, 1964.

Jones, Margaret. *Heretics and Hellraisers: Women Contributors to The Masses, 1911–1917*. Austin: University of Texas Press, 1993.

Katz, Jonathan. "Coming to Terms: Conceptualizing Men's Erotic and Affectional Relations with Men in the United States, 1820–1982." In *A Queer World: The Center for Lesbian and Gay Studies Reader*, ed. Martin Duberman. New York: New York University Press, 1997.

———. *The Invention of Heterosexuality*. Forward by Gore Vidal. Afterward by Lisa Duggan. New York: Plume, 1996.

———. *Love Stories: Sex Between Men Before Homosexuality*. Chicago: University of Chicago Press, 2001.

Kennedy, Elizabeth Lapovsky, and Madeline D. Davis. *Boots of Leather, Slippers of Gold: The History of a Lesbian Community*. New York: Routledge, 1993.

Kennedy, David. *Birth Control in America: The Career of Margaret Sanger*. New Haven: Yale University Press, 1970.

Kennedy, Hubert. *Anarchist of Love: The Secret Life of John Henry Mackay*. New York: Mackay Society, 1983.

———. ed. *Dear Tucker: The Letters of John Henry Mackay to Benjamin R. Tucker*. San Francisco: Peremptory Publications: 1991.

———. "Johann Baptist von Schweitzer: The Queer Marx Loved to Hate." In *Gay Men and the Sexual History of the Political Left*, eds. Gert Hekma, Harry Oosterhuis, and James Steakley. New York: Harrington Park Press, 1995.

———. *Ulrichs: The Life and Works of Karl Heinrich Ulrichs, Pioneer of the Modern Gay Movement*. Boston: Alyson, 1988.

Kennedy, Kathleen. *Disloyal Mothers and Scurrilous Citizens: Women and Subversion During World War I*. Bloomington: Indiana University Press, 1999.

Kinsman, Gary. *The Regulation of Desire: Homo and Hetero Sexualities, rev. ed.* Montréal: Black Rose Books, 1996.

Klehr, Harvey and John Haynes. *The American Communist Movement: Storming the Gates of Heaven Itself*. New York: Twayne, 1993.

Lasch, Christopher. *The New Radicalism in America (1889–1963): The Intellectual as a Social Type*. New York: Knopf, 1965.

Laslett, John H. M., and Seymour M. Lipset, eds. *Failure of a Dream?: Essays in the History of American Socialism*. New York: Doubleday, 1974.

Lewin, Ellen, ed. *Inventing Lesbian Cultures in America*. Boston: Beacon Press, 1996.

Lynch, Michael. "'Here is Adhesiveness': From Friendship to Homosexuality." *Victorian Studies* 29 (autumn 1995): 67–96.

Madison, Charles A. *Critics and Crusaders*. New York: Henry Holt, 1948.

Mangan, J. A., and James Walvin, eds. *Manliness and Morality: Middle-Class Masculinity in Britain and America, 1800–1940*. Manchester: Manchester University, 1987.

Marsh, Margaret. *Anarchist Women, 1870–1920*. Philadelphia: Temple University Press, 1981.

Martin, James J. *Men Against the State*. Colorado Springs: Ralph Myles, 1970.

Martin, Robert K. *The Homosexual Tradition in American Poetry*. Austin: University of Texas Press, 1979.

———. "Knights-Errant and Gothic Seducers: The Representation of Male Friendship in Mid-Nineteen-Century America." In *Hidden From History: Reclaiming the Gay and Lesbian Past*, eds. Martin Duberman, Martha Vicinus, and George Chauncey Jr. New York: Meridian, 1989.

May, Henry F. *The End of American Innocence: A Study of the First Years of Our Own Time, 1912–1917*. New York: Alfred Knopf, 1959.

Maynard, Steven. "'Horrible Temptations': Sex, Men, and Working-Class Male Youths in Urban Ontario, 1890–1917." *Canadian Historical Review* 78, no. 2 (June 1997): 191–235.

———. "Through a Hole in the Lavatory Wall: Homosexual Subcultures, Police Surveillance, and the Dialectics of Discovery in Toronto, 1890–1930." *Journal of the History of Sexuality* 5, no. 2 (October 1994): 207–242.

McLaren, Angus. "Sex Radicalism in the Canadian Pacific Northwest, 1890–1920." *Journal of the History of Sexuality* 2, no. 4 (April 1992): 127–150.

————. "Sex and Socialism: The Opposition of the French Left to Birth Control in the
     Nineteenth Century." *Journal of the History of Ideas* 16 (July–September 1976):
     478–560.

————. *The Trials of Masculinity: Policing Sexual Boundaries, 1870–1930.* Chicago:
     University of Chicago Press, 1997.

McLaren, Angus, and Arlene Tiger McLaren. *The Bedroom and the State: The Changing
     Practices and Politics and Contraception and Abortion in Canada, 1880–1980.*
     Toronto: McClelland and Stewart, 1986.

Miller, Martin. *Kropotkin.* Chicago: University of Chicago Press, 1976.

Miller, Sally, ed. *Flawed Liberation: Socialism and Feminism.* Westport, Conn.:
     Greenwood Press, 1981.

Minton, Henry L. *Departing from Deviance: A History of Homosexual Rights and
     Emancipatory Science in America.* Chicago: University of Chicago Press, 2002.

Mosse, George L. *Nationalism and Sexuality.* New York: Howard Fertig, 1985.

Morton, Marian J. *Emma Goldman and the American Left: Nowhere at Home.* New
     York: Tawyne, 1992.

Mullaney, Marie. "Sexual Politics in the Career and Legend of Michel Louise." *Signs* 15
     (Winter 1990): 300–332.

Mumford, Kevin J. *Interzones: Black/White Sex Districts in Chicago and New York in
     the Early-Twentieth Century.* New York: Columbia University Press, 1997.

Murphy, Lawrence P. "Defining the Crime against Nature: Sodomy in the United States
     Appeals Courts, 1810–1940." *Journal of Homosexuality* 19 (1990): 49–
     66.

Nelson, Bruce C. *Beyond the Martyrs: A Social History of Chicago's Anarchists, 1870–
     1900.* New Brunswick, N.J.: Rutgers University Press, 1988.

O'Neil, William. *Divorce in the Progressive Era.* New Haven: Yale University Press,
     1967.

————. *Everyone Was Brave: A History of Feminism in America.* New York:
     Quadrangle, 1969.

Oosterhuis, Harry. *Stepchildren of Nature: Krafft-Ebing, Psychiatry, and the Making of
     Sexual Identity.* Chicago: University of Chicago Press, 2000.

Peiss, Kathy. *Cheap Amusements: Working Women and Leisure in Turn-of-the-Century
     New York.* Philadelphia: Temple University Press, 1988.

Peiss, Kathy, Christina Simmons, with Robert A. Padgug, eds. *Passion and Power:
     Sexuality in History.* Philadelphia: Temple University Press, 1989.

Perlin, Terry M., "Anarchist-Communism in America, 1890–1914." Ph.D. diss.
     Brandies University, 1970.

Perry, Lewis. *Radical Abolitionism: Anarchy and the Government of God in Antislavery
     Thought.* Ithaca: Cornell University Press, 1973.

Pierson, Stanley. "Edward Carpenter: Prophet of a Socialist Millennium." *Victorian
     Studies* 23 (March 1970): 289–315.

Pivar, David J. *Purity Crusade: Sexual Morality and Social Control, 1868–1900.*
     Westport, Conn.: Greenwood Press, 1973.

Quinn, D. Michael. *Same-Sex Dynamics among Nineteenth-Century Americans: A
     Mormon Example.* Urbana: University of Illinois Press, 1996.

Rabban, David M. *Free Speech in Its Forgotten Years.* Cambridge: Cambridge
     University Press, 1997.

Reed, James. *From Private Vice to Public Virtue: The Birth Control Movement and American Society since 1830.* New York: Basic Books, 1978.

Reichert, William O. "Edward C. Carpenter's Socialism in Retrospect." *Our Generation* 14 (Fall–Winter 1987–1988): 185–201.

———. *Partisans of Freedom: A Study in American Anarchism.* Bowling Green, Ohio: Popular Press, 1978.

Reigel, Robert E. "Changing Attitudes Toward Prostitution." *Journal of the History of Ideas* 23 (July–September 1968): 445–462.

Reynolds, David S. *Walt Whitman's America: A Cultural Biography.* New York: Alfred Knopf, 1995.

Riley, Glenda. *Divorce: An American Tradition.* New York: Oxford University Press, 1991.

Robinson, Paul, *The Modernization of Sex: Havelock Ellis, Alfred Kinsey, William Masters, and Virginia Johnson.* New York: Harper and Row, 1976.

Rocker, Rudolph. *Pioneers of American Freedom: Origins of Liberal and Radical Thought in America..* Los Angeles: Rocker Publications Committee, 1949.

Roediger, David R. *The Wages of Whiteness and the Making of the American Working Class,* rev. ed. London: Verso, 1999.

Roediger, David R, and Franklin Rosemont, eds. *Haymarket Scrapbook.* Chicago: Charles Kerr, 1986.

Rosario, Vernon A. "Homosexual Bio-Graphies: Genetic Nostalgias and the Quest for Paternity." In *Science and Homosexualities,* ed. Vernon A. Rosario. New York: Routledge, 1997.

———. "The Science of Sexual Liberation." *The Gay and Lesbian Review: Worldwide* 13 (November–December 2002): 34–43.

Rotundo, Anthony E. *American Manhood: Transformations in Masculinity from the Revolution to the Modern Era.* New York: Basic Books, 1993.

Rowbotham, Sheila, and Jeffrey Weeks. *Socialism and the New Life: The Personal and Sexual Politics of Edward Carpenter and Havelock Ellis.* London: Pluto Press, 1977.

Salvatore, Nick. *Citizen and Socialist: Eugene V. Debs.* Urbana, Ill.: University of Illinois Press, 1982.

Sears, Hal. *The Sex Radicals: Free Love in High Victorian America.* Lawrence: The Regents Press of Kansas, 1977.

Sedgwick, Eve Kosofsky. *Between Men: English Literature and Male Homosocial Desire.* New York: Columbia University Press, 1985.

Seretan, Glen L. "Daniel DeLeon and the Woman Question." In *Flawed Liberation: Socialism and Feminism,* ed. Sally M. Miller. Westport, Conn.: Greenwood Press, 1981.

Schuster, Eunice. *Native American Anarchism: A Study of Left-Wing Individualism.* Northhampton, Mass.: Smith College, 1932.

Schulman, Alix Kates. "Dancing in the Revolution: Emma Goldman's Feminism." *Socialist Review* 12 (March–April 1982): 1–32.

———. *To the Barricades: The Anarchist Life of Emma Goldman.* New York: T.Y. Crowell, 1971.

Seidman, Steven. "The Power of Desire and the Danger of Pleasure: Victorian Sexuality ———. *Romantic Longings: Love in America, 1830–1980.* New York: Routledge, 1991.

Shannon, David. *The Socialist Party of America*. New York: MacMillian, 1955.

Shively, Charles. "Anarchism" in *Encyclopedia of Homosexuality*, ed. Wayne Dynes. New York: Garland, 1990.

———. *Calamus Lovers: Walt Whitman's Working-Class Camerados*. San Francisco: Gay Sunshine Press, 1987.

Sinfield, Alan. *The Wilde Century: Effeminacy, Oscar Wilde and the Queer Movement*. London: Cassell, 1994.

Somerville, Siobahn B. *Queering the Color Line: Race and the Invention of Homosexuality in American Culture*. Durham, N.C.: Duke University Press, 2000.

Sonn, Richard D. *Anarchism*. New York: Twayne Publishers, 1992.

———. *Anarchism and Cultural Politics in Fin de Siecle France*. Lincoln, Neb.: University of Nebraska Press, 1989.

Steakley, James, "Iconography of a Scandal: Political Cartoons and the Eulenberg Affair in Wilhelmin Germany." In *Hidden from History: Reclaiming the Gay and Lesbian Past*, edited Martin Duberman, Martha Vicinus, and George Chauncey Jr., 233–263. New York: Meridian, 1989.

———. *The Homosexual Emancipation Movement in Germany*. New York: Arno, 1975.

Stephenson, Billie Jean, "The Ideology of American Anarchism." Ph.D. diss. University of Iowa, 1972.

Stern, Madeleine B. *The Pantarch: A Biography of Stephen Pearl Andrews*. Austin: University of Texas Press, 1968.

Strachey, Barbara. *Remarkable Relations: The Story of the Pearsall Smith Family*. London: Victor Gollancz, 1981.

Terry, Jennifer. *An American Obsession: Science, Medicine, and Homosexuality in Modern Society*. Chicago: University of Chicago Press, 1999.

Trautmann, Frederic. *The Voice of Terror: A Biography of Johann Most*. Westport, Conn.: Greenwood Press, 1980.

Tzuzuki, Chushichi. *Edward Carpenter, 1844–1929: Prophet of Human Fellowship*. New York: Cambridge University Press, 1980.

Ullman, Sharon R. *Sex Seen: The Emergence of Modern Sexuality in America*. Berkeley: University of California Press, 1997.

Varias, Alexander. *Paris and the Anarchists: Aesthetes and Subversives During the Fin de Siecle*. New York: St. Martin's Press, 1996.

Veysey, Laurence. *The Communal Experience: Anarchist and Mystical Counter-Cultures in America.*. New York: Harper and Row, 1973.

Ward, John William. "Violence, Anarchy, and Alexander Berkman," *New York Review of Books* 15 (November 5, 1970): 25–30.

Warner, Michael, ed., *Fear of a Queer Planet, Queer Politics and Social Theory*. Minneapolis: University of Minnesota Press, 1993.

Weeks, Jeffrey. *Coming Out: Homosexual Politics in Britain from the Nineteenth Century to the Present*. *rev. ed*. London: Quartet Books, 1990.

———. *Sex, Politics, and Society: The Regulation of Sexuality Since 1800*. 2nd ed. New York: Longman, 1989.

———. *Sexuality*. London: Tavistock Publications, 1986.

———. *Sexuality and Its Discontents: Meanings, Myths, and Modern Sexualities*. London: Routledge and Kegan Paul, 1985.

Weigand, Kate. *Red Feminism: American Communism and the Making of Women's Liberation.* Baltimore: Johns Hopkins University Press, 2001.

Weinstein, James. *The Decline of American Socialism, 1912–1925.* New York: Monthly Review Press, 1967.

Wexler, Alice. *Emma Goldman: An Intimate Life.* New York: Pantheon Books, 1984.

———. *Emma Goldman in America.* Boston: Beacon Press, 1984.

White, Kevin, *The First Sexual Revolution: The Emergence of Male Heterosexuality in Modern America.* New York: New York University Press, 1993.

Wilcox, Leonard. "Sex Boys in a Ballon: V. F. Calverton and the Abortive Sexual Revolution." *Journal of American Studies* 23 (1989): 7–31.

———. *V. F. Calverton: Radical in the American Grain.* Philadelphia: Temple University Press, 1992.

Willard, Charles B. *Whitman's American Fame: The Growth of His Reputation in America After 1892.* Providence, R.I.: Brown University, 1950

Woodcock, George. *Anarchism: A History of Libertarian Ideas and Movements.* New York: World Publishing Company, 1962.

———. *Anarchism and Anarchists.* Kingston, Ontario: Quarry Press, 1992.

———. *Oscar Wilde: The Double Image.* Montréal: Black Rose Books, 1989.

Yalom, Marilyn. *A History of the Wife.* New York: Harper Collins, 2001.

INDEX

ALSO AVAILABLE FROM AK PRESS

DWIGHT E. ABBOTT—I Cried, You Didn't Listen
MARTHA ACKELSBERG—Free Women of Spain
KATHY ACKER—Pussycat Fever
MICHAEL ALBERT—Moving Forward: Program for a Participatory
    Economy
JOEL ANDREAS—Addicted to War: Why the U.S. Can't Kick Militarism
JOEL ANDREAS—Adicto a la Guerra: Por qué EEUU no puede librarse
    del militarismo
ANONYMOUS —Test Card F
PAUL AVRICH—Anarchist Voices: An Oral History of Anarchism in
    America (Unabridged)
PAUL AVRICH—The Modern School Movement: Anarchism and
    Education in the United States
PAUL AVRICH—The Russian Anarchists
BRIAN AWEHALI (ed.)—Tipping the Sacred Cow
DAN BERGER—Outlaws of America: The Weather Underground and the
    Politics of Solidarity
ALEXANDER BERKMAN—What is Anarchism?
ALEXANDER BERKMAN—The Blast: The Complete Collection
STEVEN BEST & ANTHONY NOCELLA, II—Igniting a Revolution:
    Voices in Defense of the Earth
HAKIM BEY—Immediatism
JANET BIEHL & PETER STAUDENMAIER—Ecofascism: Lessons From
    The German Experience
BIOTIC BAKING BRIGADE—Pie Any Means Necessary: The Biotic
    Baking Brigade Cookbook
DAN BERGER—Outlaws of America
JACK BLACK—You Can't Win
MURRAY BOOKCHIN—Anarchism, Marxism, and the Future of the
    Left
MURRAY BOOKCHIN—The Ecology of Freedom: The Emergence and
    Dissolution of Hierarchy
MURRAY BOOKCHIN—Post-Scarcity Anarchism
MURRAY BOOKCHIN—Social Anarchism or Lifestyle Anarchism: An
    Unbridgeable Chasm
MURRAY BOOKCHIN—Social Ecology and Communalism
MURRAY BOOKCHIN—The Spanish Anarchists: The Heroic Years
    1868–1936
MURRAY BOOKCHIN—To Remember Spain: The Anarchist and
    Syndicalist Revolution of 1936

EG SMITH COLLECTIVE—Animal Ingredients A–Z (3rd edition)
HOWARD EHRLICH—Reinventing Anarchy, Again
SIMON FORD—Realization and Suppression of the Situationist International
BENJAMIN FRANKS—Rebel Alliances
YVES FREMION & VOLNY—Orgasms of History: 3000 Years of Spontaneous Revolt
EMMA GOLDMAN (EDITED BY DAVID PORTER)—Vision on Fire
BERNARD GOLDSTEIN—Five Years in the Warsaw Ghetto
DAVID GRAEBER—Possibilities: Essays on Hierarchy, Rebellion, and Desire
DAVID GRAEBER & STEVPHEN SHUKAITIS—Constituent Imagination
DANIEL GUÉRIN—No Gods No Masters: An Anthology of Anarchism
AGUSTIN GUILLAMÓN—The Friends Of Durruti Group, 1937–1939
ANN HANSEN—Direct Action: Memoirs Of An Urban Guerilla
HELLO—2/15: The Day The World Said NO To War
WILLIAM HERRICK—Jumping the Line: The Adventures and Misadventures of an American Radical
FRED HO—Legacy to Liberation: Politics & Culture of Revolutionary Asian/Pacific America
STEWART HOME—Neoism, Plagiarism & Praxis
STEWART HOME—Neoist Manifestos / The Art Strike Papers
STEWART HOME—No Pity
STEWART HOME—Red London
GEORGY KATSIAFICAS—Subversion of Politics
KATHY KELLY—Other Lands Have Dreams: From Baghdad to Pekin Prison
JAMES KELMAN—Some Recent Attacks: Essays Cultural And Political
KEN KNABB—Complete Cinematic Works of Guy Debord
KATYA KOMISARUK—Beat the Heat: How to Handle Encounters With Law Enforcement
PETER KROPOTKIN—The Conquest of Bread
SAUL LANDAU—A Bush & Botox World
JOSH MACPHEE & ERIK REULAND—Realizing the Impossible: Art Against Authority
RICARDO FLORES MAGÓN—Dreams of Freedom: A Ricardo Flores Magón Reader
NESTOR MAKHNO—The Struggle Against The State & Other Essays
SUBCOMANDANTE MARCOS—¡Ya Basta! Ten Years of the Zapatista Uprising
G.A. MATIASZ—End Time
CHERIE MATRIX—Tales From the Clit

BENJAMIN ZEPHANIAH—Little Book of Vegan Poems
BENJAMIN ZEPHANIAH—School's Out

CDs

MUMIA ABU JAMAL—175 Progress Drive
MUMIA ABU JAMAL—All Things Censored Vol.1
MUMIA ABU JAMAL—Spoken Word
JUDI BARI—Who Bombed Judi Bari?
JELLO BIAFRA—Become the Media
JELLO BIAFRA—Beyond The Valley of the Gift Police
JELLO BIAFRA—The Big Ka-Boom, Part One
JELLO BIAFRA—High Priest of Harmful
JELLO BIAFRA—I Blow Minds For A Living
JELLO BIAFRA—In the Grip of Official Treason
JELLO BIAFRA—If Evolution Is Outlawed
JELLO BIAFRA—Machine Gun In The Clown's Hand
JELLO BIAFRA—No More Cocoons
NOAM CHOMSKY—An American Addiction
NOAM CHOMSKY—Case Studies in Hypocrisy
NOAM CHOMSKY—Emerging Framework of World Power
NOAM CHOMSKY—Free Market Fantasies
NOAM CHOMSKY—The Imperial Presidency
NOAM CHOMSKY—New War On Terrorism: Fact And Fiction
NOAM CHOMSKY—Propaganda and Control of the Public Mind
NOAM CHOMSKY—Prospects for Democracy
NOAM CHOMSKY & CHUMBAWAMBA—For A Free Humanity: For
    Anarchy
CHUMBAWAMBA—A Singsong and A Scrap
WARD CHURCHILL—Doing Time: The Politics of Imprisonment
WARD CHURCHILL—In A Pig's Eye: Reflections on the Police State,
    Repression, and Native America
WARD CHURCHILL—Life in Occupied America
WARD CHURCHILL—Pacifism and Pathology in the American Left
ALEXANDER COCKBURN—Beating the Devil: The Incendiary Rants
    of Alexander Cockburn
ANGELA DAVIS—The Prison Industrial Complex
THE EX—1936: The Spanish Revolution
NORMAN FINKELSTEIN—An Issue of Justice: Origins of the Israel/
    Palestine Conflict
ROBERT FISK—War, Journalism, and the Middle East
FREEDOM ARCHIVES—Chile: Promise of Freedom
FREEDOM ARCHIVES—Prisons on Fire: George Jackson, Attica & Black
    Liberation

FREEDOM ARCHIVES—Robert F. Williams: Self-Defense, Self-Respect & Self-Determination
JAMES KELMAN—Seven Stories
TOM LEONARD—Nora's Place and Other Poems 1965–99
CASEY NEILL—Memory Against Forgetting
GREG PALAST—Live From the Armed Madhouse
GREG PALAST—Weapon of Mass Instruction
CHRISTIAN PARENTI—Taking Liberties
UTAH PHILLIPS—I've Got To know
UTAH PHILLIPS—Starlight on the Rails box set
DAVID ROVICS—Behind the Barricades: Best of David Rovics
ARUNDHATI ROY—Come September
VARIOUS—Better Read Than Dead
VARIOUS—Less Rock, More Talk
VARIOUS—Mob Action Against the State: Collected Speeches from the Bay Area Anarchist Bookfair
VARIOUS—Monkeywrenching the New World Order
VARIOUS—Return of the Read Menace
HOWARD ZINN—Artists In A Time of War
HOWARD ZINN—Heroes and Martyrs: Emma Goldman, Sacco & Vanzetti, and the Revolutionary Struggle
HOWARD ZINN—A People's History of the United States: A Lecture at Reed
HOWARD ZINN—People's History Project Box Set
HOWARD ZINN—Stories Hollywood Never Tells

DVDs
NOAM CHOMSKY—Imperial Grand Strategy: The Conquest of Iraq and the Assault on Democracy
NOAM CHOMSKY—Distorted Morality
STEVEN FISCHLER & JOEL SUCHER—Anarchism in America/Free Voice of Labor
ARUNDHATI ROY—Instant-Mix Imperial Democracy
ROZ PAYNE ARCHIVES—What We Want, What We Believe: The Black Panther Party Library (4 DVD set)
HOWARD ZINN & ANTHONY ARNOVE (ed.)—Readings from Voices of a People's History of the United States

FRIENDS OF AK PRESS

Help sustain our vital project!

AK Press is a worker-run collective that publishes and distributes radical books, audio/visual media, and other material. We're small: ten individuals who work long hours for short money, because we believe in what we do. We're anarchists, which is reflected both in the books we publish and in the way we organize our business: without bosses.

AK Press publishes the finest books, CDs, and DVDs from the anarchist and radical traditions — currently about 18 to 20 per year. Joining The Friends of AK Press is a way in which you can directly help us to keep the wheels rolling and these important projects coming.

As ever, money is tight as we do not rely on outside funding. We need your help to make and keep these crucial materials available. Friends pay a minimum (of course we have no objection to larger sums!) of $25/£15 per month, for a minimum three month period. Money received goes directly into our publishing funds. In return, Friends automatically receive (for the duration of their membership), as they appear, one FREE copy of EVERY new AK Press title. Secondly, they are also entitled to a 10% discount on EVERYTHING featured in the AK Press distribution catalog — or on our website — on ANY and EVERY order. We also have a program where individuals or groups can sponsor a whole book.

PLEASE CONTACT US FOR MORE DETAILS:

AK Press
674-A 23rd Street
Oakland, CA 94612
akpress@akpress.org
www.akpress.org

AK Press
PO Box 12766
Edinburgh, Scotland EH8 9YE
ak@akedin.demon.co.uk
www.akuk.com